Critical Acclaim for Nick Middleton

'Genuinely funny, intelligent and refreshing travelogue ... a great read and a must for any Euro citizen, cynic and sceptic alike'
Condé Nast Traveller

'Nick Middleton writes with straightforward and relentless good humour. He is good on quirky detail and a nice turn of phrase'
Independent

'Read Nick Middleton's gloriously wry account of a trip around modern-day Europe ... this is what you really need to know about Delors et al' *Maxim*

'A very funny book ... his anecdotes are uniformly excellent'
Spectator

'Valued, rounded and unblinkered portrait' *Weekend Telegraph*

'He is good with bad weather and alcohol ... and betrays a nostalgic affinity with what a German, noted in the book, refers to as "the outskirts" of the continent' *Observer*

'An intelligent, perceptive and often hilarious view of an extraordinary place, by an author with a lively mind, and a dry sense of humour' *Good Book Guide*

'Middleton's experiences are delivered with sparky, quirky charm'
Mail on Sunday

'His tenaciously well-informed prose transcends traveloguery'
Observer

'Assiduous in his research, he effortlessly blends historical analysis with personal observations and tales of fascinating encounters'
Times Literary Supplement

Nick Middleton was born in London. As a geographer he has travelled to more than fifty countries and teaches part-time at Oxford University. When wearing his academic hat, his interest in deserts has taken him to the Sahara, the Gobi, the Thar, the Namib and the Kalahari. As a travel writer he has been accused of drug-smuggling and spying but has never spent a night in jail, although he was once fined for dropping a match in Tiananmen Square. He has been mugged in Moscow, conned in Casablanca, molested in Mexico City and kidnapped in Outer Mongolia, but he hasn't got tired of it yet. His most challenging assignment was a job editing a report on washing machine efficiency in Denmark, the initial inspiration for this, his third travel book.

By the same author

The Last Disco in Outer Mongolia
Kalashnikovs and Zombie Cucumbers:
Travels in Mozambique

Travels as a Brussels Scout

NICK MIDDLETON

PHŒNIX

A Phoenix Paperback
First published in Great Britain by Weidenfeld & Nicolson in 1997
This paperback edition published in 1998 by Phoenix,
a division of Orion Books Ltd,
Orion House, 5 Upper St Martin's Lane,
London WC2H 9EA

A CIP catalogue record for this book
is available from the British Library.

ISBN: 0 75380 159 0

Printed and bound in Great Britain by
The Guernsey Press Co. Ltd,
Guernsey, Channel Islands

For Lorraine

Acknowledgements

Many people have helped at different stages in the production of this book. In particular I would like to thank the following, who were generous with their hospitality and open with their insights: Hazel Bedford, Ole Bilde, Claire Calcagno, Clifford Dent, John Downes, Konrad Heene, Maija Saari, Keith Shannon and Steven Vertovec. Special thanks go to John Middleton for the use of his extensive library and encyclopaedic knowledge, Mark Carwardine for his moral support and usual candid reviews of the text, and Lorraine Desai, to whom the book is dedicated, for her insights, help and inspiration.

Contents

Preface

The man from the European Commission in Brussels stood up to welcome the delegates assembled around the conference table. He was an unusually large man with an unusually large beard, and unfolding his considerable frame from the chair took an unusually long time. When fully upright he must have been close to seven feet tall. As it transpired, the standing procedure took longer than his salutation. He spread out his hands, surveyed the congregation and in a booming voice said, 'Welcome.' Then he sat down again.

Everyone laughed.

'So, we must begin,' pronounced the burly Dane who was chairing the meeting. 'The first presentation is from our Dutch friends.' Down the table to my right a thin-faced man wearing a bright orange jacket shuffled some papers and rose from his chair. As he made his way to the flipcharts on the easel at the head of the table, I looked across again at the man from the Brussels Commission who was sharing a joke with the Frenchman next to him. The Commission man sounded English, which surprised me. I'd been trying to work out his nationality since he had first appeared and I would have said that his imposing presence could have hailed from anywhere except Britain. He had so much hair on his head that there was hardly room for his face, but from some angles he looked like a cross between an Old Testament prophet and a Greek Orthodox monk. He could equally have been a Left Bank intellectual who hadn't cut his beard since 1968. He resembled an Irish leprechaun that had just kept on growing, and a German professor of logic. He could have passed as a Spanish pirate or a Scandinavian swami or played a bit-part in an Italian film about anarchists. All things considered, his job as a Eurocrat was highly appropriate.

The Dutchman at the end of the table was in full swing. He was talking about washing machines. He hadn't managed to get hold of much information from Greece or Italy, he was saying to murmurs of understanding from around the table. Portugal too was a problem. More nods. Nevertheless, he continued, consumer surveys indicated that for the European Union as a whole, the ownership level for washing machines was 90 per cent, and that on average these appliances were used 4.6 times a week. 'The typical European machine is a front-loader,' he informed us, 'although in France most of them are loaded from the top.'

I'm a geographer, which covers a multitude of sins, and one of the advantages of a job like mine is that I don't have one job. At any one time, I've usually got several. Sitting at this conference table happened to be part of one of them. I was working as an editor for a Danish government agency on a European Union project. My part of the project had taken some time to get off the ground, and I'd got bored sitting around in Copenhagen. Things only started happening when I travelled with two of my new Danish colleagues to this conference in a small fishing village just outside Dublin.

The Dutchman had moved on to driers. The ownership level here was 20 per cent, he said, and these driers were used 2.9 times in an average week.

I had hit a lean patch work-wise when someone offered me the assignment with the Danish Energy Agency. Potentially interesting work, I thought to myself; see Copenhagen, I mused. I agreed to do it. Admittedly, I got some nonplussed looks from friends when I told them what I would be working on. It was an in-depth review of prospects for improving energy efficiency in European Union domestic wet appliances. Blank looks. Washing machines, dishwashers and driers, I would explain. 'Really?' said one, taking a step back as if I had taken leave of my senses. 'How interesting,' said another, clearly lying. 'You're going to Copenhagen to do the washing up?' from a slightly more imaginative acquaintance who seemed convinced that there must be an ulterior motive. There wasn't at the time, but as it turned out working on this report became the start of a book that would take me all across the European Union, although not in search of the ultimate washing appliance.

The Dutchman in the orange jacket was finishing up with his data on dishwashers. There followed a short discussion on his findings and the Dutchman made way for a French delegate who presented his institute's work on the mathematical modelling of wash performance. As the presentations droned on through the morning, I cast my eyes around the table. Here we were nearing the end of a report that had been two years in the making. Participants from government departments, research institutes and regulatory bodies, university faculties and private consultancies from all over the European Union had got together in this hotel outside Dublin to thrash out the fine details of energy-efficient washing machines, dishwashers and driers. People who to me had previously been just signatures scribbled on faxes and names printed on reports had become the faces of Europe's expertise on wet appliances. There were political conflicts over the suitability of policy measures and technical discussions on how to measure the efficiency of a dishwasher. It was heady stuff.

The Danes and the Dutch had been the first to produce their contributions and all looked rather uncomfortable wearing suits and ties. The French were debonair and charming and bent on doing things their own way. They seemed to have made up some of their own ground rules and were the only ones using an incompatible computer programme. The Irish guy was a great talker who was good at helping things along but otherwise didn't actually seem to do much. The Portuguese, however, had done nothing at all, whilst the Germans were advising because they had done it all before. If the woman in charge of the British contingent had been hooked up to the national grid, the energy she expended could have illuminated a small town, but her team was waiting for everyone else to finish before they could start. Having only just joined the Union, the Swedes, Finns and Austrians were enthusiastic new boys. The Italians had shown a complete lack of interest. No one appeared to have invited any Belgians, Greeks or Spaniards.

Slowly it dawned on me that while I had spent the past few years wandering in some of the world's more out-of-the-way countries just because they were different, I had hardly noticed that I was living slap bang in the middle of one of the greatest political and social experiments the world has known. Both in the wider perspective as a European citizen, and here and now working on a European project for a foreign government, I was playing a role, no matter how small, in the new Europe.

For a long time I had avoided the place. I had thought that while I was young and active I should concentrate on the less comfortable parts of the world. What I had seen of my own continent suggested that Europe was safe, not that different from home, and would still be there when I was old and less adventurous. But looking around the conference table made me think that perhaps I ought to get out there and see what sort of great community the beard from Brussels and his Eurocratic partners were presiding over. I have always kicked myself for not dropping everything to jump on a plane and be there when the Berlin Wall came down. The building of the European Union had been a slightly more drawn-out process, but in its way no less monumental.

An idea was germinating in my mind. As the United Kingdom was being dragged screaming like a recalcitrant child into twenty-first-century European unification, perhaps it would be interesting to see what all the fuss was about. We Brits all have some ideas on what our fellow Europeans are like: the Germans are humourless, well off and well organised; the French live on frogs' legs and look down their noses at everyone; and the Scandinavians are all morose because they drink too much. The Italians are anarchic but it's the Spanish who like killing bulls in public and throwing live goats off the tops of church steeples. The Irish are stupid and the Belgians are boring, but at least they both have an identity. Luxembourg doesn't even rate a boring tag. But did our Continental cousins really fit these stereotypes? And what did they think of European unity? Was it really possible for us all to become Eurocitizens, or would the garlic fumes simply be too much for the average Brit? Maybe I should find out.

At the same time, I thought it would be appropriate for me to take in Europe's cultural highlights. I should follow a trail of modern-day sights and experiences that every well-rounded late twentieth-century Eurocitizen should encounter. It would be like a modern rendition of the Grand Tour of Europe, the obligatory tourist finishing-school voyage undertaken by all young English gentlemen of the eighteenth century, designed to give them the wherewithal to be rounded citizens. Europe then must have been a rather confusing place to travel in. Distance was measured in several different types of mile (English, Scottish, Italian, Russian and German), and Britain only joined the rest of her European neighbours in adopting the new-style Gregorian calendar as late as 1752. Belgium and Luxembourg were called the Austrian Netherlands, Finland was part of Sweden, Danish governors ruled Norway, and Greece was still in the Ottoman Empire. I wouldn't be able to spend three years over my adventures, but thanks to the wonders of modern transportation, today's Grand EuroTour can be completed in double-quick time. As any modern Eurotraveller must, I would have to shoot through the Channel Tunnel and ride the TGV; see Venice by gondola and Vienna from Harry Lime's big wheel. I wanted a real-life version of CNN's 'Sights and Sounds of Europe'.

Back in my home town of Oxford, I burrowed into the archives of the country's oldest geography department. I was looking for an eighteenth-century yardstick to compare to my modern journey. Among the ancient tomes, I came across a two-volume reference work published in 1779. It was called *A Complete System of Geography* and covered everything from descriptions of soils and climate to customs and manners, and 'many curious and interesting circumstances concerning various places'. The book was written by a namesake, Charles Theodore Middleton Esquire, which clinched it: he would be my mentor and guide.

If I could battle my way through the camera-toting tourists, I would take in the conventional sites – the Louvres, Vatican Cities and Parthenons – but I also wanted to cover some modern musts: play 'count the banks' in Luxembourg, see what was left of that wall in Berlin and visit the underwear museum in Brussels. As well as places, I would visit pseudo-places, to sample such bastions of Euroculture as the Algarve and Euro Disney. I wanted to sample local cuisine and culture: to eat snails and horsemeat in Paris and be sneered at by a real *garçon*, to chew meatballs while doing a EuroBabewatch in Stockholm. I wanted to see a bullfight in Spain, walk the red light district of Amsterdam, and breathe the smog in Athens. In looking for community, I would be examining the contrasts. Have we really become one pizza-eating, Peugeot-driving whole? Or do we remain fifteen separate cultures, each with its own cute little identity? Have Europe's citizens become the innocent meat and drink victims of a new Euro gravy train? Or are today's Eurocrats truly visionaries with a missionary zeal?

After starting in Denmark, I thought I ought to sit down and work out some kind of itinerary, even though the idea went against the grain for me. I don't like to pre-plan much before I go travelling because it spoils the spontaneity, but I convinced myself that visiting fourteen countries would require a bit of preparation. I decided to do France early on because France was Britain's closest European neighbour and one of the prime movers in the game of European union. The other major player, mighty Germany, I thought I'd leave until last. As for in between, well ... since Belgium was where Brussels was and therefore supposedly the centre of it all, I'd go there in the middle. Logically, Belgium came with the Netherlands and Luxembourg, sort of like a sandwich. Other countries too were logically visited in groups: Spain and Portugal, and Sweden and Finland. Greece and Eire were both rather out on a limb, and Italy too for that matter. I could decide when to fit those in as I went along. That only left Austria which had to go with Germany.

I knew my task would be a difficult one. Previously, the draw for me of countries such as Mongolia and Mozambique had been their very foreignness. These European places were really too familiar, but I would try to examine them with the same open-minded approach that I had taken to the more exotic destinations. Could Europe provide as wide a cross-section of humanity? I would find out.

I had no doubt that I would expose some myths and confirm some others. Are the Belgians really boring? What makes the Finns drink so much? Can the Italians really be both great lovers and great cowards at the same time? And what have the French got to be so supercilious about?

European unity was fast becoming a political reality, and for me the time was ripe to assess the state of the Union. When I arrived home from Denmark, I gave myself a year. For twelve months, I would travel the highways and byways of Europe as a Brussels scout.

1

Danish Blues

In truth, I didn't know much about Denmark before I went. I failed the 'name five famous Danes' test miserably, never recovering from my hesitation after Hans Christian Andersen. (There are others, of course: Karen Blixen is one, the religious philosopher Kierkegaard another, but that's still only three.) Then there was Lego, and bacon, and ... Well, it was a start. A quick look in my atlas and geographical gazetteer told me that Denmark was all over the place, consisting as it does of the peninsula of Jutland – the quiff on the top of Germany – and nearly five hundred islands. But most of Denmark is in Greenland, which excited me for a moment until I read that Greenland, like the Faroe Islands, had decided not to partake of the European Union. Hence the two most interesting parts of the country were off-limits to me.

However I couldn't complain; here I was in Scandinavia's largest city and the initial impressions were good. Almost anywhere looks like Toytown when you first fly into it, but in Denmark this impression doesn't dissipate after you land. The entire country has an air of picture-book prettiness about it; it is neat, clean and orderly like a film set. I seriously expected to see Danny Kaye dance out on the pedestrian crossing in front of my swish Mercedes taxi, singing 'Wonderful, wonderful Copenhagen ...'

Everything appeared to work with clockwork efficiency. Sparkling, bright yellow buses fresh out of their boxes eased down the bus lanes, orderly files of well-oiled bicycles plied down the bicycle lanes, and neat groups of recycling bins sat ready to do their duty outside spruce apartment blocks. Even the snow, which was fluttering down to rest in delicate mounds on tree branches and atop the occasional parked car, was orderly. There was no grimy slush as in any other big city, just nice quiet flakes doing their bit to give the city a cosy Christmas-card ambience as dusk was falling.

Copenhagen is criss-crossed with waterways and unexpected lakes, and after the taxi glided across the Knippelsbro Bridge and past the green copper roofs of the old stock exchange, the fairytale dragons entwined down its central spire now sporting natty white moustaches, we turned right over another little canal. Beneath the short bridge I could just make out something floodlit below the waterline. I asked my taxi driver, who spoke perfect English, what it was, expecting him to tell me about some marine archaeological excavation. 'It is an underwater sculpture,' he said matter-of-factly. OK, I thought, something you should expect in a country with such a liberal and avant-garde reputation. Art for the sub-aqua community, why not?

The taxi pulled up outside the Hotel Christian IV on the unpronounceable Dronningens Tværgade. A sticker on the window had informed me in four European languages that tips were not expected by Danish taxi drivers because it would be included in the fare. What it didn't say was that the fare from the airport would have been a more than adequate downpayment on your own Mercedes back in Britain. Feeling a little light-headed and a lot poorer, I made a point of carrying my own bags into the hotel to check in and the taxi driver pulled away, presumably to find a travel agent and book a three-week holiday in Barbados.

The Hotel Christian IV was a fairly standard, middle-of-the-range Euro-nowhere hotel with the usual assortment of satellite channels and eco-notices in the bathroom telling you that if you used your towel more than once this was a jolly good thing for the environment because think of all the detergent that would be saved.

There were only three particularly Danish things about the hotel. One was the polite notice inside the bumf sitting on the small desk in my room, informing me apologetically that making phone calls from Danish hotels was an expensive pastime, since I would be charged whether I got through or not. Another was the appearance each breakfast time of several bottles of dangerous-looking spirits among the otherwise standard fare of bread, cereals, cheese and cold meats. Such provision appeared to be modern confirmation of Charles Theodore Middleton's observation that the 'vice of drinking to excess is almost general among the Danes; though many, sorely against their wills, are obliged to keep sober through poverty'. Although the Danes still like a drink as much as any nationality, the situation today is not quite as bad as Middleton recorded. I was told that it is traditional to down a shot of Danish liqueur with breakfast on your birthday. But then I realised that I was keeping pretty elevated company. Some of the hotel's clientele were clearly very important people. They seemed to have a birthday most days of the week.

The other Danish thing about the place was its name. King Christian IV has taken on an almost mythical status to Danes. His reign, which lasted for sixty years until his death in the mid-seventeenth century, was a golden age in which Renaissance cities, castles and fortresses flourished throughout the kingdom. Many of Copenhagen's most outstanding buildings were put up during this period and very fine tributes to his golden age they are too.

I learnt much of this on my first morning when my mentor for the editing job, a bear of a man named Ole who had a small grey moustache and fingers so thick they looked like a handful of thumbs, walked with me to the Energy Agency's office. It is a little-known fact, outside Denmark, that there has not been much variety in Danish kings' names since 1448. In nearly five hundred and fifty years, with the exception of King Hans, all Danish kings have been called either Christian or Frederik. A similarly limited number of handles characterises the Danish hoi polloi: more than two-thirds of all Danes have a surname ending in 'sen', with Jensens, Nielsens and Hansens accounting for more than twenty per cent of the population. These facts are reflected in the sense of calm and friendly community that pervades the entire country. It is almost as if everyone knows each other.

As we strolled through spectacular parks and along tranquil waterways, Ole pushing his ministry bicycle, I reflected on his casual, virtually English dress sense. He wore faded denims, scuffed black shoes and a cagoule, making me feel more than somewhat over-dressed in my jacket and tie. I couldn't quite believe that this was a senior civil servant I was walking with.

During my time in Denmark I came across two basic categories of Danes. Ole conformed to the strong silent type. Many of them look like sea captains and spend a lengthy period sizing you up as if they are about to offer you, *sotto voce*, a secret trip on their trawler to a smugglers' rendezvous on a little-known part of the Baltic coastline. The rest were pixie types, with snub noses and various amounts of facial hair where the men are concerned. The blonde women pixies are all a little too anaemic-looking, and could do with a few weeks in the sun. This was a disappointment. I had this image of Scandinavian women all being smouldering blondes, I suppose because of their reputation for illicit videos, but I never saw any Danish sexpots. Perhaps they all fly south for the winter.

Most of Ole's colleagues in the Danish Energy Agency were of the pixie type. There was the national average number of Jensens and Nielsens and all were appropriately kitted out in casuals which would result in an immediate sacking in any British government agency. Among Copenhagen's lesser-known claims to fame is the fact that it is home to Europe's largest sweater store, and most of the Danish Energy Agency's employees seemed to have been its customers at one time or another. Even the boss of the outfit wore casual gear, unless he had an important meeting to go to. This easygoing atmosphere made the office a good place to work in, but the lack of customary indicators of hierarchy threw me to begin with. A few days into my stint I found myself standing behind one of the men from the Agency in the queue at the civil service canteen. He asked me how it was going and we exchanged a few pleasantries before moving with our trays to find a table. I had been introduced to everyone, but at this stage most of the faces were still a blur. To keep the conversation going, I asked this guy what he did in the organisation. 'I'm the director,' he replied. I wanted the ground to open and swallow me up, but he was totally unperturbed by my *faux pas*.

The relaxed atmosphere notwithstanding, everyone in the office appeared to work hard. This was in spite of regular communal breaks for strong coffee and Danish cakes, including what we know as Danish pastries but which, confusingly, the Danes refer to as *wienerbrød* (Vienna bread). Everyone in the office spoke excellent English and just to prove it, on my first morning the customary meeting over a breakfast of bread and butter was conducted in English. A similar scene in a British office is impossible to imagine, but then I suppose any Dane who wants contact with the outside world has to speak some foreign language because no one is going to bother to learn Danish.

I tried rather half-heartedly to pick up some of the vernacular, but since so many seemed to speak such good English there was not a great incentive. I have often found that watching sub-titled films or

4

television programmes is a very useful way of absorbing languages, but when English TV programmes carried Danish sub-titles, the relationship between what was said and what was written was seldom clear. Danish television does run numerous British exports, including ancient reruns of 'The Tommy Cooper Show' which proved to be a helpful introduction to the national sense of humour, but the one potentially handy little Danish idiom for a crisis that did stick in my mind was gleaned from a transmission of the American film *Thelma and Louise*. When a truck driver yelled, 'Fucking asshole,' it was translated as '*Kraftidiot*', but the opportunities for using such an expletive are few and far between in any government office.

The Danish Energy Agency was housed with a number of other government divisions in an old building on Slotsholmen Island, site of Copenhagen's earliest beginnings as a religious bastion back in the twelfth century. The island is still the hub of the city. The double-glazed windows of the Agency's offices afforded fine views of the nearby Christiansborg Castle – the Danish parliament building – and most of the quirky spires that punctuate the city's skyline.

I was soon set up in my own office which unfortunately didn't have a great view. It was along the corridor and past the lifts, the last office in a section that dealt with Greenland's mineral resources. In lieu of the views, its walls were hung with photographs of wild and empty landscapes, and every now and again boxes of English-language government reports on mineral prospecting in Greenland would turn up to make interesting reading. I needed it, because a few days after settling in, it became clear that there wasn't an awful lot for me to do. I had been hired to edit a report, but the report was nowhere to be seen.

This wasn't the fault of the Danes. The project was Europe-wide, and keeping a rein on contributors from all over the Continent was a thankless task. I busied myself making ready for when the report did arrive. I was shown the stationery cupboards, and I spent an enjoyable time collecting folders, file boxes, computer disks and pens in different colours, and laying them out neatly, ready for action. I had to familiarise myself with WordPerfect in Danish and spent many a frustrating hour trying to decipher Danish computer instructions like '*Fejl under initialisering af udskriftsenhed*', which might as well have said 'Your dinner is ready' for all I knew. I was fortunate that a knowledge of Danish was not required to play Minesweeper.

There was some background reading to do, of course, but I read the project's interim report and a number of other relevant documents too quickly to be a successful civil servant. Occasionally, one of my new Danish colleagues would ask me to look over the odd letter in English, or carry some boxes from one office to another, or do a bit of filing for them. These weren't exactly the jobs I had been employed to do, but they did help to pass the time. Minesweeper was getting tedious. I suggested I might draw up a schedule for completion of the project and Ole and his colleagues agreed that this was a fine idea. Again, however, my inexperience of the pace of life in a government office meant that I completed the task much too speedily. Nonetheless, everyone at the Agency agreed that the result was a significant step forward. After due consultation and minor alteration, I faxed it out across the length and breadth of Europe and all the participants agreed that it was a fine piece of work. Other than that, no one took any notice of it.

Still eager to be constructive while I waited for something solid to do, I locked myself away in my Greenland office and compiled a set of guidelines for report writing. All the contributions were to be written in English, but English was not the mother tongue for most of the contributors. My guidelines included spelling and style conventions, and a bit of basic grammar. Everyone at the Agency agreed that this was another significant step in the right direction; it was just the sort of contribution they valued. I faxed it out across the length and breadth of Europe and all the participants agreed that it was a fine piece of work. When their contributions eventually came in, no one had taken any notice of it.

Meanwhile, I had moved out of the Hotel Christian IV and into a small flat in a northern suburb known as Svanemøllen where, sadly, people appeared to have only one birthday a year. Each morning I would pull on my heavy topcoat and brave the Scandinavian elements to wait for the number 6 bus that stopped outside the SuperBrugsen supermarket. It whisked me down the long straight Østerbrogade, past the national football stadium, circled the pretty central square of Kongens Nytorv, and headed on past the Royal

Theatre where I would jump out opposite the National Bank to walk the few hundred metres to the office.

One of the definite benefits of being a writer at home in England is not having to endure the daily grind of the commuter. Participating in the ritual in a foreign country, however, is quite fun for a while. For a week or two, there is always something new to see along the route and always someone interesting to watch clamber on and off the bus. I should point out that I have also experienced the less glamorous side of foreign commuting, but I managed to find a solution to it. I once spent a prolonged period doing research in Mexico City, where the daily forty-five-minute bus ride out to the National Autonomous University always carried five times the regulation number of passengers and never allowed me the luxury of a seat. After two weeks of being crushed while hanging from a bar, I hit on the duplicitous idea of using the sling that I had brought with me in my medical kit to get some sympathy. It worked a treat, and thereafter I always got a seat. I never had to sink to such unchivalrous depths in Copenhagen since the Danish have got their public transport provisions better sorted than most.

Throughout most of my stay in Denmark, which lasted on and off for more than three months, the weather was bitterly cold. The Danes laughed when I complained. 'This isn't cold,' one of the pixies in the office informed me from behind his beard. I got the impression that this man didn't think much of the British and he had obviously decided that I was a wimp, but I ignored his comments because he was responsible for drawing up the contract I was still waiting for. It was cold as far as I was concerned. One of the iciest days was the one on which I made a mistake with the buses and also forgot to take my hat, although the two events were not related. Looking back on it, perhaps the fact that I got on the number 14 bus instead of the number 6 was a reflection of my boredom. I don't know what I was thinking of, but half an hour after boarding the bus, when I should have been about to disembark, I realised that I had been gazing out of the window at several totally unfamiliar parts of Copenhagen for most of the journey. Small though the city is, it was clear that the number 14 bus was not going to deliver me to my required destination. I had to get off, trying to look confident throughout, cross the road and board another number 14 going in the opposite direction. I rode it until something familiar appeared and was then left with an icy twenty-minute walk to work. I was an hour late arriving at the office, but they had only just finished breakfast.

My Svanemøllen flat was on the ground floor in a street called Niels W Gade's Gade after a Danish composer. The street was composed of two neat rows of terraced houses with small front gardens. When I first moved in, I had been a bit worried that the baby belonging to the couple upstairs might be of the screaming variety, but as it turned out I had more trouble with the cats living in the apartment downstairs. There wasn't really an apartment downstairs, it was just the basement containing my shower room and another large room inhabited by the cats. Every morning, when I took a shower, I would return to find a friendly feline stretched out on the living room carpet looking sultry and asking to be petted. After what I considered to be an adequate daily stroke ration, the cat would wait until it was time for me to leave to catch my bus before initiating a prolonged game of hide-and-seek to successfully delay my departure.

Not once did I hear the baby cry. Part of the reason for its unusually peaceable demeanour was, I am sure, due to the fact that it was forced to spend long periods outside in its pram in the sub-zero temperatures. Admittedly the baby was wrapped up warm, and sometimes when I returned from work in the evening the child was enjoying the company of one or two other juniors in their prams in the front garden. But I was still perturbed by behaviour that in England would undoubtedly have resulted in a visit from the social services. But the apparently neglected child's parents seemed friendly and caring enough. Perhaps it was part of an ancient Viking character-building programme? Whatever the motivations, there was no doubting the efficacy of this Danish refrigeration technique for baby-calming. Its daily sojourns with the snowdrops kept it totally silent at night.

Of greater concern to the couple upstairs was the state of my flat. The place belonged to the baby's grandmother, who wintered in Spain, and it was let through an agency. Her daughter and her daughter's partner took it in turns to knock on my door and ask whether the flat had been cleaned properly. It had as far as I was concerned, but it was not to their liking. They seemed to delight in telephoning the letting agency and venting their spleen. The apartment had a well-appointed kitchen and living room-cum-bedroom with most of the modern conveniences. The only drawback was a distinct lack of space to store clothes. I couldn't work out for the life of me where the young woman's mother kept her clothing, until it crossed my mind that she might have been a nudist.

In an attempt to learn something about the country in which I was spending a significant part of 1995, I bought a copy of the best-selling Danish novel *Miss Smilla's Feeling for Snow*, although things never quite got dull enough for me to consider finding any Kierkegaard. The heroine of the novel, Miss Smilla, is a Greenlander, and her feelings of being treated like a second-class citizen because of her immigrant status seemed at odds with the apparently liberal and free-thinking Scandinavian image. There was only one Greenlander working in the mineral resources division where I had my office so I asked her whether the impression was a fair one. She was reticent about answering my question. 'It is not easy,' she told me as we waited for the coffee machine to stop gurgling one morning in the kitchenette next door to my office. I wasn't sure whether she was referring to my enquiry or whether she was talking about her life in Denmark. She kept glancing at the door, looking worried in case someone appeared through it. 'Everyone at the office is very friendly,' she continued carefully, and then stopped. Someone had appeared in the doorway, looking for coffee. As I was to learn later in my travels, immigrants had their difficulties in Sweden and Finland too.

It is curious to note, in this day and age, that Denmark retains huge overseas territories. All the other European countries have given back most of their empires, yet Denmark still has Greenland and the Faroe Islands. Greenland is nearly fifty times larger than Denmark and is almost the size of the entire European Union itself. Territorially this makes the Danes the rulers of probably the largest empire in the world today. But of course most of it is ice and hardly anybody lives there, so no one really takes much notice.

In practice, both overseas territories enjoy a considerable degree of autonomy, hence the fact that both have opted not to join the European Union, but there is no doubting the occasional tensions between the ruler and the ruled. When I was in Copenhagen, there was some bad feeling between Denmark and the Faroe Islands. The Faroes have a lot of fish and not much else, so when they have trouble selling them, Denmark comes to the rescue. According to many Danes I spoke to, the Faroe Islands were bankrupt. They had spent a lot of money on expensive infrastructure that they now couldn't pay for. Worse still, some of the grand projects had spawned unexpected and not entirely beneficial consequences. Several people told me stories of smart new tarmac roads being constructed through mountains and across ravines to remote settlements with just a handful of people. When the road arrived at Bumblehick, the ten people who lived there got into their station wagons and drove to the nearest town. When they arrived, they liked it so much that they never went back, and Bumblehick became the best-connected ghost town in Europe.

Iceland also used to belong to Denmark, until she declared independence towards the end of World War II. I read somewhere that the Nazis invaded Denmark by telegram. Having signalled their intentions, they occupied the country very early in the morning when the Danes were still asleep, a pretty mean trick. They didn't meet with much resistance, a fact that still seems to embarrass some Danes when they think about it. In fairness, however, this was largely a reflection of Danish physical geography. Denmark is a very flat country – its highest point is just 171 metres or 561 feet; even the Netherlands has a higher peak – which makes it a great place for cyclists but virtually useless for guerrilla warfare. When the Icelanders heard that Denmark had been invaded, they realised that they had been pushed around for centuries by a bunch of weeds, so they went their own way in 1944.

All this recent history, combined with the peaceable and law-abiding reality of today's Danes, made me wonder what had happened to that Viking spirit. A thousand years ago, the country's main exports to the rest of Europe were fear and mayhem. Today they are better known for strips of dead pig and little plastic bricks. And perhaps a few footballers. So where were the twentieth-century counterparts of the raiders and looters, the fearless descendants of the rape and pillage brigade who had terrorised the early Brits? Their demise did not appear to be a recent phenomenon. In the eighteenth century, Middleton noted that despite their 'apoplexies and epilepsies', which could be put down to hard drinking and low living,

Danes had already lost that wild edge; 'the modern Danes,' he wrote, 'are not those imaginary and ferocious people their ancestors were; who were ashamed of dying in their beds.' Gone were the days when Danes liked nothing better than a savage conflict, followed by a few celebratory beers drunk from the skulls of their enemies.

When I consulted Ole on the matter, he gave me a convincing explanation. The Vikings had left their unsociable genes in Britain, he said. 'They have all become English football supporters,' he told me with a wry smile. But my interest in the conundrum was rekindled when I heard that the Viking era has been reappraised by some modern historians. Far from being terrifying vanguards of a new era of medieval warfare who revelled in the large-scale slaughter of innocents, these academics suggest that the Vikings sailed out of the north armed to the teeth with nothing more sinister than a few Norse handicrafts and some novel ideas on agricultural innovation. Apparently, there isn't actually much evidence of the infamous Viking attack on the Northumbrian monastery of Lindisfarne in 793, and much of the fabric of the Viking holocaust story was invented by Christian propagandists and Victorian dreamers. The Vikings were more blue rinses than Blue Beards. When they turned up on the English coast, their mission wasn't to kick ass and cut throat but to weave basket and till ground.

Needless to say, not all authorities agree with this revisionist view, but if the Vikings really were nice guys it would explain a lot about how the Danes are now.

As the lack of significant action continued at work, I occupied myself establishing a domestic routine based on shopping therapy. I became a regular customer at the food hall in Illum – Copenhagen's equivalent of Harrods – buying luxury greedy-bastard dinners-for-one. I sampled every type of pickled herring and bought a Danish cookbook. Other than the Scandinavian staple of meatballs, the Danes seemed to be keen on pork, birds and fish, but to my disappointment I was never able to try out the most interesting-sounding recipe. It was for rooks in cream, but rooks were not in season. I thought about trying it out anyway, using the pussycats from the apartment below as a substitute, but it never quite came to that.

I went to the cinema and hung out in bars, checked out a few conventional museums, but was disappointed to note that Legoland was closed for the winter. I ascended Christian IV's Round Tower, Europe's oldest functioning astronomical observatory, and strolled the rococo courtyard of the Amalienborg Palace. I browsed the Danish tourist literature for other notable sights. There was a Louis Tussaud's wax museum (not Madame's as in London), a Guinness World of Records Museum, and an offshoot of a US institution called Ripley's Believe It or Not Museum. The latter offered such bizarre spectacles as the incredible light man – with a candle in a hole in his head, a six-legged calf, and an idiot called Charlie who could whistle with three balls in his mouth. (So what? I thought to myself.) I needed to visit this museum like I needed to mimic the incredible light man.

One Saturday I went in search of perhaps the best-known of Copenhagen's landmarks. I caught the bus to Østerport station, a distinctive building with a façade like one of the Louvre's glass pyramids, and ventured out towards the harbour and into a monsoonal downpour. I had been warned by a colleague at the Agency not to get too excited by the prospect of seeing the Little Mermaid. In an appropriately understated fashion, Iben had said that it was 'really quite disappointing'. It was also hard to find, especially since I had not brought my street map. I spotted a line of schoolchildren trotting through the nearby park and decided to tail them, but I gave up on the idea when they reached a car park and boarded a coach. I was already decidedly wet, but stuck to my guns, figuring that perhaps the school group had just returned from the statue. I retraced my steps and stopped a man sheltering his video camera from the rain. He turned out to be French, and didn't speak a word of English. I couldn't think of the French word for mermaid, so I carried on.

I was in the grounds of some kind of ancient fortification, surrounded by moats, and apparently nowhere near the harbour. Large, ice-cooled droplets trickled down my neck as I took stock. My shoes were sodden, my hair matted and the raindrops on my glasses allowed me to see everything as if through a kaleidoscope. Fourteen Japanese women appeared from behind a tree. I smiled. Simultaneously, they all put their noses into their guidebooks. This was my chance. I wiped my spectacles with my damp scarf and all fourteen women merged into one. The woman knew what I was going to ask immediately and gave me detailed instructions in English on the route she advised. She smiled and almost gave me a curtsy, then said finally, 'Not big, small.' I set off squelching in the direction she had recommended.

I followed a path round the moat and reached the harbour. And then I saw it, down below me, at the water's edge. The Little Mermaid was a diminutive bronze woman, perched on a boulder, gazing nonchalantly out at the gasworks across the water, perhaps in search of pickled herrings. If I'd been a Hans Christian Andersen groupie this might have been a moving moment. As it was, all I felt was a damp sense of disappointment. Like Denmark, the woman in the statue looked small, calm and really rather dull. I had been warned.

I was loath to admit it, but I was not enjoying Denmark. This worried me. I suppose it must be every travel writer's worst nightmare to be offered the chance to live in a foreign country and then be bored by it. But like the bad workman who blames his tools, I rather thought the problem might be my own. Could Denmark really be just a tedious little country, or had I lost the urge to visit new places? It looked suspiciously like mid-life crisis territory to me. Here I was, thirtysomething and supposedly in my prime. Had I missed my vocation? Should I give it all up to raise sheep in Wales, or had I just eaten too many pickled herrings? Never one to shrink from a challenge, I drank too much to forget about it.

Then my girlfriend came to see me and we avoided the issue by catching a train to Lithuania for Easter. On the way, we nearly got arrested on a trumped-up fare-dodging charge on a bus in Warsaw. Coming home, she almost suffered the same fate at the Belorussian border. She was so grateful to be back in Copenhagen that I saw the place in a new light. I was determined to give Denmark a chance.

I made some excursions out of the capital. Even when you venture beyond the city boundaries, the countryside looks spick and span. The fields were ploughed neatly, the thatch on the country cottages lovingly groomed and the whole flat landscape was dotted with graceful wind turbines. Despite the national penchant for the creatures, I didn't see a single pig. Most of them are kept inside, probably because they would have spoilt the rural scenery. What I did see everywhere I went was the red and white Danish flag fluttering atop a myriad of flagpoles. In this respect, Denmark turned out to be the most nationalistic country I visited in the European Union.

I caught the train up the coast of Zealand and visited Hamlet's castle at Helsingør, an impressive pile on the north side of a small bay. Beneath its verdigris roof the castle was dark and brooding. Unfortunately, it was also covered in scaffolding. Perhaps Hamlet did a bit of DIY in his spare time. In a nearby church the floor was covered by an art installation consisting of hundreds of shoes all painted red. Ole took me on a sortie to a garage in a place called Snaketown. Now that the last of the snow and ice had gone from the roads, he had the winter studs taken out of his car tyres.

In Copenhagen too I came to appreciate what was on offer. Spring had sprung, and I couldn't help but be inspired by the carpet of crocuses that appeared from the remnants of winter in front of Rosenborg Castle. I also discovered that there was a rebellious side to the Danish character. It was all in one place, called Christiania, a free-living alternative community a kilometre from the parliament building as the rook flies.

Since it was set up in the early 1970s, the commune has been constantly in and out of the headlines. To its detractors, Christiania was a haven for junkies and drop-outs who don't pay their taxes, but to its supporters it was an ecologically oriented, self-governing social experiment. If you can imagine *Passport to Pimlico* with Stanley Holloway playing a macrobiotic anarchist who smokes marijuana you'd get the idea. But having started out as an act of rebellion against all things conventional, the community has now become institutionalised. The collective claims to be against the concept of taxes but residents and workshops have to pay fees to collective funds, which sounds very much like taxation to me. Christiania has no laws because that's the whole point, but it has bans instead, though admittedly few of them. And whilst the place has become virtually a contradiction in terms, a sort of organised anarchy, it has also provided the Danish government with an impossible quandary. For the establishment it is an awkward example of the liberal paradox in action: they would like to send in the bulldozers, but they can't quite bring themselves to do it.

The afternoon I visited Christiania, I was almost relieved to see that there was an insalubrious side to Copenhagen. The streets were just dirt tracks, the buildings looked semi-derelict and the one bar I ventured into had an atmosphere so thick with marijuana smoke that you could hardly see any of the beards. But although Christiania had many of the hallmarks of inner city decay it still managed to be cute. It looked like Trumpton with graffiti.

Just as I thought there was no hope, things started warming up in the office. Ole was a good man to work with. He was calm and methodical and he had a dry sense of humour. The only hitch was his tendency to lose things. This wasn't his fault, it was because he had been issued with a desk that had an exceptional affinity for pieces of paper. It attracted paper from all over Denmark which became absorbed into its fabric. For the purposes of recycling, Danish citizens are obliged to sort their household refuse and Ole's office looked like the collection point for the entire country's waste paper output. The only problem was that some of it wasn't waste. Important communiqués and faxes would disappear for days, draft reports would suddenly surface after weeks in the bureaucratic wilderness, my contract went missing for more than a month. But you could never blame Ole, he was an innocent abroad, a victim of his extraordinary desk.

Slowly, the report I was working on started to come together. Contributions began to appear and at last I could get down to the job I had been hired for. Everything was behind schedule so we began working into the evenings and I no longer had time to play with the cats in the morning. The study was being conducted for the European Commission in Brussels. The brief was to assess the options for improving energy efficiency in washing apparatus and to advise Brussels on how best to achieve their aims. My job was to polish the English and make sure none of the sections contradicted each other. In the wider perspective, the project was just one small cog in the machinery set up to reduce Europe's emissions of carbon dioxide, that innocent little gas that the planet can't do without but which we in society have become too good at producing. In a small way, all this labour on washing machines would help to slow the overheating of the earth's atmosphere through the workings of the greenhouse effect. That was the ultimate driving force, but when you got down into the nitty gritty, there were rather more complex agendas at work.

The Danes were in charge because the Danes are pretty keen on being green. When it comes to being environmentally friendly, they have advanced further than most of their European cousins and they are eager to spread the word. In Britain we may have started recycling aluminium drinks cans, but in Denmark you can't buy them in the first place. They're illegal. All beverages are sold in reusable bottles instead. Elsewhere in Europe, and in many other parts of the world, lentil-eating rabble-rousers say that ultimately the world's environmental problems can only be solved if the SLOBs (selfish, loose-living, overindulgent bastards) in Europe take a cut in living standards. In Denmark, this is what the *politicians* say.

There are other fields in which Denmark seems to lead where others follow. As well as being environmentally friendly and peace-loving (when was the last time Denmark went to war? Probably those Vikings), she was one of the first countries to establish a welfare system (in the 1930s), and *the* first to allow registered partnerships between homosexual couples, effectively granting them the same legal rights as their heterosexual counterparts. In many ways, Denmark looked to me like the California of Europe: what happens there today happens elsewhere on the Continent tomorrow.

There was no doubt that the Danes are committed Europeans, although their attitude appears to be tempered somewhat by their ambivalent disposition towards Germany. They also weren't exactly bowled over by everything that came out of Brussels. One day in the canteen, over a typical lunch of open sandwiches, the director of the Energy Agency told me that the Commission had decreed that there was only one type of cheese that was properly Danish. He said it with a wry smile, but I think he was quite upset.

These were the sorts of European issues that most concerned the Continent's ordinary citizens. In the UK the national press regularly carried stories about threats from Brussels to some of our most hallowed institutions, like the sausage, the bulldog and even the prawn-cocktail flavoured crisp. As I was to learn later, some of these threats were real, others less so. But it was curious how often cheese figured in these debates. At home we had fought for a European patent on Somerset cheddar, and the Dutch likewise for Gouda. The French, of course, have always been obsessed with fromage. It was Charles de Gaulle who observed that a country with 265 kinds of cheese could only be united under the threat of danger. In a continent with more cheeses than motorways, this didn't augur particularly well for European unity by consensus. Unless you counted Brussels as the threat. But unsavoury as it might seem, this appeared to be what was happening. Nearly a year later, when I visited Greece, the banner headline in the *Hellenic Times* read 'Greek Victory of Feta Cheese Finalized'. The story related to the European Commission's agreement to grant Greece the exclusive right to use the name feta for that flaky white goat's-milk cheese. Greek feta had been under threat from cheap imitations, most of them made in Denmark as it happened. When I read the story, I smiled with satisfaction. I'd been racking my brains to think of something that Denmark had in common with Greece.

As the energy efficiency project continued, a meeting was called to assess the progress of the report. I caught a plane to Dublin with Ole. For two days we hammered our way through the intricacies of washing machines, dishwashers and driers. But soon after we started my mind began to wander. I was already planning my next sortie into the brave new world of the European Union.

2

A Mouse and Two Rats

The summer of 1995 was the summer of the bomb. While the French government was detonating harmless explosive devices of the atomic variety in the South Pacific, an irresponsible group of anarchists was letting off dangerous bombs in Paris and elsewhere on the French mainland.

With a bewildering lack of delicacy, France had chosen the fiftieth anniversary of the dropping of the atom bombs on Japan to announce a little round of nuclear testing. Most of the rest of the civilised world threw up their arms in horror which did not deter the French, though it probably hurt their egos a bit. They pretended not to understand what the outcry was about and thought it was just because no one liked French people. These tests were quite safe, they kept emphasising. Newspaper satirists across the globe had a field day. One Australian cartoon reproduced in the pages of *Libération* showed a mock postcard of a beach in the South of France above the caption: 'If it's so safe and pure, test it on the Côte d'Azur.' Francophobic rent-a-mobs turned out to throw tomatoes at French representations all over the world, but back home in France no one cared very much. Part of the reason for this was the domestic *'psycho de bomb'*, a bomb psychology that they had been forced to adopt because some group, thought to be Algerian, was in the midst of its own bombing programme. Only this one wasn't experimental. They had graduated to killing people outside the Arc de Triomphe.

None of this interested the young French woman who sat next to me in coach 16 on the 12.53 from Waterloo. I was just contemplating why it was that Eurostar had decided to put carpet on the ceiling of the carriage as well as the floor, when she struck up a conversation, seemingly with the main aim of informing me how awful English food was. Marina had been working as an au pair in Rickmansworth and had suffered six months of culinary abuse. It was the first thing she said when I asked her how she had enjoyed her stay: 'Oh, your English cooking – terrible.' (Marina was the complete antithesis of a French au pair – short and stumpy, glasses, no dress sense and very bad breath – but the way she said 'terrible' was still enough to make most Englishmen go weak at the knees.) The broccoli was never cooked properly, the petit pois were still in their cases, there were chips with everything and the stews were just appalling, which was unfortunate because stew was the only respite she got from being force-fed Marks and Spencer's chicken. But she was beginning to feel better now that she was on board a French train and the schoolboy French announcements emanating from the swish glass terminal at Waterloo had given way to the real thing here in the TGV-style carriage.

As we passed through Sydenham Hill, she began to give me details of the dinner she was looking forward to in Brittany, but my attention had been diverted by an official-looking figure in a smart blazer and yellow and blue stripy tie making his way down the compartment. I thought he must be a ticket inspector, but he was simply smiling at all the passengers in the sort of reassuring way that immediately makes you think that something is wrong. When he got close enough for me to read his lapel badge, my mind was put at rest. He was only the driver.

All the talk of food had made me hungry. Marina wisely decided to avoid the restaurant car, because it was run by a British caterer. I could tell this immediately, because the unappetising photographs of the plastic food they served were already cock-eyed in their frames behind the man at the counter and they had run out of cheese and tomato sandwiches. I returned to my seat, carrying my very own yellow Eurostar presentation paper bag, in time for the announcement that we were about to enter the tunnel. Some wag had left the old warning signs for oncoming steam trains beside the multitude of tracks leading into the hole in the wall and we were told to put our watches forward as we disappeared into it.

It was an odd sensation, because we didn't appear to be going anywhere. I did have to pop my ears, but now that the scenery had gone, the smooth ride gave very little sense of movement. There was just the odd light flashing by and a sound that was distressingly reminiscent of the surging of the sea.

Twenty minutes later the countryside returned. This time it was French. Marina perked up noticeably and began an in-depth critique of the fish finger, a food article she had not come across before, but one held in high esteem by English five-year-olds. The monologue was becoming rather tedious, so I was relieved when her topic of conversation changed on hearing an announcement over the tannoy that we were now travelling at top speed: 300 kilometres per hour, or 186 miles per hour if you are British.

'Your English trains are so slow,' she said with some self-satisfaction, 'and bumpy also.' I couldn't argue with her because she was right, and it didn't seem appropriate to launch into a discourse on the comparative sizes of government railway subsidies. I just nodded.

Marina asked me what I was proposing to do with my time in Paris so I gave her a brief run-down of the sights I was intending to visit. Top of my list was Euro Disney, a must for a modern-day Grand Tour I thought. The North American cultural invasion of Europe was everywhere to see, but I thought I'd zero in on the most blatant example. I was also interested to know how the French had dealt with Mickey Mouse and his friends. I was confidently expecting to be shown around by a Disneyfied onion seller on a bicycle. Marina thought a visit to Euro Disney was a very good idea, it was on her 'must see' list too, but she looked shocked when I told her that I would be going along on my own.

'You don't have any children you can take?' she asked, looking sideways at my bag as if I might have a couple of fold-up kids stashed inside for emergencies.

'Perhaps I can hire one for the day?' I said, a suggestion she took seriously.

'Oh I don't think so,' she replied, and she was right again, a regrettable oversight on the part of the Disneyland authorities I thought later.

Marina's giggles rang in my ears the next morning on the RER train that took me east out of Paris towards the Euro Disney site. I must say that this aspect of my visit had worried me. The thought of wandering alone around a complex designed, so I thought, specifically for the younger generation conjured up visions of being tailed by Disney security staff, probably dressed as Deputy Dawg, and being asked to leave should I so much as wink at a passing minor. But my concern was unfounded. Children were by no means obligatory accessories (later I discovered that three-quarters of all visitors to the US Disney parks are over eighteen), and although not commonplace, I was not the only lone visitor.

Or I should say that I was not the only lone 'guest', because that is what you are in Disneyspeak. Before my visit, I was amazed to learn of the lengths to which the Disney authorities had gone to promote the atmosphere of happy entertainment. Hence, in the Disneyland version of the English language, visitors were 'guests' while employees were 'cast members', queues were 'pre-entertainment areas' and shops 'retail entertainment centers'. But it is appropriate enough, when you think about it, that a place like Disneyland has developed its own language, because entering Disneyland is like entering another country. You need a Disneyland passport for a start, and they search your bags as you go in, just in case you attempt to smuggle your own food or drink into the country. There is a list of important information prominently displayed at passport control that tells you, among other things, that pets are not permitted in the theme park and that suitable dress is required: 'Shoes and shirts must be worn at all times,' although strangely it says nothing about trousers and skirts.

Once you're inside, the first thing that strikes you about Disney-land Paris is that you are no longer in France, because nowhere in France could be so pink. The mock southern-belle style buildings along Main Street, USA, are all a ghastly shade of sickly lobster, and even the pavements are pink. But it's clean and it's bright and it's happy because you've entered a fantasy film set where there is no litter or graffiti, where all the cast members are slim and use deodorant. The females all wear appropriate underwear (or so I'm told) and all the males are clean-shaven, have short hair and no visible tattoos. It is the Disney Corporation's idea of what the world ought to be like, and after just a few hours inside the compound you begin to understand why the US produces so many homicidal maniacs.

So I spent my first day on continental Europe wandering the plastic, alcohol-free world of make-believe, forever dodging in and out of somebody's video shot, marvelling at the imitation rock formations in concrete and reinforced polystyrene, admiring the topiary animals and the larger than life 'real-life' Disney characters signing autographs for their spellbound junior admirers. Besides

Main Street, USA, there are four other 'lands', each with their own attractions, entertainment, restaurants and shops. Everything is themed, so that on Main Street, USA, the cast members were kitted out in grey capes and turn-of-the-century small-town American gear, while tan-coloured Indiana Jones outfits were standard issue in Adventureland. Sadly, however, pedal-powered onion sellers were conspicuous by their absence. Old-style riverboats plied the waters of Frontierland, you could take a trip to Never Land aboard a flying galleon in Fantasyland, and be piloted through the galaxy by delinquent robots in Discoveryland. And of course the renowned mouse partnership was available in appropriate settings to guide you through a bewildering variety of retail entertainment. Inside the realistic Western General Store, Trading Post and Mining Supplies outlet, Mini modelled the latest in fetching imitation-leather squaw gear, sporting a single feather in her headband. And then, as if by magic, there she was again in veil and harem trousers to introduce you to her Scheherazade Collection inside the Adventureland Bazaar while Mickey looked on, counting your money from beneath a fez set at a jaunty angle.

Restaurants too were themed. After riding Le Temple du Péril, a one-minute high-speed thrill adventure through an archaeological excavation, unfortunately preceded by the slightly less thrilling forty-five-minute Indiana Jones Queue of Terminal Boredom, I made my way to the Restaurant Hakuna Matata, which boasted 'flavorful meat dishes and salads in an African setting'. The restaurant was 'hosted', as they say in Disneyspeak, by Maggi, the US conglomerate that makes a peculiarly tasteless form of mustard and those packet soups you always see on dusty Spanish supermarket shelves. Seemingly, they also produce numerous other substances designed to be eaten, few of which appear to contain organic material. Their African setting was certainly impressive, a mock-up of a West African mud-brick building complete with wooden pegs which adorned the upper portions of the choc-ice-shaped towers, but unfortunately Maggi's ideas men seemed to have run out of inspiration when it came to African cuisine. No doubt after extensive research, Maggi's representation of an entire continent's culinary highlights amounted to such traditional African delicacies as chicken nuggets, turkey thighs in BBQ sauce and a particularly plastic-looking 'salade chef'. But thankfully the effort to be authentically African did not end there: a real live black person was also on hand to push your chairs in under the wooden table after you had left.

Yes indeed, everything within Disneyland's control was themed, and it came as a minor relief to note that the sparrows did not fly in wearing Dumbo outfits. Everything, that is, except the toilets, because once you've passed the symbol of a man wearing a serape in Frontierland you could be in the same restroom as the one that lies behind the man in the fez in the Adventureland bazaar (I tell a lie, they resisted the temptation to be culturally offensive in the bazaar, there was no fez). This was a disappointment, and an opportunity missed I thought. I wanted to be overpowered by a wall of urinal stench as I passed that serape symbol, and piss in a real Mexican toilet surrounded by flies, or squat down over an evil-smelling hole in the ground behind the bazaar next to a cardboard cut-out of a straining Middle Eastern gentleman. Discoveryland could have had a weightless urinal where you slash on the ceiling, or space suits instead of cubicles which you put on to feel your own excrement warming your legs. The possibilities are endless once you get into the spirit of it; Fantasyland should have been equipped with bathroom fixtures shaped like the Mad Hatter's teacups while Indiana Jones hats could have served the same purpose in Adventureland, but like good clean-cut Americans the Disney Imagineers had stopped at the restroom thresholds.

One thing about the toilets was clear, however. They weren't French. Most French public loos are holes in the ground that you squat over, but this wasn't the sort of behaviour that Disney encouraged. In fact, the more I saw of Euro Disney the more puzzled I became about why it was there at all. Why should the French, so proud and defensive of their national culture, allow this wholesale importation of tacky foreign influence into their hallowed national space? Admittedly, the Disneyland theme park had simply displaced 56 hectares of beetroot fields, but you wouldn't have to be the most xenophobic of Frenchmen to believe that a Gallic beetroot is culturally more valuable than Mickey Mouse and his entourage. The French have even taken the subtle step of changing the theme park's name, from Euro Disney to Disneyland Paris, in an effort to stamp their identity on the place. Several of the non-US attractions were notably French, although they pretended to be European, but still in a Disney sort of way. None more so than Le Visionarium, in which a retarded robot takes you and French novelist Jules Verne on a simulated whistle-stop tour through the centuries in what the guest guidebook described as a 'tribute to the people and heritage of France and Europe'. The tribute was pretty backhanded in most cases. For their British Eurocousins, it consisted of a brief meeting with H. G. Wells, portrayed as a bumbling idiot complete with upper-class twit's accent.

You had to hand it to them though, since for most of the five senses, Disneyland was expert at suspending belief and whisking you away into its own sanitised fabricated reality. If ever we start colonising other planets you can be sure that Disney experts will be on hand to help create familiar living environments in extraterrestrial locations. Appropriate then that when I wandered over to Discoveryland I came upon a special space festival in which real superpower intergalactic equipment had been assembled inside the futuristic Café Hyperion, hosted by Coca-Cola. When I say 'superpower' the emphasis was very much on the USA and the former USSR. We Europeans have never really got it together to be a major force in space exploration. The park's designers even had the previously secret prototype Soviet lunar lander on display among a plethora of rocket launchers, landing modules and space suits. The Soviet machine had never been used, of course, and Disney couldn't resist a dig at the old enemy: 'In the light of the obvious progress made by the United States with the manned exploration of the moon, the Soviet lunar programme was suspended in 1974 as it no longer met the political objectives set out by the USSR government.' And once you had marvelled at human ingenuity over your hamburger and fizzy brown soft drink, it was just a short walk to Space Mountain where you too could travel from the Earth to the Moon courtesy of the Disney Corporation. The ride is a sexy big dipper with a few crashes and bangs thrown in: catapulted propulsion in a cannon at a 32° angle with three complete loops in the dark (a 360° loop, a corkscrew and a 180° horseshoe) accompanied by sophisticated eight-speaker, on-board sound synchronised with the ride circuit.

Should you, however, be an expectant mother, a child under the age of ten, or a dwarf measuring less than 1.40 metres in height, do not despair, because instead of Space Mountain you can still experience the thrills of space travel courtesy of Kodak, with a little help from George Lucas and Francis Ford Coppola. And what better

host to take you through the three-dimensional cinematic extrava-
ganza than the ultimate cross between reality and fabrication:
Michael Jackson. Yes, Monsieur Jackson, perhaps the epitome of
child-friendly superstars, is top of the bill in his very own space
adventure, as 'Captain EO' who pilots a space ship crewed by
educationally subnormal intergalactic cuddly toys. Needless to say,
the adventure is a thinly veiled excuse for the captain to dance, sing
a song and change the world (for the better).

As the day wore on, however, the extraordinary mix of fantasy and
reality became disorientating. I wasn't in France, I wasn't in Europe,
and I wasn't even really in the USA. I also wasn't sure what was real
and what was make-believe. Every gust of wind or rustling leaf had
me looking for the hidden motor or secreted fan. Was it a real live
horse pulling that streetcar or an automated replica? I sat down
beside a grassy bank near the Lucky Nugget Saloon, twangy Country
and Western music emanating from hidden loudspeakers in the
flowerbed behind me, to drink a coffee. It felt hot and looked black
and even smelt like real coffee, but when I took my first sip it became
clear that this was as far as the resemblance to the real thing
extended.

Somehow the suspended reality became sinister and even potentially dangerous. The candyfloss-pink buildings on Main Street
looked almost good enough to eat, and may well have been more
nourishing than the Maggi fare served up in the Restaurant Hakuna
Matata. But it struck me that if you suffered a heart attack in
Frontierland, or spontaneously ignited in Adventureland, the only
attention you'd receive would be from a dozen dads wielding their
camcorders and their numerous children shoving Disney autograph
books up your nose. I suppose at least you would expire on camera in
an instant of fame entirely in keeping with the late twentieth-
century theme park. When I eventually left the park and made my
way along the pink brick road to the Marne-la-Vallée-Chessy RER
station I had to pinch myself to make sure I took the police cordon
seriously. These were real French gendarmes, not authentic Disneyland replicas, and presumably the bomb-scare which had closed the
station was real too.

As I waited patiently with a growing crowd of disoriented Disney
victims, I mulled over another distinctly non-French thing about
Disneyland Paris: the fact that all the cast members have to be able

to speak English. This must have irked to begin with, until French cast members realised that just because they can speak English doesn't necessarily mean that they do. On several occasions I'm sure I baffled numerous Gallic members of the cast by beaming with a sigh of relief when my pointedly English questions as to the whereabouts of certain attractions were met with withering looks along the full length of the nose and a response in the vernacular. Indeed, from this visit, it appeared that Disneyland Paris had become the haven for all those sneering *garçons* and other public servants for which France, and Paris in particular, had formerly been so famous. I had been rather looking forward to eating snails and horsemeat under the disdainful eye of a Parisian *garçon*, but to my disappointment all the ones I came across were friendly and accommodating. It seems that the national campaign to clean up the public arrogance act (in response to the results of a survey that showed foreign visitors to France liked everything about the place except the fact that it was full of arrogant French people) had worked. It hadn't been applied in the Disney domain simply because Disneyland Paris is not France.

How things have changed. Back in the eighteenth century, French was the lingua franca for the Continent's genteel classes and Paris was a must for the Grand Tourists because France was universally admired as the centre of all that was refined in Europe. This annoyed a lot of Englishmen, of course. In his *Complete System of Geography*, Middleton was determined to 'point out the absurdity of that over-fondness which too many of our countrymen entertain for France and French fashions'. His attitude was essentially similar to that found in many British people today. France was a place to be made fun of, but the jest was mixed with a definite undercurrent of reluctant admiration. French people all had acne, Middleton suggested, hence their nascent cosmetics industry; it explained their 'nauseous custom' of face-painting. They were also conceited. 'Vanity is their predominant character,' he declared, 'and they are perhaps the only people ever heard of who have derived great utility from a national weakness. It supports them under misfortunes, and impels them to actions to which true courage inspires other nations.'

Although Middleton considered the French to be well mannered rather than well bred, he did admire their system of justice which often meant instant execution for any of the common people bold enough to steal or commit a similar outrage. This was one of the main areas in which Paris outflanked London, according to Middleton's book, although he did concede that the Louvre never failed to compare to the palace of St James's and that the Jardin des Tuileries was 'esteemed the finest in Europe'.

The Louvre was at the top of most eighteenth-century visitors' lists of things to see, and since it is still reckoned to be the 'chief ornament of the city', that is where I started my more classical itinerary back in real-life Paris. I have been there numerous times, but I have to admit that I'd never actually been inside before. I had often strolled the formal Tuileries, but just the sight of the forbidding royal palace was always enough to put me off ever crossing its threshold. The last time I was in Paris I spent quite some time taking photographs of the decaying statues outside for a book about environmental issues that I was working on. With umpteen acid-rain damaged sculptures to photograph, I didn't have time to step inside and see any of its hundreds of thousands of less flawed works of art. But this time I could avoid it no longer, it was the inside I had to see, and fortunately now that you can enter underground, straight from the Métro station, I could avoid casting my eyes over the sheer size of the place which had always deterred me before.

Everyone has to be circumspect in the Louvre. It's impossible to see it all in one sitting, so I went straight for its most prized possessions. To my surprise, there was nobody around when the *Mona Lisa* hove into view. I thought maybe I'd got the wrong room. But no, there it was, smaller than expected, and when I came to examine it, a bit disappointing. Leonardo da Vinci may have been a brilliant, truly Renaissance man, but he couldn't paint hands. I suppose everyone is too busy trying to decide for themselves whether or not she is smiling to notice, but her hands, which were painted seven times apparently, are fat and podgy. As the first tour group marched towards me, I stepped back and took up position on a grotty flesh-coloured sofa to observe the observers observing. Rapidly spoken set-piece potted art critiques in a dozen languages followed as weary rubber necks took turns to photograph each other in front of the world's most famous enigmatic smirk, virtually all with flash attachments and completely oblivious to the strongly worded request against such action on the wall next to the painting. No one seemed to care that in snapping their very own version of the woman they were all contributing to her gradual disappearance. Least of all the young attendant sitting opposite who looked supremely bored as she chewed her nails. And after a while I realised that very few people were actually looking at the picture, other than to make sure they had it in their viewfinder. As long as they had the photographic proof of their visit, that seemed to be sufficient. I suppose they could study the actual painting for as long as they liked once they were back home. And the more I sat, and the more I looked, and the more I heard of the potted histories from the passing tour guides, the less I understood what all the fuss was about. It's heretical to say so, but why is it that this painting of nobody in particular, with fat hands and no eyebrows, which is actually only the central bit of a larger canvas that has been vandalised, so famous? The Louvre is full of nice pictures. I felt quite sorry for the adjacent Guido Reni cartoons of naked strapping young lads grappling with manly tasks. During the thirty minutes that I sat watching, when several hundred people must have passed, not one stopped to look at them.

The *Venus de Milo* was more like it. Its setting was better for a start, at the end of a long marble corridor so that you could approach it from a distance. Of course it was just as mobbed by amateur paparazzi as the *Mona Lisa*, along with the usual endless succession of interesting visible objects waved by tour leaders to keep their groups from straying. Most of them were Japanese, who favoured fans and broken-off car aerials with small flags attached to their tops, although I didn't understand why they bothered because every Japanese group huddled tightly behind their leader to give the impression that Japan is a nation populated entirely by teacher's pets. British groups were usually led by a man in old clothes waving a tattered book whilst their North American counterparts had graduated beyond such behaviour because all their group members wore silly red baseball caps. The customary worldliness of US citizens was summed up by one middle-aged gentleman who took up position next to me with his Nikon and waited for ten minutes before using it because, as he explained to his wife, he was 'trying to get a shot that isn't full of Chinese people'.

The Louvre, like many large museums, is a soporific and very tiring place, and it was with some relief that I exited through the extraordinary glass pyramid that Monsieur Mitterand had decided ought to be placed in the Cour Napoléon for no apparent reason other than to remember him by. French presidents are like that, they all want to leave behind some great monument, a *grand projet*, for posterity. They are vying for a place in history to rival that of Napoleon, perhaps the most pompous of all in a nation which has had more than its fair share of conceited individuals. Of course, Napoleon did have more reason to be pompous than most. Fortunately, his form of do-it-yourself European union was ultimately his downfall, but two hundred years later he's still getting his kilo of flesh. The 'nation of shopkeepers' across the Channel has been baffled by his system of metrication ever since its imposition. (I can cope with most metric measurements now, despite starting out in life with furlongs and quarts. But my one remaining blind spot is people's height, and I'm afraid it's too late to change that. To me, a six-footer will never be 1.83 metres tall.)

As I made my way across the Seine towards the Invalides, where Napoleon lies in his undoubtably metric tomb, the innumerable public notices beside the lawns reminded me of another minor French deity, perhaps the best way to describe their curious attitude to grass. In France, it is 'forbidden' and 'non accessible' according to the small plaques designed for idiot foreigners from countries where they think that grass is for walking on and sitting on and eating picnics on. The one abiding memory of my very first adventure overseas, a trip across the Channel from junior school in Southampton, is the shocking rebuke I received when I bounded on to a manicured lawn in a public park in Le Havre. As soon as I took a step off the footpath, alarm bells rang in the heads of my teacher and no fewer than three park officials, resulting in a hail of horrified shouts that rained down on me from all directions. Until that moment, I had been coping well with France. OK, the buildings looked a bit different, the food was a bit funny, and no one spoke English, but otherwise abroad wasn't that exotic. But in an instant I suddenly realised that I really was in a foreign land. The French have gravel and dirt for walking on. Grass is for looking at.

Napoleon probably issued a decree about it. He did on most other matters. It may have been one of the things he was referring to when he said, 'Wherever the shadow of my rule has fallen, it has left lasting traces of its value.' This is just one of the many modest statements from the great man that are inscribed on the wall encircling his red porphyry sarcophagus, situated in a hole in the ground inside the Eglise du Dôme. Surrounded by puffed admirers, Napoleon sits in numerous friezes posing as a Roman emperor pointing towards lists of his great feats. How appropriate it must have been that when his remains were returned to France in 1840, from the ignoble and British island of Saint Helena, Paris was engulfed by a swirling snowstorm as the stately chariot passed beneath the Arc de Triomphe (one of the great feats) and on down the Champs Elysées.

That evening, I thought I would follow the Triumphal Way, from the Arc de Triomphe towards the Place de la Concorde, and soak up a bit of Parisian atmosphere on my way to a rendezvous with an old friend who worked on the rue du Faubourg St Honoré. Paris is rightly renowned for its beautiful boulevards and beautiful women, and the delicate yet unmistakable fragrance of eau de dog shit that hangs in the air of virtually every street. This is unfortunate, because if you're not used to it, the smell spoils the ambience somewhat. But Parisians have learnt to deal with it. For a long time I thought that it was arrogance that made them all walk around with their noses in the air. Now I realise the true reason: they're not trying to look superior, just avoiding the smell. And interestingly enough many of the smartest, most demure Parisians are among those responsible for the problem, because dogs are *de rigueur* fashion accessories. The tiniest, most idiotic-looking canines have been specially chosen to fit snugly on the forearm of the suavest women, unless they are very rich, in which case Hermès do a sophisticated little carrying vehicle that hangs decorously from the elbow. The little beasts are obviously so horribly inbred that they have lost the ability to walk, although not the capacity to use their diminutive backsides. I suppose that it is only a matter of time before someone bioengineers a version that does not produce turds, but until then Paris has a definite problem. A local non-governmental organisation has assessed its scale. They reckon that the average Parisian hound weighs 8 kilograms and produces 100 grams of shit daily. In total, they excrete no less than 25 tonnes of dog's muck on to the pavements of the nation's capital every day.

The French have of course devised their own unique solution to the problem: *le pooper scooper*, a modified motorcycle that is driven on to the pavement and delicately wiggles its hindquarters over the offending excrement. But apparently there are only enough of these vehicles to deal with a daily load of 3.5 tonnes, leaving quite a lot to fester. However, anyone who has stood behind one of these extraordinary machines while in action will know that all it seems to do is smear the crap over the paving stones, which, if anything, actually enhances the smell. Perhaps the pooper scoopers are in league with the perfumeries in an effort to boost sales. It's enough to make you wish that Napoleon was around today. What the French really need is a national edict to exterminate all dogs.

But past presidents of France have been concerned with weightier matters, such as the decree forbidding all of their loyal subjects to walk on the pavements outside the presidential palace. As I cut through from the Champs Elysées towards the rue du Faubourg St Honoré, I was rather looking forward to treading the hallowed pavement outside the Elysée Palace, since I had understood that its new resident, being a man of the people, had annulled this statute. As soon as I crossed the road towards the presidential seat, however, a gendarme signalled to me that I should reverse my decision and walk on the opposite side of the road. Monsieur Chirac had clearly changed his mind. The official reason was the danger of terrorist attack, but I rather fancy he may have been put off by the promise of eau de dog shit.

To the best of my knowledge, Keith has never owned a dog, but I think he may have underestimated the social value of such a move. I have known him for some years, but he's one of the friends that I only actually see very occasionally because he works overseas for much of the time. His most recent posting had brought him back from the delights of sub-Saharan Africa to the world's most romantic capital, but reading between the lines it seemed that he was having trouble appreciating the atmosphere. He dealt with his French counterparts on a daily basis, but outside the office things were not as simple.

'French people are actually very hard to meet socially,' he told me over dinner in a Thai restaurant in Les Halles. 'It's not that they're unfriendly, it's just that I haven't discovered where they go in the evenings yet.' Since he appeared to be finding it difficult to break into Parisian society perhaps a dog was just the accessory he needed, I thought to myself. I didn't want to say so, but I also wondered whether Keith's chances of mixing it with some chic Parisian demoiselles might be improved if he traded in his C&A suit for a slighter sharper model. 'What about clubs?' I wondered aloud. He didn't seem terribly convinced, but sipped his beer and said that we might try one later in the evening.

A fair proportion of Keith's work involved liaising with French civil servants, and I was interested to discover how he perceived their attitude to things European as we tucked into our Thai curries. 'What is good for France is good for Europe is a reasonable summation,' he told me. It was General de Gaulle, on one of his less tactful days, who described the EEC as a coach and carriage, with Germany the horse and France the coachman, but the French media are just as obsessed as their British counterparts with the supposed idiocies of Brussels bureaucrats. There were times when it seemed that the coach and carriage had been hijacked and mutated into a gravy train designed for men in grey suits who lived in Belgium. The talk of gravy trains led Keith to tell me about 'enarchs', graduates of the École Nationale d'Administration, the obligatory French civil service finishing school attended by most of France's senior figures in both public and private office. Being an enarch had almost masonic overtones, with elements of the British old school tie, and a dash of Oxbridge thrown in.

That was the moment when we were asked to leave. My attention had been vaguely drawn to some sort of incident unfolding on the terrace outside the restaurant, where it seemed that the jackbooted paramilitaries of the CRS (the French riot police), who were checking identity papers, had discovered two North African gentlemen not completely to their liking. A plain clothes employee of state security, instantly recognisable apparently by his brightly coloured jacket and casual denims, bounded in holding a walkie-talkie to announce that a suspect package had been found in the Café Banana next door. Keith wondered how they had identified the offending article because, it being a gay bar, the CRS probably considered it to be full of suspect packages.

I have always found it hard to take the CRS seriously as a riot squad, but nonetheless I grabbed my jacket expecting a rapid exit. Not necessary as it turned out. Although the CRS had obviously found a potential bomb, and presumably one which might explode at any moment, all customers were instructed to pay their bills before leaving. It's not their gear that is the problem. The handcuffs, truncheons, firearms, big boots and blousons all look formidable enough. It's when you come to the men inside that their credibility starts to waver. They don't quite live up to my image of what a crack squad of trouble-shooters ought to look like. The main entrance requirements appear to be thinning hair, a pot belly and a large collection of personal jewellery; most of them resemble a bunch of middle-aged barflies playing at soldiers, which is hardly enough to fill one with alarm or respect. This is not the case if you are not totally Anglo-Saxon-looking yourself, however, as the North Africans on the terrace were discovering to their cost. The colloquial rendition of the acronym CRS translates to Corps of Racist Bastards. No one asked Keith or me for any identification. Perhaps it was Keith's suit that got us off the hook.

As we left the restaurant and put some distance between us and the unclaimed banana, the heavens opened and we were well and truly soaked by the time we made it to our next destination. Keith had suggested that we do a short tour of the capital's British pubs and I was not expecting great things of an establishment named the Frog and Rosbif. Inside, the wooden floorboards, framed collections of old cigarette cards and strategically placed rugby shirts which adorned the walls could have been in almost any city centre pub in any British city. The place was packed with punters all tuned in to the large television screen on one wall that showed a live transmission of an England football match. This was an unusual spectacle, Keith pointed out, because despite the fact that Sky TV is thought of as a truly European satellite channel, it is not normally available to French subscribers.

A link with the French world outside was provided by the proprietors of the Frog and Rosbif in the form of the Anglo-French real ales available on tap. These included such thought-provoking brews as Parislytic, An Ale of Two Cities, and Inseine. By the time we were feeling only damp it was time to move on, and we successfully managed to get properly wet again while we searched out the nearest Métro station.

Whilst the Frog and Rosbif is largely frequented by Brits on holiday in Paris, the Cricketers is more of a haven for expatriate workers pining for such home-grown creature comforts as beer specially imported from Sussex. It is tucked away in a side street near the Bourse and is often full of city types who haven't graduated from the braces and slicked-back hair culture of 1980s London. That evening it was fairly empty, however. The main clientele were members of the British embassy football team relaxing after a match. Other than the exorbitant prices, the only other reminder of our continued presence in France was the fact that we weren't thrown out until well after midnight, and then only after Keith observed that the British ambassador's butler had finished his pint.

Interesting though it had been to observe my fellow countrymen at leisure in Europe, I was eager to see some native Parisians. We hailed a cab and drove north towards Pigalle where the lines of coaches on 'love tours' were beginning to thin out on the Boulevard de Clichy and the Locomotive night club was just warming up. But our search for real French people was to prove fruitless. After rejecting the underground portion of the club, where large amounts of ecstasy and bottled water were being consumed, we gravitated to the top floor where the music was designed for those under the influence of alcohol. Being fairly heavily under such an influence by this time, we set about our assignment with gusto. But it was a mission impossible. There were a few women who looked as if they might be French, but this was only because they had their noses straining towards the ceiling as if they were still promenading the boulevards, and because of this stance they didn't seem to notice when anyone approached to strike up a bit of conversation. After a couple of attempts, I surreptitiously checked my shoes just to make sure I wasn't a carrier. Keith did succeed in exchanging a few words with someone who turned out to be a native, although she was not from Paris. But the liaison proved to be a brief and potentially dangerous one when her boyfriend appeared from nowhere and made it clear that he was not interested in promoting the entente cordiale, never mind a European union.

After a couple more infusions of overpriced bottled beverages, we returned to the fray. While Keith settled for a woman with a broken arm, who turned out to be a Portuguese hairdresser, I got into a conversation with Sandy, a remedial blonde from Santa Barbara, California. I am not an expert on Californian blondes, but Sandy certainly did a fair impression of the stereotype. She was rather tall, mostly because of her legs, rather beautiful, and rather stupid. She had been working in a bar in Paris for three months and I asked her why she had chosen France. 'Because I got a work permit for France,' she replied.

'Was France the only country in Europe that would give you a permit?' I wondered.

'Oh no,' she said, 'I could have gone to England, or Ireland, or Germany.'

'So why did you choose France?'

'Lots of reasons,' she said, looking decidedly blank, and with just a hint of concern that I might be about to ask her a really difficult question. I had a sneaking feeling that this chance encounter would not blossom into a beautiful friendship, but I persevered.

'OK, just give me one.'

Sandy looked troubled. She wound some of her hair around a finger to play for time, shrugged, and then said rather defensively, 'Because I wanted to see the Eiffel Tower.'

It had been a long day, but I could already see that our karmas were not compatible, so I made an excuse and retired from my audience with Sandy from California, making a mental note never to go to Santa Barbara. Keith's brush with the expatriate Portuguese hairdressing community lasted a little longer, but a broken arm was not the only reason for her being temporarily incapacitated. She had obviously been drowning her sorrows in a serious way and was in danger of breaking several more limbs. Fortunately, however, her brother turned up to whisk her back to the home for disabled Iberian beauticians.

We did finally discover what young Parisians get up to of an evening. A couple of days later we found them all in a multi-level Belgian bar on the Champs Elysées, singing along to a karaoke machine.

Another place to see real Parisians is in restaurants. I did this quite a lot because it rained for much of the time that I was in Paris so I often retired early from my sightseeing for a long lunch. This was fine, since I enjoy eating, but I usually ate too much and suffered almost permanent indigestion as a consequence. But it was worth it.

The French are supposed to have invented the restaurant as an employment scheme for cooks left to their own devices by the fall of the aristocracy in 1789. You realise how seriously French people take their food as soon as you enter a restaurant because serving at table is a respectable profession in middle-age in France. If you compare the average British restaurant with its French counterpart you find a direct correlation between food quality and the attitude of those who serve it. In Britain, most waiters and waitresses are young and couldn't really care less whether you eat in their establishment or not because the food is crap anyway, whilst in France the *garçon* is the guardian of all he serves: he knows it's good and he's proud of it. OK, so this pride sometimes comes across as a condescending look which says that you should have continued another 200 metres for the McDonald's, but this is only because he doesn't want to see good food go to waste on someone who might not appreciate it.

Food also *sounds* so much better in French than in English. Your mouth starts to water at the prospect of *champignons à la provençale* in a way that it simply can't if you're waiting for a plate of garlic mushrooms. Order a cheese and ham toasted sandwich and you can smell the grease almost immediately; ask for a *croque monsieur* and you're going to enjoy it much more. But it's not just the language, of course. Pretentious British restaurants realise the attraction of French on their menus, but think that it's all they need. They don't deliver and usually overdo it. If you order *pommes frites* and you get chips, why not say chips in the first place?

It's ironic that the aspect of French cuisine most widely adopted internationally is breakfast. My heart always sinks when I check into a hotel to hear that 'continental breakfast' is served at such and such a time. Continental breakfast is French breakfast: the absolute minimum they can get away with and still call it breakfast. In France they only down a croissant and coffee because they are saving themselves for a damn good lunch. It doesn't always work like that in other countries.

Whilst the French take their food very seriously and in Britain it's a bit of a joke, these attitudes are reversed when it comes to sex. Despite France being a predominantly Catholic country, bare bosoms are pretty common currency in French advertisements and sex is not something to be embarrassed about. Another abiding memory I have from one of my early visits to France is the intense unease I felt when the family I spent a fortnight with just prior to sitting my French 'O' level took delivery of their monthly copy of *Playboy*. My English adolescence had simply not prepared me to deal with this otherwise perfectly respectable family (they had a decorating business) passing a porno magazine around the breakfast table. The French women's liberation movement has an uphill struggle because scantily clad young females are entertaining. This is probably one of the reasons that 'The Benny Hill Show' went down so well on French TV, and is certainly an important element in the continued popularity of the home-grown 'Intervilles'. Whilst 'It's a Knock-out' came and went in Britain, and elsewhere in Europe, the slapstick competition between teams of funsters prepared to do odd things involving plastic cows, buckets of water and giant Lego towers is still alive and well and regularly topping the weekly ratings in France. 'Intervilles' is presented by a sexy woman in a skirt that's too short and a T-shirt that invariably ends up getting soaked. She adds a dimension to the show that Eddie Waring and Stuart Hall could never have managed.

As any advertising man will tell you, sex sells anything, and I suppose it should have come as no surprise when I visited the small museum of the Paris sewers that I should be met by a very attractive young woman guide. In addition to the conventional European sights, I had decided to take in a few less mainstream curiosities. The success on British television of the French-based series 'Eurotrash' had convinced me that the bizarre side of modern European culture was also worth investigating. The sexy female sewer guide was actually a bit of a disappointment since the dated guidebook I was using had said that the short tour of underground Paris was conducted by pallid sewermen in blue overalls. But having been used as a Ninja Turtles film location and for a Jean Paul Gaultier fashion show, the Paris sewers are now considered to be glamorous. I only hope that the fashion show was a short one, because the sewers are hot and sweaty and, well, really rather smelly.

The visit consisted of a short tour of a few tunnels, all labelled according to the streets above, with some rapid explanations of all sorts of weird contraptions for clearing and flushing. Most of these were largely inaudible thanks to the continuous sound of rushing water, but I did catch the odd cistern statistic with which I could impress my friends. Other than the tour guides, only men are employed in the Paris sewers because it is such hard physical work (these guys remove 15,000 square metres of solids from the network each year, which is the equivalent of a six-storey building if you can believe such a thing), and the city has 26,000 manholes. These facts were followed by a series of exhibits on the sewers through the ages and a very slick slide-cum-film show to the sound of romantic music. And a quick look at a small cage that contained two rats. 'These are the only rats to be found in the Paris sewers,' my guide assured me with a smile that made my kneecaps tingle. If she'd said that the lost city of Atlantis was down there, I'd have believed that too.

From the sewers, it was just a short walk across the river to that other great monument to French nineteenth-century engineering, the tower that Eiffel built. It was quiet and drizzling and Sunday. The joggers were out in the parks and the coach tours were beginning to arrive. Their drivers stood around in gaggles looking tired and bored as they sucked on their cigarettes and chewed the cud, while a small army of men in green overalls was busy filling plastic sacks with the debris of bottles and rubbish from the previous Saturday night. The one thing that struck me about the tower itself was its colour. I had always assumed that it was a glistening black or metallic hue, but no, the Eiffel Tower is a drab brown undercoat colour that looks as if it is going to be painted properly next week.

It's not of course. Painting the Eiffel Tower is more than just a quick respray job. They only do it every seven years and it requires 40 tonnes of paint. But it doesn't really matter because all of the little models of the thing on sale at its four feet are available in a wide range of more appropriate colours, so that when you get home you can pretend to yourself that this is what the real thing looks like. And what a great time the merchandisers have had thinking up all the utterly useless articles that can be produced in an Eiffel Tower shape. There are squeezy toys that make a stupid noise, pens that you couldn't possibly write with, thermometers, perfume bottles and keyring lighters, and I'm sure if you knew where to go you could get a blow-up version for adult entertainment.

I'm surprised the merchandising men haven't made more of an effort at Versailles, but then I suppose that it's hard to parody something that is so over the top anyway. As the train climbs out of the Paris basin from the Gare St Lazare, you get an idea of just how dominant the Eiffel Tower is down there on the Left Bank. Up in the north, however, there is a small collection of more modern rivals on the Paris skyline. Tall office blocks brought to you by Elf, Ariane and Total are clustered around what looks like a new Arc de Triomphe at

La Défense. The area is designed to be an office workers' paradise, with room for 100,000 suits, but although one of the government ministries has been moved there from the centre of the city the town planners made a terrible mistake: the only place to eat lunch is a McDonald's.

It is not the sort of mishap that Louis XIV would have allowed to happen. A visit to his pad at Versailles gives you a good idea of why the French had their revolution. Back in 1661, when he finally reached the age of majority, the first thing the young Louis did was tart up his father's château. It was a minor operation, involving the diversion of a river and the draining of an area the size of Liechtenstein, and that was just for the gardens.

A walk around the palace itself is an apt tribute to that old adage about truth being stranger than fiction: no Parisian should spend good money on hallucinogenic drugs when they can pop into this place for a quick fix. Louis was ruling under the theory of divine right at the time so I suppose he could do anything, but the result is really too much for mere mortals to cope with. It is such a concentration of so many artists' endeavours that it's like sitting down to eat an entire barrel of Beluga caviar. Even the *Michelin Guide to Paris* suggests that you should only aim for a general impression on your first visit and then return 'possibly after a lapse of several years' to pick out a few special items for detailed enjoyment. During my year touring the cultural monuments of Europe, I was to take in several attempts to mimic Versailles, including Vienna's Schloss Schönbrunn and the Schloss Charlottenburg in Berlin, but none of them came even close to the real thing.

I could only deal with the State Apartments and the Hall of Mirrors, and as I reached the top of the former Ambassadors' Staircase I immediately empathised with François Lemoyne who spent three years painting the ceiling fresco in the Hercules Salon and then went straight out and topped himself. A riot of chandeliers, gilt stucco and marble tables with legs that probably took a man-year to carve hits you right between the eyes as you walk through into the appropriately named Abundance Salon. Once I had extricated myself from the all-enveloping bottle-green velvet, I staggered reeling into the Venus Salon. And so it went on, a seemingly endless succession of opulence and splendour, every ceiling a major art exhibition complete with golden frames and cherubs holding them up, each wall a dazzling display of statues and busts and outrageous clocks. I was ambushed by *trompe-l'oeil* paintings and left speechless by tapestries that must have taken a dozen women ten years to weave, literally (they are still doing it at the Gobelins workshop). The chandeliers got bigger and worse; they started sprouting stars and teardrops, flowers and petals. Every possible colour of marble was represented, and a few more besides. There were urns aplenty and scantily clad maidens supporting golden plinths with crystal candelabras. And then there was more marble, and more gold, more porcelain, more cherubs, more ceiling picture galleries, more stools with squirrels and parrots on, until I felt utterly bewildered. I suppose you could take grandeur and kitsch to further extremes but I wouldn't like to see it. By the end I didn't know whether to laugh or cry. I could only marvel at the phenomenal splendour of the French classical style, and then go and be sick.

It was a stroke of genius to sign the Treaty of Versailles in the Hall of Mirrors. They'd have signed anything just to get out of there, and it's difficult to describe the sense of relief that overwhelmed me when I got to the Princes' Staircase and there was no colour. I could only face sticking my nose into the Battle Gallery, dedicated to French victories spanning 1300 years, and just thought how much it must have really hurt that they screwed up in every armed conflict this century. Perhaps it was the realisation that they were no good at winning wars any more that made the French so keen on the idea of European unity.

Out in the grounds, the mystifying pomp continues in what is not so much a garden as an open-air architectural extension. When they're outside, cherubs are the seventeenth-century equivalent of garden gnomes, and they were there in abundance playing supporting roles to gods and goddesses lounging among the formal ponds and fountains. I ambled down the *tapis vert*, and just before I expired, slumped down beneath a chestnut tree to eat a late lunch.

I'm glad I did because it gave me enough renewed energy to forge on, away from the rigid gardens towards the area where Marie-Antoinette enjoyed frolicking with the milkmaids and playing at being a peasant. It was easy to imagine her in her custom-built wonderland as bright sunshine flooded the mock countryside. Young red squirrels dashed back and forth along the branches of a nearby tree, and down by a little stone footbridge dragonflies were flirting beside a reedy stream. The sense of wonderment was heightened still further in the impossibly pretty hamlet. Ducks floated on the pond while jasmine and wisteria climbed the wooden pillars and spiral staircases of the little thatched cottages, up to balconies festooned with pink and red geraniums. Each one was the epitome of a little girl's dream Wendy house. The Queen even had a small farm to play with.

I was well and truly pacified after the visual onslaught of the palace when reality returned in a surreal shock. Eight young soldiers, wearing full combat gear and carrying automatic weapons, marched into Marie-Antoinette's fairytale land and began patrolling. As their shiny black boots crunched on the gravel I couldn't believe that someone would attempt to blow up paradise. But then I suppose you might if you were that way inclined.

It was time to move on from Paris and I caught the early morning TGV from Montparnasse bound for Lourdes. Time constraints meant that I couldn't visit all the places I'd like to have done in all fourteen of our European neighbours, but I would definitely take in all the capital cities. People argue over the extent to which capitals are microcosms of their countries and usually come up with a 'yes and no' answer. I'd concentrate on the yes aspects, and visit some other places along the way. Lourdes seemed like a good idea for a number of reasons. It was an international centre in France and it was on the way to Spain. Besides, once I'd visited Disneyland I started seeing everywhere as a theme park. Versailles could be construed as a regal version, so I thought I might as well fit in a religious one. The EU may have been set up to encourage pan-European unity, but the Roman Catholic Church had been at it for a while longer. Lourdes was a relatively new centre for pilgrimage. It was less than 150 years old.

We glided through the French countryside past hay stacked in neat bundles and maize fields waving gently in the breeze. Outside Angoulême the sun-dried faces of the sunflowers were brown and bowed as if in shame that their yellow haloes had disappeared. Inside the carriage, the smoked glass on the underside of the luggage racks allowed you to watch people three rows ahead picking their noses upside down.

The TGV is actually only very fast as far as Tours, but it was still just three hours later that we eased past the suspension bridge over the chocolate-brown River Garonne and into Bordeaux St Jean. I fell asleep and woke to find myself in the wooded foothills of the Pyrenees where the cows were sitting in the small fields, a sure sign of rain, which started to fall from the dirty clouds as we pulled into Lourdes.

Lourdes' claim to fame dates back to the winter of 1858, when the small town's inhabitants, reeling from the ravages of cholera and starvation, were visited by the Virgin Mary. Well, she actually only appeared to one of them, a scruffy young girl by the name of Bernadette, who lived in a hovel. To cut a long story short, Bernadette saw Mary eighteen times over a period of a few months, found a spring underneath a pig-sty, upset a lot of people by crawling in the dirt and eating grass, and after four years of investigation was declared legitimate. The Church immediately set about building a basilica above the pig-sty, and the merchandisers rubbed their hands and set about producing rubbish to sell to the pilgrims.

And what a phenomenal range of rubbish they offer. After checking into a hotel by the railway station, I walked down into town towards the basilica and found myself in a holy Costa del Sol. Images of Bernadette and her celestial guest could be bought plastered across the most inappropriate objects, such as alarm clocks and cigarette lighters, penknives and thermometers. There were even ashtrays in the shape of the Virgin Mary's hand. For those seeking straightforward *objets d'art*, a range of small useless wooden implements carved to look like a heart, or a guitar, or an electric iron were available. These you could open up to reveal a picture of the immortal meeting beneath the words 'Souvenir of Lourdes'. There were also statuettes in abundance, of all sizes and catering to numerous tastes, most of them tacky. One model that caught my eye depicted Bernadette kneeling in front of the Virgin Mary who was surrounded by flashing fairy lights. But my favourite of all was a bedside lamp set to one side of a round plastic plate. Opposite the lamp stood a small statuette of Mary surrounded by plastic vegetation. The centrepiece of this monument to kitsch was a metal tap, apparently suspended in mid-air, from which a constant stream of magic water flowed to a mock pond in the centre of the plate. It was actually a fairly impressive piece of engineering, which on closer inspection gave this illusion because the water was continually pumped back up to the magic tap through a hollow tube in the centre of the ever-flowing stream.

These establishments also sold more immediately useful pilgrimage equipment at specially inflated prices. There appeared to be a significant trade in candles up to a metre long and Tupperware water containers of all sizes, each one bearing a blue transfer of Bernadette, for visitors to fill with water from the spring. I watched as an elderly Italian couple sorted through the Tupperware, discussing the pros and cons of several small containers over one 5-litre vessel. They eventually plumped for a selection of three small ones and a big one, and proceeded in the direction of the basilica. I followed, dodging in and out between the nuns pushing wheelchairs and temporarily suffocated by huge coaches as they lumbered up the steep main street pumping exhaust fumes on to the committed. We crossed a small bridge and passed through the gates of the compound where large notices informed you of the dos and don'ts and warned visitors to beware of pickpockets.

My first impression was of the sheer magnitude of the operation. Automated messageboards flashed continual information in half a dozen European languages on places to visit, and the times of services and processions, and showings of Bernadette videos. A monthly Lourdes journal, also in several languages, was on sale just inside the gate. As I walked the few hundred metres towards the basilica, I passed statues of the Virgin Mary on the grass behind railings festooned with offered bunches of flowers, and long queues of mostly old people sitting in special invalid wagons which looked like rickshaws, waiting to be pulled by attendant nurses. This was religion on an industrial scale, but my initial slight sense of disquiet was tempered when I entered the information centre and picked up a leaflet about the place. It stated that Lourdes receives no less than 5.5 million pilgrims and visitors each year. With numbers like that, they really needed to be organised.

I wandered round the basilica to a candle dispensary where notices gave you the suggested donation price per candle in eleven languages and currencies. Having bought your candle, you proceed towards the former pig-sty, now known as the grotto, past the spring where a mêlée of people were gathered to fill their plastic water containers in front of an electronic scoreboard flashing the story of Bernadette and the special waters. Behind the numerous taps, permanent notices told you to take no more than 3 litres and that the spring is closed between midnight and 6 a.m. Next along the rock face, now glistening in a light drizzle, was the grotto itself, where a long queue was slowly edging its way forward into a zone of silence. The queue passed black metal carts full of huge burning candles as tall as people, occasionally added to by a small group with their offering. Two men eased their way through the waiting line carrying one candle the size of a large cannon on their shoulders. As the queue quietly progressed towards the grotto, it passed beneath an overhang in the rock. Above the devotees' heads an assortment of walking sticks and crutches hung from a suspended washing line: symbols of the sometimes miraculous properties of the spring water. Everyone touched the smoothed rock in the little cave beside a statue of Mary in blue, before being encouraged along by silent ushers working the production line. Every now and again, the sense of silent occasion was too much for some, and whispers were truncated with a loud 'Shhhh ...' which sounded like a shot of steam emanating from the loudspeakers.

The atmosphere was sombre, reverent and moving. Outside the silent zone, people all around me were muttering prayers and toying with their rosaries. I turned on hearing the sound of sobbing to see someone crying in private grief.

Everywhere around me the old and infirm were gathered wearing their name tags, patiently waiting to be wheeled to this place or that. All want to join the ranks of people in the black and white photographs that cover the walls in the nearby small exhibition room. They are some of the more than two and a half thousand people who have been cured in a way described as extraordinary or inexplicable after a medical enquiry. Sixty-five of these have been officially recognised by the Roman Catholic Church as miraculous. Some of the photographs were accompanied by short case histories describing the medically inexplicable ways in which believers had ceased to suffer after drinking and bathing in the waters at Lourdes. There was the story of John Traynor from Liverpool, unable to walk or even stand up, paralysed in the right arm and epileptic after being shot to bits in World War I. His useless legs had trembled violently in the waters and he stood for the first time in the seven years since

Gallipoli, to shuffle away a new man. There were even the exhumed bones from the leg of a Belgian woodcutter in a display case. Smashed in a logging accident, they had miraculously fused after the doctors had given up on him and recommended amputation.

That evening I dined at the only couscous restaurant in Lourdes. It was a small place with a large Islamic mirror and several bad oil paintings of sand dunes and camels. The proprietor was an elderly Frenchman with a craggy face and a kangaroo badge in his lapel that amused the Australian couple I shared the restaurant with. As a speciality of the maison, the couscous was served with confit of duck and the wine gushed straight from a small barrel to arrive at the table frothing in its jug. After cooking the couscous, the proprietor removed his glasses to wipe the sweat from his brow and sat himself down for a rest. I commented on the relatively few customers.

'Ah yes, monsieur, it is the end of the season,' he told me, 'but the restaurant is always full at lunch times.'

'People must come to Lourdes from all over the place.'

'Yes, monsieur, from all over the world,' he gestured towards the Australians, 'but most are from Europe.'

'The European Union of Catholics,' I mused. He liked that idea and gave me a little snort of approval. 'And this European Union doesn't tell us our cheese is no good,' he added with an ironic look. The proprietor's craggy face then broke into a smile and he asked, 'How old do you think I am?'

Slightly nonplussed, I said, 'Fifty-five?'

'Ha!' he exclaimed in delight. 'I am eighty-three.'

The couscous man's joy echoed in my mind the following day as I continued my perusal of the basilica and surrounding sights. Although this was a place for the devout and faithful, and an air of gravity pervaded the area, it was not without its lighter side. I suppose it shouldn't have surprised me, but it did. Pilgrims, like any visitors, laughed and joked as they lined up with their church banners for team photographs in front of the towering statue of the Virgin Mary surrounded by offerings of fresh white dahlias sprayed the light blue colour of her robe. While waiting to be called into position, a young boy did occasional wheelies in his wheelchair.

There was certainly an infectious carefree holiday atmosphere about Lourdes. That evening, while I finished my dinner at a terrace restaurant beneath the fort that towers above the town on a rocky outcrop, the table behind me was occupied by six elderly German ladies wearing slacks and jumpers and horn-rimmed spectacles. All were sixty years old if they were a day, but they laughed and giggled like teenagers as they tucked into ice cream sundaes with small parasols and finger biscuits.

The light had faded and the mountain air had a fresh snap to it as I made my way back to the basilica for the evening open-air service. Processions of wheelchairs were proceeding along the special red wheelchair lanes in the streets towards the magical occasion. The strangeness of public worship which for each person was at the same time a very private experience was enhanced by the light from a thousand hand-held candles, each flickering in a cardboard cover printed with the words of the 'Credo' and 'Ave Maria'. I was standing in the middle of the European Union of Catholics. For these people their faith was enough to bring them together across the boundaries of nationality. It struck me that Brussels had its work cut out to compete with God as a uniting force.

No one turned to stare when an ambulance glided noiselessly into our midst, lights flashing, but sirens silent. There was one worshipper who might not see the night through.

3

The Man with No Voice

When I awoke the following morning the clouds were so low they threatened to engulf the whole town. They had sent a gentle drizzle as an advance party. The fort had already gone and the basilica was a misty memory as the train pulled out of Lourdes station bound for Pau. Just two carriages were waiting at platform 3 for my connection, but I knew immediately I was on the right track when I heard the hard machine-gun Spanish accents.

I broke out a fresh notebook, a red one. After years of experimentation, I had found a design and size that I was completely happy with. This one opened at the top and was small enough to slip into a pocket. It had feint blue lines just the right distance apart, and the covers even came in a range of colours which satisfied the pedantic side of my character. I had chosen colours according to national flags: a blue one for France, the red for Spain, and I had a green one tucked away in my bag ready for Portugal. To cap it all, the brandname was Europa.

They had given up on the railway after Orloron, but French railways provided a bus for the final 50 kilometres to the border. As the bus wound its way upwards along the shiny new tarmac, we passed the rail track several times. It was overgrown and had not been used for some time. It was raining hard by now and the shaggy sheep took no notice of us from their fields.

I was headed for Bilbao, industrial city of the North and the engine room of the Basque country. I had fond memories of the place. At least I think I did. It's all a bit of a blur now. Some years ago I worked for a small publisher that printed its books there, and on one occasion I had been sent to oversee the process and encourage the printers to do it speedily since, as usual, we were late on delivery. The work was hard but the drinking was harder. Bilbao was a marathon of eating and drinking. Everyone seemed to eat as if there was no tomorrow and drink as if they didn't realise that beer and wine are alcoholic.

The Pyrenean valley we were driving up was heavily wooded with elegant conifers draped in lichens, and birch trees with trunks that were a furry, bearded mass. Then the slopes became so steep that they made me tired just to look at them. At Bedons the bracken was turning into golden-yellow and rich honey-brown colours. We passed the peremptory French border control and climbed up to a zone of red slate and purple heather where large signs adorned with yellow EU stars announced that we were entering Spain.

My memories of Bilbao were a mix of thumping German printing presses and long sessions wading through the knee-deep rubbish that lurks beneath the counter of every tapas bar. Each morning, suffering from the excesses of the night before, a group of us would troop up the road from the printers to a workers' caff where we'd down a tiny cup of black coffee that was so strong the locals called it heroin. It pepped you up immediately, and we would emerge from the bar, fill our lungs with the grime of the city, and return refreshed enough to continue until the first bottle of wine at lunch time.

Bilbao was also my first trip abroad on expenses, and I remembered the shock on everyone's faces at the printers when I arrived late on a Monday morning after a long weekend in southern France. I had missed the last bus back to Bilbao the night before, and had been forced to stay the night in San Sebastián. I walked into the nearest hotel, the Maria Cristina, and flashed my company credit card. The place looked terribly posh but the man behind the desk didn't bat an eyelid at my jeans and T-shirt and even offered to carry my luggage up to my room. Since it only consisted of a briefcase, I didn't think it was necessary. The bill was enormous. After the initial shock, the printers thought it was a huge joke because this was where the King of Spain stayed on his holidays.

My reminiscences were interrupted when the bus finally came to a halt at Canfranc, not so much a town as a large railway terminus surrounded by a few shops tucked into a gash of a valley. The terminus was built like a French château maybe 400 metres long. It looked huge and imposing and rather out of place. It was also dead.

'*Nous sommes abandonnés,*' cried a short Frenchman as the small group of remaining bus passengers struggled across the tracks with their luggage to be met by bricked-up doors and boarded windows.

The scene had the atmosphere of a *Marie Celeste*, the whole complex a victim of the end of border controls in the European Union. I peered through the cracks in the boards to see the customs halls with their long tables draped in dust sheets and dust, a magnificent waiting room with marble columns tapering to a high vaulted ceiling and wooden ticket booths in the style of confessionals. There was even an international hotel, its grimy white stuccoed ceiling now crumbling and in pieces on the parquet floor, and further down the platform a room for delousing less wholesome travellers. And yet a diesel train sat waiting at the platform, its engine pumping noxious fumes into the crisp mountain air; although there was no driver and no station official of any sort. Eventually, one of the ill-fated passengers found a grubby timetable pasted to the wall at one end of the platform. It indicated that there were two departures a day from Canfranc to Zaragoza. We had a two-hour wait before the train was due to leave.

There was something immediately more appealing about Spain: rougher at the edges and less intimidating than France. When the train eventually chugged out of the Canfranc terminus we passed through three tunnels before the driver remembered to turn on the lights. We proceeded at a very stately pace down on to the plains of the Ebro and gradually the jagged horizon was replaced by large slabs of sky as the landscape flattened out and became anaemic-looking. Pieces of agricultural machinery in strong primary colours appeared out of place in the sun-bleached panorama.

From the hot and sticky confines of Zaragoza's new rail terminal, I jumped on to an express that came from Barcelona. It was smart and clean and its carriage ceilings were lined with video screens. You could even move the seat backs so that you could always face the way you were going.

Bilbao was just as I remembered: dirty, prosperous and full of energy. It was how I imagined the industrial towns of northern England must have been fifty or a hundred years ago. Stand anywhere in the city, surrounded by factories and grand railway stations and a stagnant river, and you can raise your eyes to see green fields rising vertically all around you. Look up from the industrial heartland and see a cow, or a man wearing a beret, in a field.

I checked into a *hostal residencia* next to the cathedral in the Casco Viejo, the old part of town where the paint on the wrought iron balconies and room-high wooden shutters looked as if someone had taken a blowtorch to it. Inside, the Hostal Roquefer was full of rich dark wood and musty carpets that pre-dated the Hoover. My shower curtain looked as if the last person to use it had been a mad scientist with a penchant for breeding exotic bacteria.

My mentor during my previous visit to Bilbao had been the printers' export manager, an Italian named Pietro, and it was with slightly mixed feelings that I rang him soon after my arrival. The publishing company I had worked for was run by a cowboy who was rather better at spending money than at earning it. When it came to printing his books, he practised a type of financial shifting cultivation across Europe: he would cultivate a large print bill and then shift his activities to another company. When he had been through a number of printers in one country, he would move to another. When I first started working for him, he was printing in Italy. Shortly afterwards, he shifted to Spain, leaving a trail of irate Italian creditors behind him. By the time I left, he had dabbled in Portugal and Eastern Europe and moved his attention to Singapore. Pietro's printing company had been left with a rather large unpaid bill, and I wasn't sure what sort of a reception I would receive.

I needn't have worried. Pietro now worked for a different company, and he welcomed me at the factory gates like a long-lost brother and proudly took me on a tour of his new print works. Here again was the repetitive rumbling of the huge Heidelberg presses – more expensive than Japanese machines, he shouted above the din, but they last longer – and the rhythmic chatter of folding, stapling and binding machines. As we passed a pallet of new Bibles, Pietro informed me that according to one of his Irish customers, the very lightweight paper they are printed on is excellent for rolling joints.

Pietro had lived and worked in Bilbao for longer than he cared to remember. He fitted in well. Like most Basque men, he had a barrel for a chest and a stamina that could have been used for running up and down mountains, but instead had been turned to working, smoking, eating and drinking. He also had an interest in women.

In fact, Pietro was a jet-setting equivalent of the sailor with a girl in every port. His customers were spread all over Europe and wherever a major contract lay, his dusky good looks had also made a conquest. It seemed that each star on the plastic EU flag that sat on his desk represented one of Pietro's amorous triumphs. We sat down in the quiet of his office and he surveyed a line of six attaché cases sitting in a row behind his desk. He selected one and looked at the combination lock. 'Shit,' he said, 'I can't remember the number.' He thrust the case back in line and grabbed another. He looked at me as if I might be able to give him inspiration. 'No,' he said, shaking his head. 'I wanted to show you some photographs of my girlfriend in Paris.' He methodically picked up each of the cases, but couldn't remember the combinations for any of them. 'She is a model,' he added casually, 'there is one picture of her in this book.' He leapt out from behind the desk and riffled through a pile of hardbacks to produce a photographic volume on health. 'Page forty-seven,' he said as he picked up the telephone. 'I must call her.'

I sat gazing at an image of the woman in question with a white towel on her head as Pietro left a brief message in French on the machine in her Paris apartment. Pietro was off on a business trip the following day, and he would have time to rendezvous. Before we left his office for lunch, he had left a similar message with a woman in London, brushed off an incoming call from a randy divorcee who he said had been chasing him for some months, made a dinner date for that evening and introduced me to his beautiful assistant. When she closed the door, he just smiled at me in a way that didn't need translating. The man was a phenomenon.

We drove into town, past the towering apartment blocks that march up Bilbao's network of valleys and the high bridges that sweep across the gushing river. Every road sign was a bilingual reminder of the proud Basque nation that doesn't really have written records, but often turns up in other people's histories as a bit of a pain. Possibly the original European aborigines, with a bizarre, unique language full of Xs and double Zs, the Basques have never done what they're told. The Romans didn't tame them, neither did the Moors. They backed the wrong side in Spain's Carlist wars and did it again in the Spanish Civil War. In the latter case, Franco's mates in the German Condor Legion thought they needed teaching a lesson, so they invented saturation bombing and tried it out on the sacred Basque oak tree at Guernica. Picasso painted a picture about it. The tree survived but a lot of Basque people didn't. The world was shocked, but not as shocked as it was a couple of years later when Hitler invaded Poland.

Since the end of Franco, relations with Madrid have been much improved, but the Basques continue to pride themselves as a nation apart and don't take kindly to being pushed around. The home-grown terrorist group, ETA, still lets off bombs and kidnaps people every now and again in protest. The most recent generation of would-be rulers was represented by a *Guardia Civil* vehicle that had stopped on the hard shoulder to change a wheel. It was surrounded by nervous-looking guys standing guard in bullet-proof vests clutching automatic weapons. They clearly didn't feel they could flag down a passing driver for help. The sooner the *Guardia Civil* left Basque country the better, Pietro said.

Over lunch, Pietro intermingled his accounts of recent sexual conquests with a few of his latest funny stories gleaned from a network of Italian doormen stationed at hotels all across Europe. His life seemed to be smoothed by an extended family of compatriots. Everywhere he went he appeared to have a friend. If he didn't, his ardent manner made him new ones soon enough. He was amusing, compassionate and lovable in every sense of the word. Even I wanted to have his babies.

One of the things I liked about Spain is that it is still full of butchers' shops with real meat in them. Restaurants too usually have a wide assortment of dead fauna on display in their windows, because in Spain they still think that their customers would like to know what species of recently deceased wildlife there is on offer. Britain isn't like that any more. Eating meat has become such an ungodly pastime that we have to disguise the fact that it comes from dead animals. Such self-deception doesn't apply in Spain.

I had a long time to ponder this as I waited patiently in line for a table at the world's earliest restaurant, down in the old part of Madrid in the lee of the Plaza Mayor. I knew the Restaurante Botín was the 'earliest' restaurant because there was a certificate to that effect from the *Guinness Book of Records* on one of its knobbly walls. It was founded in 1725, and would have been an ideal pit stop for Grand Tourists if they had come to Spain, but they didn't. I wondered why the place wasn't referred to as the oldest restaurant and concluded that it must be an oblique reference to the length of time one had to hang around before securing a table. It's the early bird that catches the waiter's eye.

The house speciality is a Castilian dish: suckling pig roasted in an oven fuelled by evergreen oak. The window was full of dead piglets. These are pigs of the young and small variety, pigs at their cutest: tiny and squealing as they trot around the farmyard. Only the one that they bring you isn't, because they have killed it and cooked it, and you are about to eat it. They've left the feet on, and the tail, and they've slit its throat so that it'll slot on to the side of the terracotta plate and look at you, because they want you to know what you're eating.

This was too much for some of the Americans who squeezed in through the tiny door to be met with an entire carcass being whisked into place in front of some eager carnivore.

'Oh my,' exclaimed one US citizen when her horn-rimmed spectacles had demisted. 'Arnold, it's a whole pig,' she shrieked with devastating simplicity. Arnold, who had pictures of ants on his tie, was clearly a husband of the long-suffering variety. He sighed knowingly and confirmed his wife's astute observation. 'Yes, dear.'

'We can't eat here,' the horn-rimmed spectacles announced as she turned on her heel to be followed by Arnold whose face had the longing, hunted look of a frustrated meat-eater.

The Spanish do have a special attitude towards animals. When they're not eating them, they are participating in all sorts of curious animal rituals, many of which involve the creatures' premature and unnatural demise. Much has been written about this topic, but I still can't really understand why Spaniards continue to labour under the odd delusion that throwing live goats off the tops of church steeples during religious festivals somehow makes God look more kindly upon them. As one Spaniard put it to me, it's all part of their culture, which apparently makes it all right. It certainly makes the job of Spain's European cousins, many of whom consider this sort of behaviour to be uncivilised, more difficult. Meddling in other countries' culture is a tricky diplomatic issue, and I suppose if the Spanish went to the Costa del Sol for some tips on what we regard as civilised behaviour they would be just as perplexed.

Traditional pastimes involving quadrupeds are not without their Spanish critics, who see them as throwbacks to an old Spain which is best forgotten. It is all tied up with that crucial Hispanic need to prove their manliness, with a dash of artistic flair added in the case of bullfighting. This is why Hemingway felt so at home in Spain. I couldn't quite bring myself to find a bullfight while in Madrid. I thought I'd try the Portuguese version instead because they don't actually kill the bulls as the Spanish do.

I spent a few days wandering the streets of Madrid, brushing shoulders with considerably more American tourists than I'd seen in Paris. They had probably been driven south by the bombs, whilst the Japanese, a more fearless race, were just as numerous as they had been up north. The warmer weather in Spain also brought out another aspect of the Japanese that was new to me: their fondness of English-language T-shirt slogans. Judging by the selection I came across (e.g. 'greengages are lucky', 'hospitals and cheese', 'talcum powder crabcake') they don't care what the slogan says as long as the writing is in English.

I liked Madrid. It was bustling and energetic, but in that relaxed sort of way that seems to come with being closer to the Mediterranean. Charles Theodore Middleton liked the place too, but writing in the late eighteenth century, he gave a good indication of why so few Grand Tourists had ventured south of the Pyrenees: 'Madrid was formerly a very dirty disagreeable town, but has been greatly improved of late.' The houses were now all numbered, he recorded, there were as many lamps as in London, and the streets were as neat and clean as those in Holland, 'whereas 10 years ago Madrid might have vied with Edinburgh in its former state for filthiness'. Neat and clean it still was, and as I was to discover later, it still keeps pace with Holland.

From my lodgings, slightly further than a goat's throw away from the Plaza Mayor, it was a short walk along the neat and clean streets of Madrid to the Prado. Having wimped out on a bullfight, I decided to concentrate on the artistic side of Spanish culture. Early one morning I made my way towards Madrid's answer to the Louvre past the old men in cloth caps working as shoe-shiners and the amusement arcades full of only slightly younger men working at losing their money on the fruit machines.

Spain boasts a phenomenal number of great artists of all types, though curiously, despite all the flamenco and guitars, no great composers. Diego Velázquez is considered by many Spaniards to be the greatest painter of them all and the Prado rooms devoted to his work are always busy. Spain's golden age was on the wane when Velázquez was around, and it's a shame he missed out on the opportunity of painting some of Spain's earlier Habsburg monarchs. One of the Habsburgs' family traditions was incest, and they produced some notable royal idiots as a result. Philip IV was not quite in the same moronic league as his father, but his portraits make him look stupid enough. Some of the earlier pictures show him as a pallid young man with bulbous red lips, little kiss curl sideburns and a Tintin quiff. In other portraits he can be seen trying to grow a moustache; attempting to look manly with a lion at his feet; and on horseback wearing a nice pink sash. In *Philip IV as Huntsman* even his dog is thinking, what a prat. If he hadn't been a king, he would have been beaten up a lot at school.

It amazed me that Velázquez had been allowed to get away with such candid portraiture, despite a Spanish tradition for unflatteringly realistic royal portraits. A hundred and fifty years later, Goya was at it again. By most accounts, Charles IV was also a twerp, and Goya depicted him as such, while his wife María Luisa looks just like the evil witch that she was supposed to be. Mind you, Spaniards have a long history of rulers whose pet names reflected their insalubrious qualities. The last king of independent León, for example, was known as Alfonso the Slobberer. Other medieval rulers include such characters as Wilfred the Hairy, Bermudo the Gouty, Enrique the Impotent and Sancho the Fat. Add to this general irreverence towards many of their rulers the fact that Spain had not long been one country, so regional feelings must have been strong. Velázquez was born in Seville and Goya was from Zaragoza. Perhaps they thought that these Castilian nobs needed taking down a peg or two.

Spanish regions still have a remarkable sense of identity and a considerable degree of autonomy. Several people I spoke to in Bilbao referred to Spain as if it were a foreign country, and you can come across the same sort of attitude in Catalonia. Though less independently minded, perhaps most distinctive of all the regions is Andalucía. The morning I left Madrid, bound for Granada, I scoffed a quick breakfast in the Museo de Jamón close to the Puerta del Sol. This is the dead-centre of Spain, and there is even a small metal plaque in the pavement to prove it. The Spanish entry into the EU in 1986 has brought a few changes, such as the virtual extinction of the mid-afternoon siesta for the urban professional classes – they found they couldn't compete with their northern European counterparts who stayed awake all day. But within a period of just a few minutes I was struck from two directions by a feeling that there is still more than just a whiff of old Europe in Spain.

The first was inside the Museo de Jamón, a cross between a bar and a delicatessen, and not, as its name suggests, a museum. Most of the Madrileños crowded at the central bar were puffing away on cigarettes beneath multiple lines of hams dangling above their heads. It struck me that there aren't many other places in Europe where this sort of behaviour would be tolerated, and I wondered whether the yellow-brown tinge on the hoofed slabs of meat was a result of the official smoking process or owed more to the endless waves of nicotine to which they are subjected before being brought down and delicately carved. Although my guidebook informed me that the Spanish authorities have moved with the rest of Europe in banning smoking from most public places, no one seems to have told the Spanish people this. It still appears that you can manage a smoke anywhere in Spain, and everyone does.

The other time-warping experience came after five minutes of trying to hail a taxi on the Calle Mayor. It took me that time (it *was* early in the morning) before I realised that none of the small 'taxi' pimples on the taxi roofs was illuminated because they can't be. In Madrid they haven't graduated to putting lights in them. The drivers manually flick a '*libre*' notice in the windscreen instead. Admittedly, these were just little things, but they did rather symbolise the state of the country. In many respects Spain lagged behind most of the rest of the Continent. It was a feeling that was reinforced when I moved on to Portugal, as if those Pyrenean peaks acted as a barrier to the flow of modern ideas. This was by no means a bad thing, I decided, because among other things it meant that the Iberian peninsula is the last good place in Europe to drink spirits. Ask for a shot of any hard stuff here and the barman brings you a glass bucket full of icebergs, which, with considerable flourish and from a great height, he proceeds to fill with about a litre of your favourite tipple. Everywhere else they barely wet your glass.

A *sine qua non* of any trip to Spain is the Alhambra in Granada, and that was where I was heading in my bus. Even Middleton, who generally disapproved of the Moorish incursion into Europe, agreed that the Alhambra was 'one of the most entire, as well as one of the most magnificent of any edifices which the Moors erected in Spain'. For hour after hour we sped south towards it through the parched flat landscape of La Mancha with an eternal promise of something more interesting in the hills on the horizon that never seemed to materialise. The driver played a video of *The Bodyguard*, mainly for himself to watch, but I was hypnotised by the endless rows of vines flicking by like lines of falling dominoes. Occasionally the black silhouette of a bull would appear to break the monotony. Then we ran out of motorway and the vines were replaced by olive trees.

By the time we had slipped down and into the foothills of the Sierra Nevada, dusk was falling and it took me the best part of the next half-hour to find a hotel that wasn't full of coach parties. Having been properly trained in late-night eating during my time in Bilbao and Madrid, I waited until an appropriate hour before venturing forth to find some fodder. This was a mistake; Granada was the one city in Spain that doesn't wait until 10.30 before thinking about dinner. I eventually settled for a *bocadillo* in a greasy joint in one of the narrow souk-like streets by the cathedral, where the mustard was of the kind that if you squeeze an entire bottle on to your meat it still doesn't taste any different. As I chomped away on the hunk of bread and meat, a curious sense of *déjà vu* came over me. I couldn't work out why until I took another bite and a large blob of yellow mustard oozed out of my sandwich and landed right in the middle of my T-shirt. Then I realised. The brandname on the plastic mustard dispenser was Maggi, the firm responsible for the African Restaurant Hakuna Matata in Disneyland Paris. Maggi products the Continent over had obviously been made aware of my opinion towards them and were out to get their own back at every opportunity.

Next morning I awoke bright and early for the trek up into times past. I spent the day in the *Arabian Nights* world of the Alhambra, which seemed to be able to absorb endless numbers of sightseers and still remain serene. Hard-boiled historians and archaeologists may shake their heads at the romantic image visitors have of the ochre castle, but Washington Irving's version was OK by me. I wanted to wander a mysterious realm of caliphs, eunuchs, alchemists and spies. I wanted to imagine emirs lying on carpets spellbound by the ceilings, to picture them listening to poetry as harmonious as their surroundings.

The gentle trickle of water unites the whole complex of palaces, medina and gardens; it is a lifeblood that flows along channels in the floor and along paths between endless pools and fountains. I followed the sparkling rivulets, down the avenue of cypress trees cut to resemble arched battlements, and into the Generalife, a garden of gardens, summer palace of the Nasrid kings on the mountain of the sun. Oranges and limes, jasmine and passion fruit exuded tranquillity as the fuzzy shadows of the wisterias softened the sharp edges of mud bricks. Rosebeds, now past their best, still echoed the delicate Islamic arches and their intricate yet simple carving, creating a perfect harmony between curves and straight lines, subtlety and strength. Figs and custard apples were approaching their prime, the walnuts and horse chestnuts already bursting from their shells. The pomegranates were large and green and ready to ripen.

I came across a small bush with multi-coloured flowers that I'd seen before, in the grounds of the fort at Lourdes. It looked to me like a type of buddleia and I'd been tempted to steal a few seeds when in France, but a watchful gardener had put me off. Here in the Generalife I cast furtive glances all around me and then pinched off a few of the seed-filled heads. Content in my role as an ecological vandal, I sat and feasted on the shimmering landscape below, closed my eyes and drank in the delicate fragrance of jasmine wafting up on the gently cooled breeze.

I raised my eyelids to see the back of a head with a New York baseball cap shading its neck. The figure turned on its Nike pumps to reveal a T-shirt emblazoned with the words 'When the bulls start running the brave go drinking' above a picture of a bull and 'Pamplona' written below. The figure took a seat on the bench beside me and was joined by a compatriot. He lit up a cigarette, exhaled a small cloud of pollution, and said in a loud North American accent, 'Well, you figured out where we are yet, Mac?'

'Somewhere in the General Life,' said Mac. If I'd been in possession of a firearm I would have blown them both away on the spot.

Down below the magic mountain lie the remains of Ferdinand and Isabella. It was Ferdinand who finally completed the reconquest of Moorish territory in 1492 by capturing Karnattah, renaming it pomegranate (Granada), and deciding that this was where the happy couple ought finally to be laid to rest. Fat gypsy ladies were selling sprigs of rosemary, and a man was shouting the odds over his prickly pears in the higgledy-piggledy streets around the cathedral. Beneath a custard apple tree a municipal employee in bright yellow overalls was cleaning between the cracks in the paving stones with a Medvac machine.

Having effectively united Spain, kicked out the Moorish infidels, expelled a few Jews, and commissioned a man named Columbus to discover an entire new world, Ferdinand and Isabella felt justified in spending a large sum of money on their chapel and mausoleum. Inside is an impressive collection of treasures, including Ferdinand's sword, Isabella's personal art collection and her surprisingly plain silver crown complete with several patches (the signs of mending) around the inside rim. The most poignant sight, however, was to be seen below the grandiose sarcophagi where their unadorned lead coffins were laid out in a bare stone crypt.

I'm not sure what Ferdinand and Isabella would have made of the most recent invasion of Andalucía, this time by holidaymakers who come to burn their skin on the garish Costa del Sol. I made the mistake of taking a bus that appeared to be stopping at every lamppost along the 100-kilometre stretch between Málaga and La Línea. The itinerary read like a holiday brochure for Spanish sun, sea and sand: Torremolinos, Fuengirola, Marbella, Estepona, each one merging into the next. The march of high-rise and low-rise, British pubs, paella bars and multi-lingual exchange bureaux stretched like a concrete rash along a grotty coastline that forty years before had been a miserable string of malaria-ridden fishing villages. Now it is a memorial to twentieth-century popular Euroculture, and selected vanguards of *Homo suntans* stumbled on to our bus to ask, in every European language but Spanish, whether this was the bus to where they wanted to go, which it invariably was not. Each time, the driver was unable to bring himself to look at his fellow Europeans from behind his reflecting shades. He just sneered. Few, if any of them, seemed to realise that they were in Spain. Fascinating though this part of the country no doubt was, I didn't dally because I was intending to stay in the Portuguese equivalent on the Algarve instead.

As we neared Algeciras, Arabic lettering began to appear on the road signs and migrant descendants of the Moors could be seen herding their families into ancient Peugeot wagons. The huge rounded rock of Gibraltar, which had been gradually enlarged with every kilometre driven since Málaga, now dominated the skyline as a Pillar of Hercules ought to do. But I wanted to see the other one, the enclave of Ceuta, one of the Spanish anachronisms across the way. It is one of the few remaining shards of an empire that was largely broken up more than a hundred years ago, and is today one of the small bits of the European Union on the African continent. Given a bit more cash, I would gladly have visited all the far-flung parts of 'Europe'. There are several EU outposts in the Atlantic (the Azores and the Canaries), a couple on the edge of the Caribbean (Guadeloupe and Martinique), one in the Indian Ocean (Réunion) and even a piece of South America (French Guiana). But publishers' advances being what they are, Ceuta was the best I could manage. I was keen to visit it both because it was a piece of Europe in Africa and because it was a last outpost of the Spanish Empire.

The ferry was followed for the first half-hour out of Algeciras by a school of twenty to thirty dolphins. They were pointed out to me by a North African who stood at the rail. He told me they lived in these straits. He smiled and said what beautiful, happy creatures they were, before turning and leaving me to watch their playful jumps. Some time later, I realised that this was the first stranger who had talked to me for no reason other than friendliness since I had left England several weeks before.

It should come as no surprise that Spain continues to hold on to Ceuta. Its strategic and symbolic significance go hand in hand, because it was from here that the Moors invaded Spain. They were sent by the unlikely-sounding Count Julian, to avenge his daughter who had been ravished by a Visigoth lout with the even more unlikely name of Roderick. Julian's small force liked the land they saw, and within three years they had returned to take the lot, as far as Narbonne in France.

Today, the whole of Ceuta is a Spanish military zone, my young taxi driver told me as we drove up from the port in the direction of Monte Hacho, the other Pillar of Hercules. Perched on the summit was a large sprawling fort. This would be interesting to visit, I thought aloud to the driver. Impossible, he told me, it belongs to the army. Since the fort was out of bounds, and the only other attraction in Ceuta seemed to be an endless succession of crappy duty-free shops, I couldn't see me staying for long. Although it wasn't in my remit, I asked the driver how easy was it to cross the border into Morocco. He looked at me in the rear-view mirror as if I had just farted.

'What do you want to go there for?' he asked incredulously.

'It would be interesting, different,' I replied, almost apologetically.

'No,' he said shaking his head emphatically, 'you shouldn't go. It is full of Moroccans. They are not civilised. They will rob you, kill you perhaps.'

I smiled, but this just aggravated him. 'Truly, I tell you. It is not like Spain.' He had now decided the rear-view mirror was not direct enough, so he turned round to convince me. 'Have you seen these people? They do not have our standards.'

'Are there many Moroccans here in Ceuta?' I asked, pointing out of his windscreen, trying to avoid a traffic accident.

'Yes, too many,' he replied, 'they come here to take our jobs.' Thankfully, he turned his eyes back to the road in time to swerve and avoid an oncoming military truck. 'Morocco,' he was shaking his head again. 'Dirty, dangerous. Don't go.'

We arrived at a *casa de huéspedes* on the Calle Real and I paid the man off. As he picked my bag out of the boot, he looked at me like an anxious friend, genuinely concerned for my health. 'Enjoy your stay in Spain, but don't go to Morocco.'

This hostile attitude was somewhat at odds with my experience of North Africans. I've spent a fair bit of time in Morocco, and always found the people to be hospitable and friendly. In fact, the only difficulty I've ever experienced in that part of the world was excessive friendliness, and that was my own fault. For anyone who shares the same Christian name as me, never use your diminutive when introducing yourself to an Arabic-speaker. In Arabic, Nick means the same thing as another four-letter word, but one that begins with an F and ends in a K.

But it wasn't just the taxi driver who detested Moroccans. The allegorical significance of Ceuta as an outpost of fortress Europe was confirmed to me by the woman behind the desk in Ceuta's tourist information bureau. She didn't think I should go to Morocco either. Perhaps I should wait until Morocco came to Ceuta, I suggested. When did she think Spain would give it back? Never, she said simply. Ceuta was full of Spaniards, it would always be Spanish.

Rather like Gibraltar to the English, I teased. That was different, she replied. Perhaps it doesn't matter now that we are all part of the European Union, I told her, but she didn't seem terribly convinced.

The woman gave me a photocopied street plan of the main part of town, circled a couple of museums, and told me that I ought to go shopping. The shopping didn't interest me, although I had noted that if ever I needed any duty-free artificial limbs Ceuta was the place to come. Every third shop seemed to be selling them. I headed instead for the one museum that sounded as if it might be of interest. It was for the Spanish Foreign Legion whose motto is 'Long live death'.

The museum was just across the road from the police station. A policeman looked me over from behind his dark glasses and pointed it out. This was just as well, because I would never have believed it was the place. Inside the main gate, I had to pass a small ornamental pond to get to the museum entrance. The pond was surrounded by several large plastic frogs, a giant turtle and a garden gnome playing a saxophone.

Behind a long counter inside the building stood three legion-naires: a Sikh sergeant flanked by two raw recruits who looked very bored. They were stiff at attention. For a moment I thought they too were ornamental, until the Sikh blew his nose. I asked if I could visit the museum and all three looked me up and down as if I were presenting myself for a selection board. It was possible to visit the museum, but first I would have to sign in, the sergeant told me, pushing a book across his counter. I filled in the columns: name, status (military/civilian), nationality. Stupidly, I stopped at the passport number column and admitted that I hadn't got my passport with me.

The sergeant eyed me suspiciously. 'You have to give us this number,' he ordered. He scrutinised the columns I had filled and, perhaps because he saw that I had written 'civilian', he added in a more conciliatory tone, 'It is for our records.' I shrugged and told him again that I hadn't got my passport with me. 'But we need it for our records,' he urged, in English now. 'You can return another day, with your passport.'

It took me five minutes to persuade him that I should look now and return later with my bloody passport. He was very concerned lest his records be incomplete, but eventually he gave in. One of the recruits would escort me, because although the serg[...] English, he couldn't leave the front desk as long as h[...] officer was not on duty. He had a conspiratorial loo[...] Moroccan invasion was clearly expected at any mom[...]

I was marched around the museum's three floors o[...] subjected to a recorded message relayed through the[...] who accompanied me. There was all the usual military [...]ags, old firearms, medals and an assortment of uniforms draped on tailors' dummies whose faces had been roughly painted all different skin colours. The Legion was formed in 1920. It had earned a reputation as a band of cut-throats during the Spanish Civil War, and had furthered its notoriety while fighting in the then Spanish bits of the western Sahara. Its third commanding officer was General Franco, the young recruit told me proudly.

My mind had begun to wander a bit in the rapid stream of Spanish, but I was woken from my daydream when my guide offered me an ashtray. This was unexpected because I wasn't even thinking about smoking. I looked at him with a puzzled expression on my face. 'Millán Astray,' the young man said again, and he offered to write it in my notebook. This was the name of the legion's first commanding officer, a fearless man apparently. The young recruit was showing me Astray's uniform with four red stripes, each signifying a loss or serious injury to a vital body part. One was for the loss of an arm, another for the loss of an eye, the other two for critical wounds. I was proudly shown Astray's artificial arm, with attached fork for when he was feeling peckish, and then led to a display case in the centre of the ill-lit room. The recruit pointed to a small glass bottle. 'Commander Astray's eye,' he announced, as if he was pointing out his knapsack.

As we returned to the entrance desk, my visit officially concluded, the recruit and the Sikh suddenly stiffened and saluted. I was perplexed. Had I unknowingly been admitted to the Spanish Foreign Legion? I looked around for an alternative explanation of their abrupt change of attitude. For a sinking moment I couldn't see anything. Just as I was preparing myself to tear off an arm and gouge out an eye, a tiny man appeared. He was about five feet tall and six feet wide, a cross between a mini-fridge and a demented dwarf. He looked like the type who would enjoy walking all over your face just exercise. His open-neck shirt revealed a nasty scar just below chin.

While I was checking all my body parts were still in order, the pantomime continued. The little man mouthed a few words to the Sikh, who shouted his response. The dwarf screwed up his face in thought and thrust out an arm to point at a row of shelving behind the Sikh. On the shelves were commemorative Foreign Legion items for sale: tapes of the Foreign Legion band and disposable cigarette lighters with a portrait of Millán Astray on the front. I consulted my notes; perhaps his name was Ashtray after all. The Sikh took a lighter off the shelf, flicked it to make sure it was working, and handed it to the man. The man shouted another order, and the Sikh jumped. It was only then that it struck me that the little big man wasn't actually making any sound. I checked my ears. How could any serious fighting force operate when it was made up of men without the full complement of senses? It would take an entire division of the Foreign Legion just to make a Spanish omelette, let alone fight a rearguard action against Moroccan rebels. It brought new meaning to the phrase 'Hear no evil, see no evil, speak no evil'.

I must have smiled as I thought this, because the dwarf became aware of my presence and slowly turned his head to give me a glacial stare. On second thoughts, perhaps legionnaires didn't need all the customary body parts. This man looked as if he'd been trained to kill with his eyes. He held his stare just long enough to make me feel like a verminous insect, before barking another silent order to his frigid underlings and marching out past the plastic frogs and the saxophone-playing garden gnome.

The Sikh turned to me. 'That was my commander,' he said. 'He has been de-voiced.'

As the bus neared Seville, we passed a road sign from the old Spain. The Spanish tend to avoid walking whenever possible, but the sign marked a pedestrian crossing and showed a snappily dressed man trotting along in a fedora. A little further on, its modern equivalent showed an androgynous matchstick striding purposefully towards the twenty-first century. Apart from the Costa del Sol and an uncanny knack of providing the names for every other model of motor vehicle in Western Europe (Granada, Cordoba, Marbella, etc.),

Andalucía has another claim to late twentieth-century cultural fame. The city of Seville, inventor of the tapas bar and flamenco dancing, was chosen to host the 1992 Universal Exposition. This was partly because prime minister Felipe González originally hailed from Seville, and besides, he wanted to put his city on the map with a flash high-speed rail link to Madrid.

As I approached my hotel in a taxi, a less fortunate aspect of the modern era was being demonstrated against by large numbers of noisy Sevillanos. The Avenida de la Constitución was packed with a slowly moving throng of people carrying green and white flags, and banners emblazoned with trade union handshake logos above words like 'workers' and 'shipyards' and 'economic policy'. Ringleaders led chants through their megaphones while television presenters in jackets and ties and jeans clutched their brightly coloured microphones as they waited to go on camera. On the roadside, plain clothes men jabbered into their walkie-talkies and above their heads police helicopters buzzed the scene.

Somehow, the Seville of the future hasn't quite worked out in the way that the planners had hoped. Destined to be a watershed in this process, 1992 was a year when the new Seville, and the new Spain, could be showed off proudly to the world. It was the five hundredth anniversary of Christopher Columbus's voyage and the year of the Seville Expo. They built a full-size replica of Columbus's ship to celebrate and launched it into the Guadalquivir River. It sank. And now the Expo site looks like an industrial wasteland.

It still seems impressive from a distance, but when I crossed the Puente del Cachorro and got up close, the site looked like the morning after the night before. Having invited the world to come and marvel at the slick new architecture, most of the Expo site was now fenced off, sad and run-down. I crunched my way across the broken glass that littered a temporary lorry park, where three years before visitors had disembarked from their luxury coaches to gaze at the wonders of modern Spain. The specially built new footbridge across the river was fenced off, the cable car was defunct and through the windows of the boarded-up nature pavilion I could see the half-dead tropical vegetation of the Selva Amazónica. Chest-high grass had grown up around a giant sand-coloured bullring of a building while the greenery hanging from the aerial horizontal trellises had given up and died. Weeds thrived in the cracks around the specially forged Expo '92 manhole covers.

If this was symbolic of the new Spain it wasn't terribly impressive. As I strolled up one of the roads, unable to walk on the pavement because of the long grass, I wondered whether it would be too harsh to think of this wilderness as an emblem of the new Europe. I stopped outside a building that looked as if it had been designed to rust away quickly and saw an ominous answer to my question. Over the still-visible outline of its original sign that read 'Expo '92', the building, which sat slap bang in the middle of the wasteland, was now labelled 'Institute for Prospective Technological Studies Joint Research Centre of the European Commission'.

Depressed by the desolation, I wandered back through the rubbish and beer bottles along the riverbank of the Triana suburb. I came across a bizarre avant-garde statue of a naked young man clutching a deformed dog. The inscription at the foot of the plinth said that it was a present to Seville from the Romanian government. The graffiti and fresh excrement smeared on the plinth implied that some Sevillanos didn't really appreciate their kindly gesture.

Back in the centre of town, the slightly more ancient architectural monuments were in rather better shape. The cathedral is the largest Gothic building in the world. It stands on the site of a great mosque, of which only a towering minaret remains. The whole complex is surrounded by stumpy Roman columns linked by thick chains as if the authorities are afraid of Moslem suicide car bombers.

You get a better idea of its sheer size inside the cathedral. It doesn't have a nave or a transept, so it just seems enormous and empty. Over on one side, beyond the main altar, is the tomb of Christopher Columbus below a clock stuck permanently at the eleventh hour. It seems that Columbus so enjoyed crossing the Atlantic that he kept doing it even after his death. He was first buried in Valladolid, but then sailed to Santo Domingo and lay there until the Dominican Republic became independent. Then he moved to Havana. After Cuban independence, he was moved again, this time to Seville. His tomb is supported by four larger-than-life pallbearers. The back two look very weary, as if they have carried him all the way from the Caribbean.

I spent the evening doing what Sevillanos do: roaming the tapas bars of Santa Cruz, an impossibly pretty maze of narrow streets and whitewashed houses, trying to catch the eye of the señoritas for which the city is justly famous. The ability to flirt is an essential skill for any traveller, a pleasant way to get involved in local culture. Standing alone in an olde worlde bar, I wasn't doing too well, but just listening to the señoritas' voices was a turn-on. Even their lisps were sexy. As I stood at a battered old counter and tucked into a pickled aubergine, I wondered about Spain. In most other countries a lisp is considered an impediment. It is not as bad as a stammer, more like a boss eye. You can carry on life as normal, but you're noticed and your lisp marks you out to everyone you meet. Everyone with a lisp should come and live in Thpain, I thought to myself. I learnt my Spanish in Latin America, where they don't have lisps. Although I'm no Don Juan, I wondered whether my lisplessness was proving an impediment to the task at hand.

I signalled to the barman who moved over to add up my tab which he had chalked on the mahogany counter, and I moved on. Tomorrow I was heading for Portugal. Perhaps I would have better luck there.

4

Where's the Beef?

Eight-thirty came and went but the bus didn't. All around me vehicles growled in and out of the departure bays beneath the swish new Expo bus station, but bay number 27 remained steadfastly empty. There was a small group of us waiting for the bus to Lagos in southern Portugal. Two smart middle-aged Spanish women stood out from a motley collection of backpackers. Most of them were English-speakers: British students and three North American women. There was also a young German couple: slobs in grubby T-shirts, grotty trousers, matted hair and nose studs. They were both extraordinarily ugly and lucky that they had found each other.

This collection of human packhorses vied for the dubious distinction of largest backpack in the world award. Some of them couldn't even make do with one, despite its size, so they carried a second, smaller rucksack on their fronts. I have often wondered what these people carry inside their gargantuan packs. It wasn't clothes in the Germans' case because they had clearly been wearing the same attire for the last two months. Anyway, the weight of these things usually suggested something more substantial, like a complete set of encyclopaedias, or a couple of dead sheep, or a steel girder suspension bridge. I don't like backpacks and the shoulderbag that I usually carry is always as light as possible, because I know that I'm the one who is going to have to carry it and I know how lazy I am. Hence I pare everything down to the bare minimum. I would have thought that most sane individuals would follow the same logic, but apparently the average backpacker has a dire need for some very large and rather heavy objects.

After two hours, the bus arrived. When the Spanish women started to complain, the driver looked at them as if they were accusing him of murder. 'I'm here now aren't I?' he asked menacingly, and the Spanish ladies stopped their complaining.

The journey was uneventful. We soon crossed the Río Guadiana and entered Portugal to proceed along the Algarve, an endless succession of drive-in potteries and political posters for the forth-coming elections. All of the candidates were grey men with moustaches, none of whom would you feel happy to leave alone with your children.

We stopped briefly at Albufeira where a van with a megaphone on its roof was slowly touring the streets encouraging all foreign visitors to attend the evening bullfight. The announcer's little spiel was in English. I heard it half a dozen times before we moved on; each time it ended with the words, '... and remember, the bull ees not keeled'.

The bus finally arrived in Lagos in the mid-afternoon. The Spanish tourist industry is well organised and regulated, but it has nothing to compare to that special breed of late-middle-aged Algarve ladies who hawk their 'clean rooms' at every bus and rail station in southern Portugal. Go with one of these ladies and there will be no form filling and no hassle, just a longer than expected hike to a small apartment block in some back street. The lady who picked me up was knee-high to a grasshopper and wore a straw hat with a flower in the band. Over her tiny forearm she carried a wicker basket with nothing in it. She led me to an apartment where the room was clean and airy and there was a wide view across the bay from the roof.

Lagos has a long and illustrious history as a port dating back to the Phoenicians, Greeks and Carthaginians, and as modern-day resort-cum-fishing ports go it didn't seem to have been messed about too badly. There were no high-rise hotels and real Portuguese people mixed with the foreign tourists. The usual beer-sponsored parasols lined the parade of outdoor eating places, but the knick-knack shops were not too awful. As in most of the rest of southern Portugal, much of the town's ancient architecture was destroyed by the 1755 earthquake which flattened Lisbon, but the small square fort at the harbour entrance survived, as did large chunks of the sixteenth-century walls that used to completely surround the town.

Dotted around the place are statues to various famous Portuguese associated with Lagos. Henry the Navigator, father of the great age of Portuguese exploration and discovery, sits in his own little square with his back to the afternoon sun, soberly surveying the harbour from beneath his wide-brimmed hat. Henry set up his school of navigation down the road at Sagres, the mythical end of the world until his protégés started venturing out into unknown portions of the Atlantic Ocean. Fellow navigator Gil Eannes has a similarly appropriate bronze likeness, but pride of place, in the town's main square, has been given to Dom Sebastião, the king who sailed from Lagos in 1578 and managed to obliterate almost the entire Portuguese nobility in one fateful battle against the Moors across the way in North Africa. Dom Sebastião's youthful statue is in the style of Bill and Ben the Flowerpot Men. It makes him look like a gormless girl dressed in pink for an American football match.

The municipal authorities have been more reverent in their approach to restoring some of Lagos's old buildings. One of the interesting things that Henry the Navigator's pupils found in the unknown parts of the world they 'discovered' was large numbers of black people, and consequently Lagos became host to Europe's first slave market. The small building still stands near the waterfront, and is now used as an art gallery. Across the square and up the road from the old slave market stands the church of Saint António, which looks like a standard-issue whitewashed Mediterranean place of worship from the outside but explodes into a riot of splendour as you step through the door. Sprawled across the walls between the pink and blue painted ceiling and the *azulejo* tiles that hemmed the bare stone floor were the writhing bodies of a thousand cherubs. Supporting pillars, peeping through vines, offering up plates laden with fruit, or just doing a regular cherub act with a pair of golden wings, these chubby pink chaps swarmed everywhere across the gilded walls. The church of Saint António is not the only place in Lagos to see cherubs, however. Hordes of their real-life counterparts paraded the cobbled streets of the town dressed in fluorescent green Lycra shorts and orange dungarees, transported sedately in pushchairs or waddling along with their puppy-fat knees. But cherubs should be seen and not heard, because as soon as they open their mouths to reveal that they are from Leeds or Hamburg, all their charm disappears.

Away from the cherubs, I spent a pleasant few days wandering the rocky coastline around Lagos, a long chain of secluded sandy beaches edged by precipitous cliff faces. It was late September and towards the end of the season, so the sun-worshippers were not so thick on the sand. Elderly German ladies sat sipping their lunch-time half-litres of beer at the beachside cafés and British 'yoofs' carried plates of greasy chips and tomato sauce down to eat on their towels. At the end of each day, red-faced tourists perused the multi-lingual menus set out on the white cobbles of the pedestrianised town centre. The place had an untroubled, family atmosphere. When you tired of the Portuguese staple of grilled sardines and salad there was always a wide variety of other seafood on offer and it didn't appear to be any effort to get it on to your plate. Down by the harbour wall, large fish just lolled about in the warm water waiting for the next order.

Apart from the cherubs, there was one other drawback to eating out in Lagos. It was a problem that comes back to haunt the single traveller every now and again; a phenomenon often encountered in family-type resorts like Lagos. I call it the 'table for one routine', and it goes something like this. You walk into a busy restaurant and stand looking eager for about five minutes while all around you waiters brush past carrying piles of plates destined for large groups of customers. If the waiters register your presence at all, it only results in a terse request to step aside because you're in their way. When one of the staff does finally realise that you are waiting to be seated, rather than just standing there gawking at the scenery, he sidles over to you with a knowing glint in his eye. He looks behind you to feign surprise that you are alone, and then asks a question that he already knows the answer to. 'How many?' You tell him and in an unnecessarily loud voice he shouts across the restaurant to a colleague, 'Table for ONE.'

All around you, diners stop briefly with their forks halfway to their mouths to throw a glance in your direction. Anyone who has queued at a supermarket checkout with a pile of sad-bastard meals-for-one will know what I mean. Everyone, including the person at the till, looks at you. It's never more than a brief glance, because since you are so clearly on your own you must have a personality disorder and you could be dangerous. If they catch your eye they always look away.

In restaurants, I used to hate this. Sometimes I wanted to play up to it and say loudly that I had just been released from Psycho Ward One and the only reason I wasn't with my friends was because I had chopped them all up into small pieces. On other occasions I wanted to ingratiate myself by stating, just as loudly, that 'My girlfriend and her family and their friends and the dog all decided to eat in tonight, so I'm alone, which is pretty unusual and actually rather a relief.' But any waiter worth his tip would know you're lying because they can recognise the slightly hunted look in your eyes that betrays your solitary status and the fact that you'd really rather have someone with you. Either way, the result is the same: they put you at the crappiest table in the house. This might be next to the smelly toilet or in front of the kitchen so that the waiters all trip over you when they emerge carrying multiple servings for large groups, or by the door so that the back of your chair gets knocked every time someone comes into the restaurant. When they get around to taking your order, they do so with an attitude that implies you're lowering the tone of their establishment and they'd really rather you weren't there at all.

After a few doses of the table for one routine I took to eating outside beneath the parasols where this attitude was not so prevalent. It was here I realised that there was actually a fair sprinkling of single males in the town of Lagos, and most of them were on the fringes of society. There was one eccentric young Englishman who looked as if he was dressed for a winter in Hyde Park, despite the fact that during the day the temperature was well into the eighties. Every now and again, this character was to be seen leaning against a wall shouting nonsense at anyone that passed in an accent which suggested his parents had wasted a large sum of money on his education. The two policemen who regularly patrolled the centre of town, whose only apparent duty was to confront situations like this, would gently scold the young man and ask him what he meant by it. His usual response was to try and sell them some of the waste paper from his overcoat pockets, and the policemen would send him on his way.

The streets of Lagos were also home to several drunks, of indeterminate nationality, who staggered about the place being harmless. Early one evening, I was waiting for my dinner to arrive when one of these resident dipsomaniacs sat down at the table next to mine. He was a short, red-haired man, dressed in an ancient bomber jacket and blue painter's smock. He brought with him a small black dog that he called Abdul and a powerful odour of unwashed body which, in turn, was accompanied by a significant following of house flies. In a few minutes, he was joined at his table by a tall, thin man wearing dark glasses, a bush hat and cut-off jeans. They sat in silence, staring out towards the harbour mole, while

Abdul busied himself trying to catch flies. The restaurant management took no notice of their two most recent guests. They didn't offer to take any orders, but they didn't attempt to move them on either.

After some minutes, the red-haired man said loudly, in accented English, 'I don't go tonight, I go tomorrow.' His tall companion said nothing. The redhead added, 'But don't tell to your wife that I speak anything.' Abdul the dog had grown tired of trying to swat flies, and turned to the tall man's plimsoll lace which offered a more satisfying subject for his attentions. My fish arrived and I began to tuck in. Apropos of nothing the tall man said, 'Today is my birthday. I am sixteen years old,' which seemed very unlikely. The man was fifty if he was a day.

The drunks' conversation continued as if they were reading a medley of lines taken at random from a phrase book. Their voices became muted and I strained to hear something that sounded like, 'Hey, I can take the best bus to the bus station, with your rich wife.' They were either former English-language teachers indulging in a bit of reminiscence about their favourite idioms, or they were rehearsing a newly discovered play by Samuel Beckett. Drunks the world over converse in this same hybrid language, as if they are the human remnants of the attempt to promote Esperanto. The international language never took off and the trainees are still trying to get over it. They have been relegated to the streets where they can only communicate with each other.

The vignette ended when the tall thin man announced that he was 'sick and tired of this foreign food' and he stood up to walk away. The dog chased after the lanky figure, but his master, the redhead, shouted, 'Abdul, how much is a taxi to the airport?' and the dog returned. The two of them then left in the opposite direction.

Everyone who has looked at a map of Spain and Portugal knows that Portugal looks like the face of the Iberian peninsula head. I took a bus that ascended the country's chin and disappeared up its nose to Lisbon. Both literally and metaphorically, Lisbon is the closest a European capital comes to the Third World. You notice this immediately because its streets are lined with shoe shiners and lottery ticket sellers and large numbers of beggars with less than the average number of limbs. Tiny wizened old ladies who should be tucked up in bed sipping cocoa are out in their slippers, bent double beneath the weight of their black headscarves, selling Lotto tickets. Blind people with large black money boxes attached to their long white sticks hassle you for spare change as you pass. For the more morbid passer-by, a black man on crutches will show you his leg wound in return for a donation. Able-bodied street operators exploit a thriving niche market in car parking. The long Avenida da Liberdade is divided up into sectors, each worked by a man or a boy who flags down passing cars and directs them into his part of the kerb. For a few escudos these characters won't scratch the paintwork.

Lisbon's resemblance to a developing country's capital betrays the fact that Portugal is one of the poor men of Europe. There are many other indicators of the country's position a few steps behind most of her European cousins. One of these is the money. While every other EU country (except Eire) now issues tiny lightweight coins that look as if they were designed for a kiddies' board game, the Portuguese are still using seriously large coins bearing pictures of boats that went out of date hundreds of years ago. Portugal was keen to join the Union when she did in 1986, and it's not surprising. The entire country was designated a 'less favoured area' (EU-speak for backward) and they started throwing money at it. Brussels is providing Portugal with a staggering 12.8 million US dollars a day for the rest of the century to help her catch up. Imagine taking Manchester's Moss Side and a couple of depressed Welsh valleys, roll them out to the size of a whole country, spread with a bit of sunshine, garnish with olives and you'd get more or less the same thing.

The country has been at the bottom end of the European development scale for a long time. Portugal's period as a major world power, ignited by Henry the Navigator in the fifteenth century, was already fading towards the end of the sixteenth century, when Spain walked in and took over for sixty years. In the nineteenth century, Portugal virtually fell apart. When Napoleon's army turned up the Portuguese royal family took an extended leave of absence in South America, and left the British to sort things out. For a time, the country looked like a cross between a Brazilian colony and a British protectorate. The monarchy returned to preside over a century of muddle and mayhem before they were finally deposed in 1910. The sad state of affairs to which Portugal was reduced is symbolised by the statue of Dom Pedro IV which stands in the central Lisbon square named after him. It is a bargain basement adaptation originally cast for the Austrian Emperor Maximilian of Mexico. The statue just happened to be in Lisbon when news of the emperor's execution reached Europe in 1867. Portugal's last king, Dom Manuel the Unfortunate, sailed away to a life of exile in England. He died in Twickenham in 1932.

Worse was to come. Portugal got republicanism instead. This lasted for sixteen years, during which time the country went through 8 presidents, 44 cabinets, 24 uprisings and revolts, and 158 general strikes. These were turbulent times. In the first five years of the 1920s, Lisbon police records show that no less than 325 bombs exploded on the streets of the capital. Then the military took over. While the rest of Europe got involved in World War II to fight off the threat of fascist dictatorship, Portugal and Spain didn't. OK, the Spanish had tried and failed, ushering in Franco, but Portugal got Salazar, who ruled the roost for nearly forty years before he fell off his deckchair. He landed on his head and took two years to die from the resulting brain damage. It was only in 1974, after a series of colonial wars in Africa had all but bled the economy dry, that a coup led to the modern era of democracy in Portugal.

The Portuguese are still recovering from the effects of the military dictatorship according to Luis de Jesus, a young travel agent who started talking to me in a bar in Lisbon's Barrio Alto one evening. He was killing time before he had to make the trek out to the airport to chaperone some of his clients on to their flights. Like his namesake, Mr Jesus seemed intent upon spreading goodwill to all men. He sat down at the table next to mine, gave me one of his cakes, and miraculously offered to buy me another glass of wine.

When I enquired as to why it was that you see so few Portuguese backpackers in Europe, he explained that apart from not having a lot of money, Portuguese youth were a bit wary of abroad. The gospel according to Mr Jesus made a lot of sense. Closed minds had been passed down from the generation that still remembered the days of the Salazar dictatorship, he said. Most of his clients were middle-aged, self-made people with little formal education who wanted to see Europe but did not have much confidence and didn't speak any foreign languages. Most of them travelled on escorted tours. When I asked him what had happened to Portugal's pioneering spirit, all that he could come up with was a couple of Portuguese teams that regularly enter the Paris–Dakar motor rally.

There is, however, one arena in which the Portuguese can still stun the world with their bravery and fortitude, but you have to come to Portugal to see it. I'm referring to that quintessentially Iberian public display of machismo, the bullfight. As a spectacle, the Portuguese version of events is marginally preferable to its Spanish counterpart because, as the megaphone van in Albufeira kept emphasising, '... the bull ees not keeled.' Well, not publicly anyway; apparently most of the unfortunate bulls are slaughtered later.

Nonetheless, I couldn't really come to this end of Europe on my modern-day Grand Tour and not see one of the most distinctive aspects of regional culture, so I duly bought a ticket for the Campo Pequeno and jumped on to the clean and litter-free Lisbon metro in good time to find my seat for the 10 p.m. start. I knew I was getting warm when I disembarked at the station where the marble walls were emblazoned with stylised images of bulls and matadors and, believe it or not, prancing naked women.

Above ground, the night was buzzing with crowds milling past the mobile burger vans towards the stadium entrances where fully dressed combatants were nervously pulling on their final cigarettes. A strong smell of urine pervaded inside, beneath the grandstands, where two large moustaches in elaborate eighteenth-century costumes sat upon two huge chestnut horses. The horses wore black blindfolds over their eyes, and heavy padded blankets hung down over their flanks. Their riders' legs were encased in suit of armour leggings below the knee and their feet fed into heavy, wooden box-like stirrups. The riders looked tense and expectant, their mounts supremely unruffled.

Up in the arena, the evening's events were heralded by a short burst from a brass band, a signal for the spectators to stand up and almost immediately sit down again on the concrete benches. All the participants paraded around the raked pink gravel ring and paid their respects to an important-looking character in the main stand.

A Portuguese bullfight is divided into two main parts. The arena was cleared and a bugler sounded off to announce the arrival of a rider on a white horse without any protective blankets, flanked by the two chestnut mounts I had seen behind the scenes earlier. It was the job of the white horseman to taunt and provoke the bull, while the two chestnuts, their riders carrying long pointed poles like boat hooks, stood by in case of any unexpected developments.

An immense black bull was released into the ring through a gate in the blood-red boards and the *toureiro* on the white horse proceeded to dance around the glistening beast. The aim was to avoid the bull's charges while planting spikes in its back. The bull's horns were wrapped in sacking but if it had made contact, the horse would have been an instant dog's dinner. At first, the bull looked dazzled by all the lights and attention but when it focused on the white horse it made a special effort. After three or four charges, and having hardly noticed the prongs now hanging from its back, the bull looked bored and wandered around to see how it might get out of this stupid situation. When it realised that it couldn't, the bull got cross and resumed its charges with a new determination.

If you could conveniently forget the unnecessary public humiliation of this noble creature, this bit of the bullfight was an exhibition of astonishing equestrian prowess based on an incredible understanding and trust between rider and mount. The second half of the bout was more extraordinary.

The white horse left the arena to loud applause and two matadors jumped into the ring to occupy the half-tonne of irate black muscle while a group of men emerged from the toilets stubbing out their fags. The eight-man team vaulted into the arena and lined up behind their leader who produced a floppy green joker's cap from his tunic and pulled it on to his head. This front man was standing near the centre of the pink gravel ring and started to call the bull. The bull appeared to be enjoying himself with the two matadors and took no notice. (This was unlikely, of course. I don't think enjoyment would be very high up on the list of emotions running through my head if I was placed in a ring surrounded by hostile spectators, with half a dozen spears hanging out of my back, to be faced by a couple of half-wits waving coloured blankets at me.) After a few more attempts to capture its attention, the animal turned its huge head towards the joker trying to confront him and you could almost hear the bull thinking, piss off, little man, I'm playing with this cape.

But the men with the capes exited and the joker persisted. He stood with his head held high and his thumb tucked in his tunic pocket. He stamped on the pink grit, gesturing defiantly at the bull.

At last the bull took interest in the line of psychopaths standing opposite him. It charged.

If I hadn't seen this with my own eyes I wouldn't have believed it. The joker at the front of the line just stood there. Apparently, this was what he wanted. The bull went straight through him and several of his colleagues. All of them were tossed into the air like ... well, like men who had just been hit by a charging bull, to come crashing down heavily in various unceremonious positions. The rest of the madmen scattered.

The cape-wavers were on again immediately, to entice the bull away from finishing off the wounded, who gingerly picked themselves up, visibly shaken by their close encounter with a half-tonne of steak. But they weren't fast learners. Limping, the lead idiot checked his ribs, tweaked his moustache, replaced his joker's cap and went for it again. This time he went under the bull as it charged and was trampled, leaving the chap immediately behind him to be flipped head over heels through the cool night air. The crowd took a sharp intake of breath.

Again the cape-wavers were quickly on the scene to cause a diversion as a team of medical advisers piled over the side of the ring to come to the prostrate joker's aid. He lay motionless, a victim of his own effrontery. A stretcher appeared and the figure was carried away, presumably to live out the rest of his days in a prolonged vegetative state.

I must say that I wasn't quite sure what to make of this wanton display of Iberian valour. But it wasn't over yet, because the next applicant for vegetable status pulled on the joker's cap and the whole procedure began again. Everyone around me could sense the nervousness of the new lead idiot. He must have been thinking to himself, Silvano was a pretty macho kind of guy and look what happened to him. The bull charged a third time. The joker didn't flinch. He just stood there, held open his arms and took the bull's forehead full on the chest. The crowd roared, the lead idiot's mates were suddenly behind him and all around the bull, grabbing hold of the creature and struggling to avoid being trampled. For a few seconds the danger of further human casualties was a very real one, until the seven men finally stopped the bull in its tracks. There was a markedly relieved air to the loud cheer that went up from the spectators.

Later, after the bull had been pacified by the cunning ploy of flooding the arena with half a dozen girl cows wearing sexy cowbells, who then led him out of the stadium, the walking wounded made a victory parade. Those survivors of the eight-man team who still had the use of their legs limped around in their blood-stained tunics taking bows before the audience. The ovation appeared to be in celebration of the fact that some of the men were still alive. Flowers and hats were thrown into the ring and some wag added a walking stick.

And that, as they say, was that. There were several more such bouts, but when you've seen one Portuguese bullfight you've seen them all. And what I had seen was a display of phenomenal virility and courage, but also an indication that Portuguese men do not know the difference between bravery and a lack of common sense. Stupidly, I asked the young man sitting next to me what it was all about. 'It is a show, a spectacle,' he told me. 'It is part of our culture.'

Calouste Gulbenkian wasn't Portuguese. He was an Armenian oil magnate who made lots of money and spent some of it putting together a world-class art collection. He then auctioned it off in the 1940s to the highest bidder among the nations of Europe. Portugal made him an offer that included complete exemption from any taxes and won herself one of the century's most generous patrons of the arts. The Gulbenkian Foundation sponsors an orchestra, concert halls and galleries as well as numerous cultural projects.

Gulbenkian had an eye for a deal, and his museum and foundation complex in Lisbon seems to act like a magnet to all sorts of lesser operators with an eye for a scam. The 200 metres between the metro stop and the museum consisted of a dangerous multi-directional road junction which demanded total concentration to avoid adding to Lisbon's traffic casualty figures. Hence the zone was ideal territory for the small army of freelance peddlers, hawkers and charlatans which patrolled the area. I was offered umbrellas by three different umbrella salesmen, a young woman asked me if I could change a good forgery of a 500-escudo note for her urgent telephone requirements, and a man wearing an orange jacket approached with a weak sob story about being the victim of urban crime and could I spare him the fare to get home? Judging by the size of his request, he was normally resident in Brazil. Later, when I was entering the museum café, three gypsy kids pushed by me and did a quick round of tables demanding handouts and grabbing handfuls of sugar sachets before being chased out of the building by a security man.

The museum itself was purpose-built, but unfortunately at the time when the multi-layer concrete square box approach to architecture was in vogue. Its inside, however, was serene. Dapper grey-suited attendants glided across the marble floors to usher you noiselessly into the complex of spacious galleries which contained the most beautiful collection of art I have ever seen.

Greek coins don't usually turn me on, but the small number of gold specimens in the first gallery were awe-inspiring. Ancient Egyptian bronzes of cats gave way to stunning vases and carpets from all over the Middle East, phenomenally beautiful Islamic wall tiles, and illustrated books from Armenia and Persia that you would kill for. Tiny intricate Japanese lacquer medical boxes rubbed shoulders with Chinese porcelain that looked delicate enough to be made of rice paper. Each gallery had just enough in it to keep you fascinated, but not so many exhibits that you felt exhausted. And mid-way through the collection, just when you feel that you might be fading, you come across a sitting room where you can rest up in all-enveloping leather sofas before moving on.

Then there was a small collection of pre-fifteenth-century European books of hours. I could almost smell the wild strawberries on the page of one Italian specimen, but reeled when I got closer to discover a fluorescent multi-coloured three-headed devil lurking behind the foliage. From beneath a fifteenth-century Venetian parasol in red velvet, even a room full of French Regency furniture looked pleasing. Beyond the outrageous Louis XVI clocks, there were Monets and Manets, a couple of Turners, and an entire room devoted to the exquisite Art Nouveau jewellery and glasswork of René Lalique. Other than this room, which was dark to highlight the intricate spotlit details of orchids and insect wings, every gallery was complemented with views of the landscaped gardens inviting you to let your troubles seep away and become a lotus-eater for the afternoon.

I had never before been in a museum where I felt so totally in tune with the collector's taste. The exhibits were exquisite and I wanted them all. If I had limitless funds and decided to start a collection of expensive nice old things from all over the world, from virtually every conceivable period, this is the sort of collection I would put together. I can't remember the last time I had such a good time in a museum.

To celebrate, I went out for dinner. I'd grown tired of eating seafood in Lagos so I had been experimenting with other forms of Portuguese cuisine. But tonight I was in the mood for something conventional after an unfortunate experience with *cozido a Portuguesa*. I had ordered the dish for lunch one day in the Baixa and was rather pleased with myself because the waiter gave me a smile of approval when I did so. Usually when I order blind like this it turns out to be tripe, but on this occasion the waiter brought me a couple of boiled carrots, a piece of vinegary blood sausage, and several unidentifiable chunks of boiled pig's flesh all laid out on a bed of boiled cabbage. To me this was not very appetising, but what really made me lose my enthusiasm was the one piece of pig which I could identify, because it was half of its snout. Not one to shrink from a challenge, I downed a few carrots and dispatched the sausage before turning my attention to the former pig's nasal apparatus. I skewered the article with my fork, popped it into my mouth, and started chewing. It tasted like boiled pig's snout.

Hence, that evening I went to a restaurant called the Bom Jardin which had been recommended to me by a friend not noted for his culinary adventurism. 'You have to order chicken,' he told me, 'because it is *the* place to eat chicken in Lisbon.' The Bom Jardin was tucked away off a street lined with disabled beggars and dodgy characters trying to sell you hashish. It was like entering a motorway service stop: clean, too bright and plastic-looking. The only clues that you were still in Portugal were the orange-tree motifs on the wall tiles and the hum of the air conditioner. The place was almost empty. I sat down and a waiter shuffled over. He was fat, fortyish, and wore thick heavy glasses halfway down his face. The buttons on his shirt were open below his chest because the formerly white material (now a sort of tie-dye effect of brown gravy stains) could not manage to encase his ample tummy. He was carrying a white ceramic plate which he sneezed over before placing it on the tablecloth in front of me.

I said, '*Boa noite*,' and the waiter didn't reply. He just pushed his spectacles up his nose with the back of his hand. I looked around the restaurant as the glasses began their slow descent down the waiter's nose. 'Do you have a menu?' I asked. The waiter stood there motionless for a few seconds, as if we were speaking over a long-distance telephone line. Without a word, he turned and shuffled away.

A good ten minutes later he returned, carrying a laminated menu card. This time he handed it to me before sneezing. He muttered something and waddled over to the air conditioner to switch it off. I examined the menu. It was full of fish, entrées, meat dishes and desserts. Chicken did not even appear to get a mention. I looked across the restaurant again. The couple in the far corner were tucking into what looked like a former farmyard inhabitant, as was the young chap sitting at a table against the wall. Maybe it was just that every dish was served with a free fried chicken.

I returned to the menu, and this time I noticed the word '*Frango*', scribbled like an afterthought in the bottom right-hand corner. The waiter was hovering and I caught his attention. He began the long trek across the quarry tiles towards me, sneezing twice on the way. He was raising his hand, in preparation for a third eruption, as I asked, 'Do you have chicken, *senhor*?' His hand stopped abruptly and he gave me a broad grin.

'*Si, senhor*,' he said proudly, as if I had said the password. Then his face screwed up, his head wobbled and he let forth an almighty blast down towards my leg. '*Batatas*?' he asked, as if nothing had happened. I nodded. '*Salada*?' I nodded again. I asked him to bring me some white table wine to go with it.

I had ordered chicken and that's what the man brought me. An entire chicken, cut in four, with only the head and feet missing. It arrived with a knowing smile on the waiter's face which I mistakenly thought said, 'Here it is, and this is one area where us fatties are winning, because there is no way you're going to eat this entire chicken *and* this plate of chips.'

What his smile really said was: 'You think you can't eat all this, but just you wait and see ...' And of course he was right, it was so good I did eat the entire chicken. It was crisp where it should be crisp, succulent where it should be succulent and overall much tastier and more real than any British chicken. This was probably because it hadn't spent a miserable life pent up in a little wire cage being force-fed fishmeal. There were definite advantages to being what the EU describe as 'less favoured'. This was one occasion when I was glad to be eating alone, so that I wouldn't have to share it, and there were no witnesses to my piggery, or should I say fowlery?

Having enjoyed Europe's best chicken dinner, I took the lift back to my hotel. I know this sounds impossible but believe me it isn't in Lisbon. Like Rome, the city is built on seven hills, and one hundred years ago Gustave Eiffel, the French engineer, came up with an ingenious and bizarre method for transporting people up and down between the Baixa and the Barrio Alto. The lift goes straight up into thin air in its iron skeleton and you get out to stroll the 200-metre walkway which connects it to the hilltop. Depending upon your mood or intoxication level the lift shaft looks like a piece of church, or a giant candlestick or a turn-of-the-century science fiction beast which is about to come alive and chase you. It was way before its time architecturally, a post-modern contraption that pre-dates modernism. The Parisian Pompidou Centre is hailed as an inside-out building, but Lisbon's *elevador* is an inside part of a building without the building at all.

I went to Sintra, Lisbon's celebrated hill station, summer residence of the city's Moorish lords and later of Portugal's native royalty. It is a world away, but just a forty-five-minute ride on the train. So much has been written about its cool and wooded charms that the superlatives tend to pale. It was a youthful Lord Byron who famously likened the place to Eden, although the Portuguese poet Gil Vicente had called it paradise on earth nearly three hundred years before. In his *Complete System of Geography*, Middleton was too concerned with the 1755 earthquake and the scandalous activities of the Inquisition to pay much attention to Sintra, but he did note that it was 'supposed to have the most salubrious air of any place in Portugal'. Like Spain, Portugal was not on the itinerary of many Grand Tourists. The few travellers who did venture that way complained about everything. The worst dog kennel in England was a palace compared to the best Portuguese inn, the food was terrible, and you couldn't move in Lisbon without being exposed to a succession of misshapen limbs, huge tumours and carefully exposed wounds (not much change there, then). Those who made it to Sintra, however, were more than compensated.

83

As it happened, Sintra's charisma was not immediately apparent the evening I arrived. The small town centre was actually more like Bedlam than Elysium because things were warming up for a visit from the Social Democratic Party's prime ministerial candidate.

I had to ask a spectator what was going on and when he told me I swallowed my pride and enquired as to the man's name. In Britain, we pay attention to a change of government in Germany or France, we make jokes about it when it happens in Italy, but no one takes any notice when it happens in Spain or Portugal. We just go there on holiday. The candidate's name was Fernando Nogueira, and judging by the photographs of him on all the campaign literature which was being handed out, he was an instantly forgettable grey Hispanic John Major look-alike.

A jam of horn-blaring traffic had clogged the narrow winding street and a band was playing ear-splitting drum rolls. When the musicians paused for rest, a repetitive campaign jingle took up the slack from a loudspeaker mounted on the roof of one of Senhor Nogueira's orange campaign vehicles. Girls in campaign T-shirts and team neckscarves were handing out bright orange campaign souvenirs designed to enliven Mr Grey's image. Favourites with the children in the throng were hand-sized polystyrene oranges which appeared to be very satisfying to squeeze. There were also small flags to wave and stickers of oranges to apply to anything you felt needed an orange sticker (I put one on my green notebook). Less obvious in their symbolic significance were the plastic aprons being doled out by another campaign man in a smart suit. Each carried a picture of three parrots.

And then, as if by magic, Senhor Nogueira's convoy appeared from around the corner. It looked as if one of his campaign managers had carefully chosen the vehicles to give his motorcade a pan-European flavour: there was a Rover, a Citroën, a Fiat and a Volvo. Portugal doesn't have a car industry, but there was also a notable absence of Spanish vehicles. A bit of minor jostling took place as a press photographer and a TV cameraman pushed forward to capture the moment when the candidate stepped out of his Citroën and into Eden. Rapturous cheers went up, there was a blast of the mind-numbing campaign jingle and then the band took over again. The man who would be prime minister dashed around with a fixed grin on his face, shaking hands and waving V for victory salutes to the crowd while the band played on. Then, almost as quickly as he had appeared, he gave a final wave and jumped into his car to edge through the crowd along a cordon of helpers in sleeveless jackets. Parping their horns, the convoy whisked their charge away down the hill. The band stopped and cleared away leaving a ragged crowd and a street full of rubbish for someone to clear up.

Now that the streets of Sintra were mine, I took stock. I had decided to spend the night in the town because several people had told me that Sintra was too pretty for its own good in this day and age and therefore crawling with coach parties during the day. I had got the place more or less to myself, but the light was fading quickly and soon all I could see were the overpriced restaurants and the tacky souvenir shops. I had the cool, clean mountain air, but that was actually rather chilly. I persevered and wandered away from the main square, up and down the network of narrow streets that criss-crossed the hillsides. It got better. The dim light from the wrought iron street lamps illuminated a world of quaint villas, or *quintas*, with terracotta roofs and colonnaded balconies, hanging vines and creeping ivy. Lichen and moss grew in splotches on every stone wall, echoing the piebald bark of the plane trees which in Lisbon had looked pock-marked and diseased but here were just atmospheric. Cats slunk in and out of the shadows on the smooth cobbled pavements and up above was a sky full of stars.

I was sufficiently inspired to be up early the next morning to walk. Just behind the town you can disappear into the forest which clings to the Serra de Sintra. A winding path climbs through the fairytale woods of sweet-smelling eucalyptus, pine, ash and chestnut. Huge granite boulders were furry with moss, and curly green ferns sprouted from every crevice. Birds flitted in and out of the dappled sunlight, tweeting their appreciation. Now I could really see what all the fuss was about. Although Byron was in a stroppy mood when he came to Portugal in 1809, he couldn't help but be spellbound by Sintra. He just thought it was too good for the Portuguese.

Despite the fact that Portugal is England's oldest European ally, and we share the same patron saint, not many Englishmen had anything good to say about the Portuguese 200 years ago. Middleton considered their chief characteristics to be 'craft, treachery, malice, haughtiness, cruelty, avarice, and a disposition totally vindictive'. Other than that, they were really nice people. He summed them up as second-rate Spaniards, and about the only complimentary thing he could say about the Spanish was that they didn't drink too much like everyone else in continental Europe. An exception to this general rule, however, was William Beckford, an extremely rich Englishman who took up residence in Portugal towards the end of the eighteenth century. He liked Portugal and he liked the Portuguese, which was just as well because he couldn't go home. Beckford had been driven to Portugal from England by his scandalous sexual proclivities. Being a homosexual, he didn't really fit in in Wiltshire. I had brought a copy of his book on Portugal and read bits of it in my hotel room the previous night.

For Beckford, it was love at first sight when he arrived in Sintra. He set up shop in a *quinta* and indulged his penchant for playing the oriental sultan, a whim which his enormous wealth allowed him to enact to the full. Modern-day backpackers may carry around a lot of luggage with them, but they aren't a patch on William Beckford. He brought an entourage of valets, footmen, chefs and confectioners, his own physician and artist, a tailor, a hatter, a barber and a harpsichordist. Whenever he went on tour, he brought his own bed which had to be erected for him each night. He liked Sintra so much he even had a flock of sheep sent out from his Wiltshire estate to keep him company.

Beckford made friends with a local marquis who had fifty table servants and ate thirty-five-course dinners. He borrowed a selection of musicians from the Queen of Portugal, violins and a wind section to accompany 'delicate warblers, as plump as quails and as gurgling and melodious as nightingales', and placed them at strategic intervals behind orange and bay trees. He passed hours listening to them, being aesthetic, and I could see why.

Since this had all the attributes of a fairytale forest, it made sense that towards its summit there should be a magic castle, and there was. Actually there were two: one in ruins, the other well preserved thanks to the Portuguese government with a little help from its EU friends. The first I came upon was the ruined Moorish version, its walls growing organically out of the boulder-strewn granite hillside. From the ramparts which snaked across the slope, you could look down almost vertically into the town of Sintra. Within the castle walls, as in Granada's Alhambra, narrow water channels ran throughout the complex to distribute life-sustaining liquid like veins through a body. Evergreen oak trees had now taken up residence to provide a secluded and shady respite from the precipitous views. Every stone, trunk and branch came in a battleship-grey veneer of lichen. Once the mountain-top retreat of Moorish conquerors, the castle was now the realisation of a thousand childhood dreams of princesses with long golden hair.

I continued my ascent to the more recent Palácio da Pena, an architectural riot of a castle put up in the 1840s on the site of an old monastery. It looks as if it was built by the Romantic movement after experimenting with psychedelic drugs. From the outside, its turrets and domes are all lemon-yellow and terracotta, set off here and there by walls decorated with sparkling blue *azulejo* tiles and crocodile heads sticking out from unexpected places. It was built on the orders of Queen Maria II's Bavarian prince of a husband with the help of a Prussian engineer named Ludvig von Eschwege, whose vast statue in warrior-pose stands guard over the mock-medieval structure from a nearby crag.

Inside, the castle was no less bizarre. Four life-sized turbaned Moors brandished candelabras in the pink stuccoed ballroom, and the Queen's favourite room for taking tea was decked out like a subcontinental brothel with a Bohemian chandelier and horribly overcarved teak furniture. One of the bedrooms had plaster walls painted to simulate wood panelling, there were swanhead taps in the bathroom and a throne-sized wooden toilet. Apparently, the whole complex has been preserved as it was when the Portuguese royal family, headed by Dom Manuel the Unfortunate, hurriedly left the country in 1910 bound for England and a life in exile. Twickenham must have been rather a come-down.

I munched my late lunch-time sandwich in the grounds of the Palácio da Pena on the highest point in the Serra de Sintra. Perched on the hilltop, I had no need of William Beckford's army of musicians because Sintra provides its own natural harmony. Crickets played the accompaniment to the occasional bee which buzzed solo to suck the last drops of nectar from the fading gorse and heather. Pairs of butterflies danced like acrobatic lovers in the sunlight and a bright black beetle landed on a stunted pine. I feasted my soul on the marvellous vistas. Down to the left and behind, Lisbon sat on the banks of the Tagus, its suspension bridge shimmering in the midday haze. Beyond the fantastical Palácio da Pena to the north lay the heights around Torres Vedras, where, while Byron scowled his way through southern Portugal, Wellington was putting up a line of fortresses against the French which were eventually to prove a decisive move in the Peninsular War.

Straight out in front of me sat Cabo da Roca, the westernmost point on the European mainland, and beyond that the endless expanse of the Atlantic Ocean. Being on the edge of things is good for the sense of perspective it can bring. As for most of her European cousins, Portugal's heyday of adventure and empire had been and gone. Now it was just a has-been stuck out on the far end of a continent which is itself but a knobbly afterthought to the vast tracts of Asia. It struck me that the whole EU idea was our communal attempt to avoid the ignominy of becoming a Continental has-been, now that the rest of the world could stand up for itself. My mind wandered to other attempts at European unity. I suppose the first to manage it had been the Romans. I'd do Italy next.

5

The Italian Job

The relaxed air of chaos that is Italy began as soon as we arrived in front of the Alitalia check-in desk. I was standing with my friend Cliff, studying the careful comb grooves set in the black marcel wave of the head confronting us. The young man was deep in conversation on the telephone and oblivious to the growing line of passengers awaiting his services.

'On the phone to mother again,' said a very English voice from behind us. The Alitalia man was gesturing vigorously at the telephone, attempting to force his words into the mouthpiece.

'They'll never get it right, will they?' came the voice from behind again, which was emanating from a business suit with attaché case attached. Just as the telephone was replaced, an Armani type appeared beside me at the counter and quickly launched into a rapid account of his requirements.

'Hey, there is a queue you know,' called the English suit behind me. The Italian raised his hands in a gesture of tranquillity.

'I just pick up my boarding card,' he said, which was what we were all trying to do. The phone rang again and Mr Comb Grooves handed the boarding pass to his fellow countryman as he lapsed back into a rapid exchange of verbal fire.

'Bloody chaos,' said the English suit again, casting an anxious glance at the flight monitor on the wall beside us and shaking his head. 'Twenty minutes before my plane to Rome goes.'

The phone receiver was replaced in its rest once more and the young man took our tickets, glanced at them and tapped a few things into his computer terminal. He looked up at me quizzically, as if he was about to ask whether I wanted extra buffalo mozzarella on my pizza or a contract put out on my grandmother.

'This flight may be quite late,' he said with a knowing look, 'I put you on the one before.' Cliff and I looked at the departure information screen. There was another flight to Milan, scheduled to have left thirty minutes ago, but still flashing as boarding.

'Will we still make it?' Cliff asked.

'Look, I'm sorry, but my flight leaves in fifteen minutes,' butted in the voice from the suit behind, 'would you mind terribly if you just gave me my boarding pass.' We let the man past as we considered the situation.

'Your flight is maybe three hours late,' Mr Alitalia said to Cliff and me as the English suit bounded off for his flight to Rome, 'you can make the one before if you hurry.'

Hurry we did, only to sit on the delayed plane for another thirty minutes before it eventually took off. There was no eagerly humble apology from the captain, and the slightly geriatric cabin staff were supremely unconcerned. No one complained. The passengers seemed to expect to be treated like a nuisance. I wondered whether the Roman Empire was as befuddled; did Julius Caesar shrug and say, 'OK, we won't be invading you today because the forage man hasn't turned up to feed the horses'?

Given this introduction to Italian ways of doing things, I should not have been surprised that when we finally presented ourselves at the Hotel Majorca in Milan, where rooms had been booked for us by a friend, the management had cancelled our reservations. It was my problem; I hadn't yet fully adopted the Italian frame of mind.

'But why did you fly with Alitalia?' demanded Laura. 'They are morons.' We were sitting around the dinner table in a second-floor apartment on Viale Piceno on the east side of Milan. I had barely unpacked my horribly unfashionable British abroad gear before Cliff whisked me away to dine with representatives of the Milanese glitterati.

'They always get it wrong,' Laura went on, 'they are always late. I always fly with British.'

Our hostess was a leading Italian literary figure, one of Cliff's Italian network of friends. Cliff and I had known each other for many years, but our friendship had been punctuated by long periods of silence. Usually due to circumstances that were beyond his control. He had often told tales of his antics in Milan and suggested that we go together. Finally we appeared to have made it.

We sat with an interesting set of people. There were two sharp members of the Milanese fashion set, a representative of the Italian women's pipe smokers' union, and a publisher. The air was thick with tobacco smoke and the after dinner drinks were flowing. Marco, the publisher, whose life of long lunches had resulted in a tummy that looked as if he had swallowed a basketball, informed me that the lady with the pipe had just returned from the international women's conference in Beijing. Since I knew that the conference had ended more than a month before, I wondered whether she too had flown with Alitalia.

'Never,' she declared as if her life would depend upon it, which it may well have done. I was impressed with the candid lack of patriotism when it came to flying the national carrier.

'British Airways have said they want to buy Alitalia,' Laura announced. 'This will be a good thing.'

A home-made citrus liqueur, made by Marco's mother, was going the rounds. This was partly a decoy to conserve the bottle of whisky that Marco was using to pour himself healthly long measures. It was an apt conclusion to a fine dinner, the first course of which had baffled the British contingent sat around the dining table. We had begun with pasta served in a sauce that had tasted damn good, but saying as much had turned into an embarrassing exposé of our culinary ignorance. 'What do you think it was?' asked Laura smiling. Cliff suggested turkey. Laura shook her head. I thought maybe aubergine. She shook her head again. 'Tuna?' said Cliff. 'Tuna!?' cried Laura and she laughed a deep laugh that turned into a cigarette-induced hacking cough. 'It couldn't be tuna because we never eat Parmesan with fish,' and she screwed up her face. 'Aagh.' The sauce turned out to be curdled milk flavoured with veal, a speciality from some part of Italy that I hadn't heard of. Not wanting to expose us to more ridicule, I didn't ask for any further details.

Marco lit himself another Camel and launched into an explanation of Italian regional variations. Things were simply very different in the South, he said. There had been a phase of mass migration from the South in the 1950s and 1960s, of people to work in the industrial North. They had not been well received, facing a racism that in most other European countries is reserved for immigrants from Africa and Asia. But then most of the South is closer to Africa than to Milan.

What of Romans, I wanted to know. 'Yes, let us speak of Romans please,' said Laura with a wry smile, 'it is the only time we ever won.'

'Rome,' dismissed Marco with a wave of his cigarette, 'it is everything and nothing.' He asked me if I'd ever been. 'Yes,' I replied, 'I had lunch there once. Perhaps that is enough?' Marco smiled into his whisky and nodded. 'I think so,' he said.

Ricardo, a man in his mid-thirties who was in the fashion industry, had worked in Rome for some years. 'The mentality is different,' he declared. 'From my point of view Rome is politics; they talk a lot about work but don't do anything.' Ricardo resembled an eccentric English squire in his tweed suit with wide lapels and bulbous silk tie in what could have been old-school coloured stripes. Somehow, because he was a Milanese, he managed to look slick rather than like a twit. 'And I also worked in Naples for one year,' he continued. 'In Naples you always look out for your back. They always think, let's get the man from Milan.'

Since there were such internal differences within the country, did Italians feel European, I wondered. Laura shook her head. 'Italians don't really care about Europe,' she announced. 'Talk about the ways the countries differ in your book,' she added, 'but this is nothing to do with the European Union.' Everyone seemed to agree, although Ricardo was obviously concerned about Italian attitudes to the EU. He thought that Italy may be missing out on an opportunity. But for himself, he had had enough: he wanted to emigrate to New Jersey where he could make lots of money fast and then retire. He was not discouraged when we told him that that state was considered to be the armpit of the USA.

'Outside Italy we are only good for making silk ties,' he said, 'we are lazy, not interested in making business.' Laura scoffed, 'Oh Ricardo, always business, this is Berlusconi talking.' The English turned to Italian and the hands began to gyrate when the talk moved to politics. Laura had already aired her views on the former Italian prime minister. He was a slick, plastic businessman, a new Italian stereotype whose consumerist mentality was affecting too many Italians in the wrong way.

The conversation had fragmented. Whilst politics Berlusconi-style inspired much gesticulating, others around the table began to reminisce about colleagues they had loved and lost to the clutches of Class A illegal substances. Laura's son had spent time in a drug rehabilitation community near Oxford some years before and had written a book about his experiences. The book's success had inspired a stream of Italian residents to go in search of reconstruction. Several of the rehabilitation centre's British residents had subsequently died of their self-abuse, but no Italians. Laura put it down to the stronger sense of family in Italy. The Italian residents were buttressed by the family fortress when they ventured back into the outside world.

My mind drifted away. I couldn't follow the political discussion because it was in Italian and I knew nothing about drug rehabilitation. Either way, the average Brit doesn't stand a chance when the Italians get their talking trousers on. I began to play a variation on that childhood game where you have to imagine all your teachers are animals. Marco the publisher looked like a soporific rabbit on William Lawson's whisky, Ricardo most closely resembled a piglet, whilst his wife looked like a giraffe. She was long and graceful, a former model with legs up to her neck, and a long thin nose. Her mane was a mass of blond curls, the ends of which provided her with continual fascination. I broke from my reverie when talk had turned to Italian views of the English. Laura was saying that she liked English food, especially onion rings. She liked English people too because we were respectful, but our pedantic views sometimes aggravated. She had once sat on a train leaving Brighton and asked someone in the carriage whether this was the right track for London.

'This man looked at me and said, "Track? We do not say track in England. This is an American word."'

Just to keep the ball rolling, Laura added another interesting aspect of the English: our occasional tendency to become serial killers. The Italians all laughed. Italy had only seen one serial killer, the 'monster of Florence' who was thought to have dispatched no fewer than sixteen victims in the Renaissance city. All the newspapers said that he must be an Englishman.

The dinner party was breaking up, and Ricardo announced that he would take us to a club. Cliff insisted that it should be the Killer Plastico and we all embraced each other before falling out of the door of Laura's apartment. Several long whiskys notwithstanding, Ricardo backed his car off the central reservation abruptly into the stream of oncoming traffic, nearly causing a major pile-up. 'It's OK, I know how to manage these people,' he said with only the slightest slur. He put his foot down hard on the accelerator and we shot off past the teams of streetwalkers along the Viale Abruzzi.

A small crowd of would-be revellers was gathered outside the Club Killer Plastico. They were held at bay by a sharp-suited character with a pigtail and half a dozen earrings lined up along his earlobe. This turned out to be Wolf, who greeted Ricardo like a long-lost friend and proceeded to usher us past the line of hopefuls into the bowels of the Killer Plastico. We made our way into a room within, presided over by a large lady perched astride a tall stool. Her hair was short and platinum blonde and she amply filled her double-breasted grey jacket. She looked at us as if we were dirt in her fingernails as she allowed us to troop in behind Ricardo, who strode with head held high like the king of Milan.

Cliff had prepared me for our foray into Milanese nightlife, but I was still surprised. Ricardo said that Killer Plastico was a timeless venue. Other 'in' places came and went, but Killer Plastico was always the place. It may have been the preferred haunt of the fashion set, but it was the complete antithesis of the expected stylish venue. As Cliff had said, when you go to Milan and find the place to be, you expect it to be like stepping into a Martini ad. But the scene inside this inner sanctum was more like a tacky college disco than a high class hangout. Screen-printed zany reproductions of classical paintings adorned the walls and plastic globes dangled on pieces of string from the ceiling. Beside the bar, a bank of TV screens showed a permanent image of the Taj Mahal between video footage of fashion catwalks which later gave way to silent reruns of 'Happy Days'. The clientele were also disappointing. I expected beautiful sexy people in super-sharp fashions. Everybody knows the Italians dress better than anyone else in Europe and this was the country's fashion capital. But instead all I got was the average number of shaven heads and dark glasses, berets, tracksuit tops and leather jackets, a new romantic and a Humphrey Bogart look-alike sweating profusely in his camel-hair coat. Beside the dancefloor, two girls who looked about sixteen lounged on low square cushions, perhaps because their PVC trousers matched the transparent plastic covers. Some time later, the bizarre array of fashion types was augmented by Milan's well-known population of *viados*, Brazilian transvestite prostitutes looking to relax after a night working the streets.

We danced awhile as Ricardo's wife, the giraffe, fended off all boarders, many of whom turned out to be lesbians. Conversation was difficult, and although I was happy to be in Milan with a friend after plodding my way round Iberia solo, it is sometimes a strain talking to other people's acquaintances. I wandered into some of the club's other areas, to find the ecstasy zone, where the strobe lights flashed only every fourth frame because everyone danced that much faster and behind the bar they sold bottled water and Chanel No. 5. But garage music is bad enough in English, let alone Italian, so I soon returned to the screen-prints and the Taj Mahal. I ordered a Campari because that seemed to be what everyone else was drinking. I nursed it for the rest of the evening, mainly because I would have needed a bank loan to acquire another drink, but also because it tasted so ghastly that I couldn't bring myself to drink it all. Ricardo materialised to tell me that it was a shame it was Friday because all the real big guns leave town for the weekend. If I really wanted to see the fashion elite at play, I should come back during the week. Somehow I couldn't see that happening.

Although I was to hear Milan's claim to be the country's engine room asserted many times during my stay in Italy, the city's proclaimed efficiency isn't quite borne out by its cathedral, the Duomo. It was commissioned way back in 1386. In the late eighteenth century Middleton noted that it was a 'vast pile, all of marble' but that 'though something has been doing for near 400 years towards the outward or inward ornaments thereof, it is not yet finished'. They finally managed to complete it in 1958. I suppose these things are all relative, but I think that six centuries is a long time to put up a building. Still, it's an impressive piece of architecture, its higher reaches a multitude of spiky pinnacles, pillars and statues that rise up from its marble façade to shimmer in the eternal smog that shrouds the city. One advantage of finishing the thing so late is that they managed to incorporate a lift which takes you up to the roof where you can wander the forest of stone pinnacles and gaze out over the yellow-brown haze. From far below, the only distinguishable sounds above the murmur of the city are the tinny strains of the Lambada emanating from the battery-operated dancing bootees sold by lines of black Africans all around the piazza.

The Piazza Duomo is a gathering place for tourists and Italians alike, a wide open space ideal for the locals to catch up on the latest gossip over their mobile telephones while ducking the kamikaze pigeons who do their best to keep the crowd moving by conducting low-level aerobatics at head height. Here at least the Milanese lived up to their reputation as inhabitants of the fashion capital of Italy. Everyone was elegant, sophisticated, sharp and debonair as only the Italians can be. Even the babies were pushed in designer prams and clothed in designer kiddies' outfits straight from the pages of *Vogue Bambini*. The traffic police too looked slick, the females among them well groomed and glamorous despite their white helmets that looked like up-turned buckets. Designer gear languishes behind every shop window, beckoning to be purchased and added to your sumptuous wardrobe, while for those unable or unwilling to fork out hundreds of pounds on a handbag created by Louis Vuitton or Coco Chanel, the African street traders can do you a somewhat cheaper version from their blankets on the pavement beneath the porticoes. Continually on the look-out for passing officialdom, these graceful figures stood in small groups overlooking their wares, apparently immune to the soul-destroying Lambada tune issuing forth from their brothers' musical footwear offerings. We sat at a piazza café for a half-hour after our sojourn on the Duomo roof and the repetitive tinny music nearly drove me demented. During this time, I didn't see one person stop to inspect the tiny flashing toe-caps and I wondered how many batteries these guys would have to get through before they graduated to the designer bags.

For a long time, many of the world's most spectacular buildings were put up for religious worship, but now most of the western world is more obsessed with shopping. When we could stand the Lambada no more, we wandered through the Galleria Vittorio Emanuele II, a magnificent nineteenth-century arcade full of shops and cafés, in search of lunch. I was always hungry in Milan; perhaps it is a little-known side-effect of smog that it gives you an appetite.

Adequately resuscitated, we moved on towards Milan's canal zone and the street market on the Viale Papiniano. As Cliff pointed out, even the waiter who served up my *osso bucco* and fried risotto rice was dressed more smartly than either of us. When he removed his pinny at the end of lunch, he looked like an executive in a top merchant bank with his braces, well-cut shirt, silk tie and smart trousers. The market we were headed for was one of the best places to buy low-priced designer attire; we couldn't very well come to Milan and return without something to remember our visit by. If I'd had the money, I'd have bought an entire new wardrobe. I still wasn't quite tuned in to travelling in Europe. I'd brought too many old T-shirts that I wouldn't be seen dead in at home. They were fine for roughing it in Asia and Africa, but here in Italy they just attracted suspicious looks. Fortunately, when I opened my mouth and people heard I was English, their suspicions usually disappeared. I don't think they expected any better from an Englishman.

Laura had told us that legitimate *haute couture* from previous seasons could be bought at bargain prices along the central reservation of the Viale Papiniano, but I suspect that many of the stalls were also dealing in less legitimate produce. The long stretch of table-tops was crammed with eager customers sorting through the cashmere sweaters, endless piles of shoes, shirts, suits, soft leather gloves and the inevitable silk ties. Unlike a similar street market in London, virtually all the stuff looked to be of good quality.

There is no doubt that Italy has a problem with fake goods, most of them near-perfect imitations of the real things. This is not surprising since in many cases counterfeit products are said to be produced in the same factories as their legitimate counterparts; they turn out legal handbags during the day and produce fake Fendis at night. Naples is traditionally thought of as Italy's counterfeit capital, but as with everything else in Italy, there are regional differences. Shoes and handbags come from the central regions of Tuscany and the Marches where there is a long tradition of leatherworking, whilst in Trento they specialise in sunglasses. There are no statistics on where the dancing Lambada bootees come from. It's not just fashion goods that are systematically counterfeited; in Turin and Milan they are said to be expert in producing false spare parts for cars. In total, the Italian *industria del falso* is thought to be worth billions of pounds, and the country is reputed to be Europe's number one producer, third only in the world rankings behind South Korea and Thailand. But as the crowds at the Viale Papiniano seemed to indicate, Italy does not just produce and export the stuff; it is also a major consumer.

One of the difficulties of combating the counterfeiting business, apart from the age-old problem of the inevitable involvement of organised crime, is that Italians don't really think buying this stuff is morally wrong. The longer I spent in Italy, the more I realised that moral values, and the general attitude to rules and regulations, were rather different to my own. Ricardo had mentioned the Italian lack of respect for municipal society: 'If you ask people whether they want to pay ten thousand lira and receive a receipt, or pay five thousand for cash, they always say cash,' he told us with a shrug. Others I spoke to said that when Italians were faced by a new regulation they tried it, and if it didn't suit them they then set about finding a way to avoid it. Corruption scandals in Italy are as common as pasta, and since everyone seems to be at it, why not have a go too? While I was there, Giulio Andreotti, seven times prime minister of Italy, and the man who helped coin the catchphrase 'Better ruled from Brussels than by the Mafia', was sitting in a Palermo court room accused of having colluded with the boys from Sicily all along. At the grassroots level, thousands of would-be invalids were also being exposed as alleged frauds, benefiting from special pensions and jobs reserved for the genuinely disabled. 'Blind' men were found to be working as chauffeurs. Not all were as quick-witted as one apprehended while window-shopping in a Sicilian town, who explained to the policeman that his sight had just been miraculously restored after a visit to Lourdes.

What to an Englishman seemed to be a disregard for authority that verged upon the anarchic appeared to permeate every level of Italian society and was evident in almost every act, from shooting a red light to bribing the government. But then, Italy does appear to be a little bit different from most other European countries. In how many other countries would a man hold the post of prime minister *seven times* and then be tried for corruption and murder? Even their currency, with all its noughts, looks as if it should be circulating in the Third World. For the British, the lira presents an additional confusion because it is often represented by the same sign as the pound. This takes a bit of getting used to; when the bill for £72,000 came after lunch, it seemed for one horrible moment that the proprietors thought Cliff and I had made a bid for their restaurant.

I bade farewell to Cliff and set out for Venice. A long weekend together had been just about enough for both of us. We could seldom agree on when to eat, where to go next, or how much we were prepared to spend when we got there. Travelling alone does have its advantages.

Riding the metro, it struck me that not even in Milan could they keep their decoration up to date; it all looked very 1970s in brown and orange. One of those linguistic quirks that turn up every now again during foreign travels appeared on a large poster at each station towards the railway terminus: the poster advertised a new large dishwasher manufactured by an Italian market leader. The caption read 'Big Smeg'.

Above the big smeg sat a big smog. The dull, grey miasma enveloped the Stazione Centrale, a huge, imposing and rather austere building. It reminded me of the Moscow underground and like most of Moscow in recent times the terminus was surrounded by vagrants and delinquents. Although it was early in the morning, the smog did not look as if it would ever clear, and its ashen pallor made the city look like some kind of futuristic industrial hell-hole. Inside, however, the arrivals board indicated that I was still in today's Italy: every single train was noted as late.

The fog continued to sit in the northern Po valley for most of the journey, only outside Milan it became fluffy and white. A few wooded hills turned up around Brescia but disappeared just as quickly into the flat, green and agricultural landscape. The youth sitting opposite in my carriage was obviously aware that there was no restaurant car on the train because he had brought a huge supply of sandwiches. He ate throughout the entire three-hour journey. He was only saved from my mugging him for his final mouthful by the sight of water. The train trundled the last 4 kilometres across the lagoon and we entered Venice.

It was exactly as I had imagined: full of men wearing stripy T-shirts and boaters working the gondolas, with gnarled and crumbling buildings in pastel shades lapped by the waters of the canals. I was immediately struck by how quiet the place was thanks to the absence of cars. Even on the busy main thoroughfare, the Grand Canal, the motor boats weren't really loud, they just made friendly chugging noises. *La Serenissima*, the Most Serene Republic, was a totally apt name for the place. Even in Italy all that water has a very calming effect.

Yet it took some time before I could take it all seriously. The canals looked like streets that happened to be full of water, the rough wooden poles for tying up your boat like remnants of submerged fledgling roadside verges. I had to keep reminding myself that this is what it has always been like. But it was still difficult to get my head around, to appreciate that this was a working city that was built on more than a hundred small islands. The people in those boats weren't on holiday, they worked here. There were taxi boats and blue and white 'panda' police launches, long low boats carrying cargo and luggage, and a large number 15 bus boat. It made me want to start a fire just to see the fire engine boat speed on to the scene and douse me with canal water.

Although many of the locals have moved out to live across the lagoon at Mestre, and sightseers from the world over take it in turns to wander the back streets, my initial impression of Venice as a theme park was not appropriate. This was not how the Americans would do it. Venice needed cleaning up and painting, most of its buildings needed refurbishing and the graffiti removed. If Milan was a sharp and dashing businessman, Venice was a cracked and wrinkled old lady. The municipal authorities also needed to find a solution to their sewage disposal problem, reminders of which wafted up from the waterways every now and again to spoil the romantic view. But the smell has been a problem for a long time: visitors on the Grand Tour used to refer to Venice as the 'Stinkpot'. The authorities have always had more pressing problems to deal with. Today, they have their work cut out just to keep the place above the waterline.

The city is an easy enough place to get lost in, but I only had a day to weave my way through the winding streets, hop from islet to islet across the multitude of little footbridges, and look longingly up the narrow side canals at the washing hanging out to dry. Piazza San Marco appears suddenly gigantic when you emerge from the maze. Despite being one of the most famous squares in the world, it was not disappointing. But this was not because of the fluted columns and glittering façade of St Mark's Byzantine basilica, or the ornate blue law courts' twenty-four-hour clock tower where crowds stand and gaze at bronze Moors striking the bell each hour. For me, the splendour of the piazza was made by the 99-metre square brick tower of the *campanile* because it seemed so out of place standing in the corner of the otherwise classical symmetry. Although it looks like an afterthought, the tower was put up in the tenth century. It collapsed in 1902, so they had to rebuild it.

As its bells boomed a deep and resonant echo across the piazza, temporarily drowning out the dulcet tones of a piano and accompanying strings which were set up in the near-zero temperatures outside one of the small tea rooms, I ducked into the Caffè Florian. The Caffè Florian has been in the same place beneath the porticoes on the north side of the piazza since 1720, and like Byron and Henry James before me, I sat and drank overpriced coffee served in porcelain cups on a silver tray. It was like being inside an eighteenth-century padded chocolate box. The walls were a riot of ornate painted scenes showing maidens and he-men, Moors and milkmaids amid oriental drapes and rugs and tranquil rural backgrounds. Plum-velvet fitted couches lined the walls and crisp waiters glided across the well-worn squares of the parquet floor. Like most of Venice, the *caffè* has seen better days. Its golden wood frames are chipped and its large mirrors are losing their reflecting ability in places, as if they have been eaten away by patches of lichen. But if you can screen out the honeymooning English couple opposite and the thoroughly modern fat Italian family through the door in the next room, you can still sit back and absorb the Vivaldi and pretend you are doing the original Grand Tour. But today's visitors come just to look at the floating city. Two hundred years ago they came because Venice was known as 'the brothel of Europe'. Today that distinction has been transferred to Amsterdam.

Othello look-alikes are featured in the ornamentation all over the place in Venice. They even popped up as light-bulb holders on an otherwise pure-white opaque Venetian glass chandelier in another of the piazza's tea rooms. During its 1000 years of independence as a republic, Venice grew into a powerful city state that dominated the Adriatic, the entire Mediterranean and the trade routes to the Levant. It was from here that Marco Polo set out on his voyage to China. This was the place where East met West, where Europe came face to face with exotic Asia, and the city still retains traces of that mystique. As dusk began to fall, and the better-lit streets started to come alive with the early evening bustle, elsewhere the poky blind side alleys took on the crepuscular shadows of the city's more menacing side. Death and decay, mouldering rot and violence, dwarves in little red capes and other images from *Don't Look Now* crowded into my imagination after I had seen the Bridge of Sighs and decided that the replica at Hertford College in Oxford is actually more impressive than the original. It's difficult to say why exactly, other than because it's bigger. The feeling of menace was enhanced by the musky smell of damp, decaying buildings and the *Carnevale* masks that hung from every shop front smiling at me in a sinister way. As the *vaporetto* from the Rialto Bridge chugged along the Grand Canal towards the railway station, the murky waters lapped at the steps of classical buildings that looked forlorn and empty.

Rome worried me long before I arrived. It had too much history for one city. Despite the northern aspersions cast upon the place, it was still the hub of Italy and although past its sell-by date, the country was still the former 'mistress of the world, the chief of empires, the seat of the muses, the nursery of the arts, and the centre of opulence', as Charles Theodore Middleton put it. And an awful lot of it was in the capital. In preparation for my visit I had bought a pocket-sized *What to See in Rome* in a second-hand bookshop. The volume assumed the reader would arrive at the main railway station, which I did. On the first page it told me that the antiquities would begin as soon as I stepped out of the terminal. The big ruins visible on the left were the remains of the walls of King Servius Tullius dating from the sixth century BC. Opposite the station were the Baths of Emperor Diocletian, completed in AD 305. And so it went on. There were 2500 years of history in a living architectural palimpsest. I was terrified.

I needn't have been. What the book hadn't told me about were the modern Romans. Although they inhabit perhaps the world's greatest concentration of history, legend and monuments, they don't seem to notice it. Early on in my visit, I was being driven into the city by some Italian friends who had lived in Rome for much of their lives. Fabrizio pointed out a long stretch of pink-coloured ruins that ran alongside the road we were speeding down. 'You said you wanted to see some monuments,' he said waving a hand at the collection of ancient columns, pieces of wall and other bits of ruin. 'There you are.'

'Ah, yes,' I said, trying to sound intelligent. I paused, not really wanting to admit my ignorance, but finally said tentatively, 'What's that one?'

Fabrizio shrugged. 'I don't know,' he said.

Later I discovered that it was the backside of the Palatine hill. This was only the cradle of Roman civilisation, the most important of the seven hills of Rome, where Romulus traced the *sulcus primigenus*, the first furrow around which he built his first walls. It was only the most significant archaeological site on the planet, which includes the Forum, the commercial, political and religious centre of ancient Rome, the very heart of the empire which controlled almost the entire world known to Europeans at the time.

The episode made me feel much better. I felt the pressure of cultural obligation lift from my shoulders and I took to the streets of the Eternal City a new man. Everywhere I went the locals' irreverent attitude pervaded. From my base halfway up the Janiculum hill I waded through a sea of plane leaves to the vistas from Piazzale Garibaldi. Snogging couples lined the ramparts behind the white forest of pedestals supporting busts of stern Garibaldinos with their twiddly moustaches and flashy bow-ties. Down through the bustling medieval streets and squares of Trastevere I crossed to Tiber Island where the wide riverside walkways were unkempt and overgrown, the weeds and ramshackle bushes jostling for position between the scrawls of graffiti. A large rat scurried along past a pile of broken rocks and an idle Turbo 4×4 digger. It looked as if the authorities were trying to clean up, but Rome wasn't built in a day, and anyway it was lunch time.

The Spanish Steps were closed for renovation, Bernini's Fountain of the Rivers in the Piazza Navona smelt of bleach, and the Pantheon was covered in scaffolding both inside and out. The Colosseum had been taken over by cats. Although it's well over a thousand years since the last meet at the Circus Maximus, would-be charioteers now race the surrounding highways in their Fiats and Alfa Romeos. The Trevi Fountain looked spectacular enough but its square was too small. It looked as if someone had airlifted it there temporarily. Meanwhile, its riot of god-types, struggling to keep their troublesome horses in order, were covered in idiot pigeons which thought the coins being thrown into the water were for their entertainment.

Beside the Capitol, you could buy cigarette lighters shaped like grenades, and cardboard cut-outs of Disney cartoon characters which danced on stringy legs to a cassette player. These were in addition to the rather more appropriate knick-knacks such as mini-busts, carvings and columns in mock-marble. Such trinkets have a long history. Back in the eighteenth century, several Englishmen were involved in rackets selling fake Roman coins, cameos and intaglios to unsuspecting Grand Tourists. But like the more discerning Grand Tourists, I was after the authentic article. Middleton's assessment of Italy in general and Rome in particular is as apt today as it was then: 'With respect to their genius and taste in architecture, painting, carving, and music, they excel greatly, and leave the other nations of Europe far behind them.' Rome is still the place to come if you want to set foot on classical ground. I sat down in the spot where Edward Gibbon first conceived his history of the Roman Empire, hoping to be struck by an equally remarkable inspiration to help me. At this stage, the exact nature of my mission still eluded me. Was it to be The Decline and Fall of the European Union, or The Revenge of the Killer Directives starring the Boys from Brussels? But there were no barefooted friars chanting Latin litanies from the top of the hill, so I gave up and bought a greasy burger from a street vendor instead.

Time-warped reminders from my school Latin textbooks also popped up in unexpected guises. Everywhere I walked I saw the initials SPQR, immortal cipher of ancient Rome, inscribed on lampposts and manhole covers. Then a real classical manhole cover turned up, beneath the portico of the first-century church of Santa Maria in Cosemedin. The large round marble slab is carved to form a great face with open mouth, the Mouth of Truth, which was used as a lie detector in the Middle Ages. The piazza in front of the church was a place imbued with superstitious dread and the threat of tragedy, formerly fronted by an eighth-century prison and a public execution site. In those days, if you told a lie while your hand was inside the marble mouth, it would shut tight, cutting off your fingers. Like any old person, the mouth now looks as if it needs dentures. Stick your hand in there today and your fingers would get a gumming which would be caught on the film of a thousand Japanese camcorders.

There was not a cloud in the sky on the day I visited the Vatican, the world's smallest state and headquarters of one its largest religions. Rome was warmed by a bright autumn sun that was refreshing after the misty shrouds that had enveloped most of the

North. It was an odd feeling to walk up the wide Via della Conciliazione and into St Peter's Square without passing through customs. It was impossible to see where Italy ends and the Vatican City State begins, yet I had some idea that I had entered a new country when I saw my first member of the Vatican Swiss Guard. The young man was resplendent in floppy black beret and billowy costume of multi-coloured stripes. Unfortunately, he was about four foot two and looked as if he still collected football stickers in his spare time. I concluded that his costume was billowy in order to hide the fact that he was probably still wearing nappies.

Considering that it's a whole country, it was surprising to learn that half of the Vatican's national land area of 44 hectares is garden. On the other half, they have crammed a bunch of palaces, chapels, halls, offices, apartments for its thousand or so inhabitants, a radio station and the largest church in the world. It has its own bank, which they call the Institute for Religious Works, and it runs its own postal service, newspaper and train station. Its library is one of the few I know of that has a bar.

I braved the crush of humanity all trying to enter the Sistine Chapel at once and was duly impressed to note that the attendants were unique among the everyday guardians of Europe's cultural treasures in that they were actually trying to enforce the ban on photography. I was also impressed by the stamina of a man who could spend four years of his life lying on his back, single-handedly painting 900 square metres of ceiling. Just trying to take it all in for twenty minutes made my neck ache. The best-placed person in the chapel to see Michelangelo's handiwork was a bald baby in a pushchair, but his response to the world's most famous ceiling mural was to scream and kick anyone who happened to be standing near him. He would probably grow up to be a vandal.

Still reeling from the Sistine Chapel, I sought out the Vatican restaurant where I was hoping they would serve up hot-cross buns and Christmas cake all year round. They didn't. I had to make do with lasagne instead.

I emerged from the world's cutest sovereign state and nearly got run over in its most deranged traffic. I had been forewarned about many things Roman before I arrived, but the two main pieces of advice that stuck in my mind concerned the traffic and the threat of robbery, possibly with violence. By this time, I had grown accustomed to the men in bullet-proof vests outside the banks in Milan and the elaborate electronic doors which made entering such buildings a major logistical challenge. But I had been somewhat perturbed to see prominent signs outside hole-in-the-wall banking machines in Venice advising you not to withdraw money whilst carrying a firearm. On my previous visit to Rome, I only had time for lunch while gazing at the Pantheon in the Piazza della Rotonda. The occasion had been marked by a flurry of activity in which half a dozen of my fellow diners had taken a call on their mobile and suddenly piled into two waiting Alfa Romeos. My companion and I had looked at each other in disbelief when the sharp-suited young men pulled automatic weapons from beneath their seats as the cars screeched their way around the fountain and off up the Salita dei Crescenzi. No one else took a blind bit of notice.

Happily, I managed to avoid any brushes with gun-toting undesirables on this visit to Rome, but unless you sit in your hotel room and watch CNN all day, avoiding the traffic is a physical impossibility. When I first arrived at the Stazione Termini the lunch-time rush hour was in full flow. As the number 75 bus plied its way through the midday throng, I was treated to a full introduction to *la dolce* traffic. After a few days, I decided that one of the reasons for this apparent chaos is the fact that there is no clear demarcation between areas safeguarded for pedestrians and those set aside for motorised vehicles. In other cities the pavement kerb serves this purpose, but it doesn't work like that in Rome. Where pavements exist, mopeds and scooters drive on them. Cars park on them, across them and up them, as well as beside them. Indeed, it struck me as surprising that the authorities were making such a fuss about the fraudulent invalid scam in which supposedly blind people were working as chauffeurs. Why weren't they taking action to stop the thousands of real blind people from parking their cars all over Rome?

Since pavements are not the sole preserve of pedestrians, people take to the roads. It comes as a terrible shock the first time you see a little old lady laden with shopping bags ambling across a four-lane highway with high-speed car chases zooming past her elbow. But Romans clearly begin their on-foot training at an early age, because the little old ladies never look fazed by any of it. For a foreigner it's a different matter, partly because we aren't used to it and partly because Roman drivers can't see foreigners. I believe this is literally the case. Roman roads are beset with invisible obstacle courses and slaloms, and drivers continuously weave in and out of them at high speed. Each driver has his own course and occasionally this course lies at right angles to most of the other courses. Zebra crossings appear to have been placed at haphazard intervals to make visitors feel more secure, but they shouldn't be, because the drivers can't see them either. Try crossing the road in Rome and you will have some understanding of why they call it the Eternal City. You'll either wait for ever for a gap in the traffic, or venture out and never reach the other side.

Traffic problems are not new to Rome. The congestion in the city centre got so bad back in the first century BC that Julius Caesar banned all wheeled vehicles during daylight hours, with the exception of VIP chariots. The city had its ups and downs after the end of the Roman Empire, but to the Grand Tourists it looked like a ghost town because there were so few residents. According to Middleton, you could walk round it in three or four hours because it was only 13 Italian miles in circumference. I read somewhere that a root cause of modern Rome's frenetic traffic and lack of planning is the fact that since becoming the capital of Italy in 1870, the city has grown so fast that no one has been able to keep up with it. This is nonsense. Rome is a city full of bureaucrats and it's their job to keep up with it. What else are they there for? The truth of the matter is that the bureaucrats are bored stiff sitting behind their desks all day and the only excitement they get is on the roads. Making things more orderly would spoil their fun, so they are never going to do it. They can't wait to jump into their cars and pretend they're racing drivers.

Rome really is a city full of bureaucrats. It doesn't have any industry to speak of, just pen-pushers. They work for the many levels of Italian government: national, regional, provincial and commune, as well as a few international organisations such as the UN's Food and Agriculture Organization. Everyone in Rome has their favourite story about the labyrinthine bureaucratic procedures. My host had a good one. It concerned her parents' flat on the Janiculum hill. They bought the place in the early 1970s, with an average dose of bureaucratic wrangling, plus a series of disputes and some minor changes in the law governing sitting tenants. As a consequence, they had to wait twelve years before they could move in.

The only way to get things done is through the system of mutual patronage, a reciprocal use of favours that in my northern European mind I had previously only associated with developing countries. If you want to get a telephone line in less than a year, or your grandmother into a home, or your child into hospital, you need to find a friend. Failing that, an associate of a friend, or an acquaintance of your first cousin twice removed, just so long as they work in the appropriate institution. If not, your grandmother moves in with you, your kid gets meningitis and you won't have a phone to tell anyone about it.

I was lucky. I had keyed into the network without knowing it. I had written to an old friend who now lived in the Eternal City and she had set the wheels of patronage in motion. As soon as I arrived at the flat on the Janiculum the phone started ringing and a series of complete strangers began to offer me advice and interviews. Within hours, a man arrived to take me out to dinner.

His name was Paulo, and he was Polish. But he had lived virtually all his life in Rome, and he told me about it as soon as we jumped into his car. 'So, what do you want to know?' he asked me, and without waiting for a reply he launched into his complete life history.

Paulo was a multi-lingual freelance radio journalist who when he wasn't being a journalist turned his hand to freelance tour guiding. He had had enough of Poland by the time he was two years old, so he left and went to Rome. Actually it was his parents who had had enough of Poland, but he was probably precocious enough at two to give them the idea. Paulo had been in Rome ever since, except for a two-year stretch studying in Paris. 'Oh, and I went to Florence for two weeks,' he added, just to get the record straight. Everything seemed to come in twos in Paulo's life.

We were speeding out of town somewhere, towards his home on the outskirts of Rome. Paulo drove with one hand on the wheel, one hand continually gesticulating, and both eyes on me. By the time we arrived at an *autostrade* I was dripping with nervous sweat.

Paulo's hour of glory had come in the late 1980s when Eastern Europe was emerging from the grip of communism. His Polish roots had served him well. He understood what was going on and everything he did was broadcastable. But when attention turned away from the East, Paulo's maverick approach did not go down so well. He had an idea for a live radio programme to mark the inauguration of the single European market in 1992. People from all over the European Community would have a discussion that would be broadcast simultaneously in every European country. It sounded like a good idea to me. Everyone would speak their own language without translations, he explained. Ah, I thought to myself, perhaps not such a good idea. Paulo's boss thought the same. They eventually ran a pilot, with Italian, French and Spanish participants. The programme was broadcast live in Italy and Spain, but the French recorded it and ran it with translations a few weeks later. That was as far as it went.

'Now the radio people say it is boring; "We are not interested in Europe." There is no possibility to make such programmes,' he said with a dismissive wave of his hand. 'Europe is a fact only for journalists who write about it; it does not exist in Italy,' he went on, eyes still dangerously averted from the little business of driving. 'The average Italian: he has no opinion about Europe. The European Union is about changing the colour of taxis from yellow to white because Brussels says so. Nothing more.'

We had reached Paulo's home, a new block of apartments on the outskirts of nowhere. Miraculously, we hadn't hit anything on the way.

As he made dinner, Paulo continued lecturing in his intense Polish-Italian sort of way. I was interested to hear his views on Italy as a whole country, which by now I had realised didn't really exist. As Prince Metternich, the 'architect of Europe', once said, 'Italy is a geographical expression,' and it still seemed to hold true. Allegiances were to family and friends first, secondly to a city. Italy as a nation state was a poor third, Paulo thought. Whilst the British make jokes about the Irish, the French poke fun at the Belgians, and the Swedes laugh at the Finns, the butt of Italian jokes are the *carabinieri*. 'Why?' I asked him.

'Because they're stupid. Why do you always see them in pairs? Because one of them can read and the other, he can write.

'Italy is the country of a hundred capitals,' Paulo summed it up simply. But there were perhaps three, or maybe four Italies: the North, the central region of Umbria, Tuscany and Emilia, long a bastion of communism, and the South. Then there was Rome. 'Other places think, Rome: they bastard, they do nothing. They just talk politics. Rome is the mother of all the faults.'

And then there were the islands. Paulo paused for thought while cutting the tomatoes. 'Sicily is a little bit Mafia,' he said prodding the air with the large knife in his hand. 'No, first, it is something very special, with an identity; second Mafia; third holidays.' He put the knife down and continued the survey with his thumb. 'Sardinia is known for kidnapping people and holidays. Third,' his thumb had been joined by two fingers now, 'the forests are burning in summer.' He went back to the tomatoes satisfied. 'And it is an island where the people are shepherds,' he added finally as he sliced another tomato.

We were joined for dinner by Paulo's small son, Tommo. Chicho, a tabby cat they were looking after for some friends, made an occasional walk-past.

Later, as Paulo drove me back through the night into the Eternal City, I asked Tommo which countries he had been to in Europe. Leaning over between the two front seats, he gave me a careful list of five countries on his fingers. Since we had talked a fair bit about identity, I wondered whether Tommo felt more Italian or European. Or Polish, his dad added. The little boy's brow furrowed as he considered the question. Then he answered simply, 'I feel normal,' and he stretched out on the back seat and went to sleep.

You can usually rely upon small children to put you straight. Here I was, a third of the way through my search for European unity, and the logic of a six-year-old was telling me not to waste my time. But I couldn't really return to England and give up my mission on the advice of a Polish-Italian kid. I decided to go to Sweden instead.

6

Villas, Volvos and Valium

My visits to Copenhagen were my first to Scandinavia, and if Denmark didn't exactly set my pulse racing, my initial brush with Sweden augured for an even less exciting outpost. The Danish attitude to their cousins across the water seemed to be summed up in an advertisement for the Copenhagen–Malmö high-speed ferry link. 'When in Copenhagen,' the flyer screamed, 'don't miss Sweden.'

I took the advice and crossed the narrow Øresund strait to have a look at Malmö. It looked just like Denmark. 'That's because it is,' my Danish mentor Ole told me. 'Malmö is a Danish city.' Actually, Malmö has been Swedish since the mid-seventeenth century, but all Scandinavians seem to enjoy this friendly rivalry, probably because most of them have been ruled by their neighbours at some time or another during their history. Denmark and Sweden have long been the major powers in this northernmost part of Europe; this is where the Vikings came from. Norway was governed by Denmark for several hundred years and then by Sweden until 1905, and the Swedes owned Finland for nearly five hundred years before they gave it to the Russians. But the Viking culture and ruling other people are things of the past. Today they are just one big happy Nordic family bonded by a common history. In modern Sweden they have put their energies into being nice to each other and their neighbours instead; the country has a peaceful reputation that stretches back for nearly two centuries. In the meantime they have concentrated on building a welfare state that is the envy of Europe and regularly topping the world league of suicide rates. All in all, I thought that I wouldn't be staying for very long.

However, I was under some pressure to have a good time in Sweden. A friend of mine named Ashley, who has lived and worked in Scandinavia for a large part of her life, was distressed when I told her about Copenhagen. 'Then you've got to enjoy Stockholm,' she commanded. I had my doubts, especially since the Danes had constantly told me how boring the Swedes were. My mind kept returning to all those Ingmar Bergman films that I could never watch for more than half an hour. But Ashley was determined that I should appreciate her favourite part of Europe; and she kept mentioning all those blonde women, which did awaken some interest. She said she could fix me up with somewhere to stay, with a friend of a friend, whom Ashley thought was a countess. I was bound to have a great time.

I arrived at Anki's flat, a few stops up the underground line north-east of the centre of Stockholm, late on a Saturday morning. It was mid-December and the city was like the twilight zone. It was hazy, dark and shrouded in snow. I took the lift to the eighth floor of the apartment block and found her front door. A large envelope, addressed to a Mr Englishman, was taped to it. Inside the envelope was a note on a piece of blue card. The note read, 'Hello Mr Englishman, I'm sorry I forgot your name. I can't remember if I told you about the key – it is in the shoes. See you later, Anki.'

At the foot of the door frame was a pair of furry boots. I picked a key out from one of them and let myself in.

Inside the flat another note with arrows on it directed me to my room. It had pink wallpaper and a view of a power station out of the window. On the windowsill was a pot of wooden tulips and a triangular candelabra with seven electric candles stuck in it, three on each side rising to a single one at the apex of the triangle. I was to see these advent candelabras in virtually every window in Sweden. A huge old TV set sat on a side table and a very grotty chair sat beside the bed. The room was comfortable enough, although not quite what I had been expecting from a countess. But then, this was probably just her town pad. I had been told that most Swedes have a country villa too. That was probably where the real opulence was kept.

Having got up at four in the morning for my flight, I felt somewhat weary, so I lay down and closed my eyes. Several hours later, Anki was still nowhere to be seen. I had a rendezvous with an American friend who happened to be in Stockholm attending a conference and I was due to meet him for dinner, so I began the laborious process of dressing for the cold outside.

I don't have a great deal of experience of cold places. I prefer the heat of the tropics, so when planning my visit to Sweden and

Finland it was tempting to make it in the summer time. But I had a strange fascination to see what it was like in a country where winter means just a handful of daylight hours each day, if you're lucky, and temperatures that are regularly well below zero. I had taken advice and raided the cupboard of a friend who works up mountains a lot. I had borrowed two hats (one wind-proof, the other woolly), two scarves, wind-proof gloves and felt mittens, thermal trousers, a ski lift operator's wind-cheater and a pair of rubber boots with leather uppers and felt insoles. To these, I had added a couple of thermal vests. Pulling on this lot every time you wanted to go out made a trip to the corner shop feel like an Antarctic expedition.

I took the underground south to Gamla Stan, Stockholm's oldest part, a maze of narrow medieval streets on one of the city's fourteen islands. It was 3.30 in the afternoon, but already the night had closed in. Paraffin lights in small round tin cans flickered in the piercing wind on the pavements outside shops and cafés, to signify they were open for Christmas business. In the Stortorget, a small square tucked away behind the royal palace, a Christmas market was in full swing. Smart new wooden kiosks were huddled together beneath the towering time-worn façades in copper red and peppermint green. I stopped at a stall to buy a shot of something called *glögg*, which turned out to be a hot alcoholic fruit punch, served with raisins and an almond at the bottom of a small plastic cup. It went straight to the pit of my stomach, which needed warming. Nearby, a Santa Claus figure in a Michelin man suit that covered the entire human body was smiling at children beneath his red floppy hat as he doled out candyfloss. Other stalls sold gloves and furs, hot sausages and pickled fish, haunches of reindeer and elk salami. Intricate Christmas decorations woven origami-like in corn were everywhere. In Sweden, you are more likely to see corn-dolly goats and pigs hanging on Christmas trees than angels and stars. Presents aren't delivered by Santa, but by a gnome riding a goat.

I met my friend Steve and found myself invited along to his conference farewell dinner. His meeting had been part of a UNESCO programme on social transformation, so Steve had spent the last couple of days locked in a room talking about 'management of multi-cultural and multi-ethnic societies' and 'cities as arenas of social transformations'. Unlike many European countries, Sweden did not have the remnants of a developing world empire to supply

113

them with immigrants in the late twentieth century (that's not entirely true – the French gave them a small Caribbean island in the eighteenth century, but they sold it back to them a hundred years later), so after an influx of immigrant workers from Europe in the 1960s they started welcoming refugees from South America, Africa and the Middle East. Today, one in ten Swedes has either been born abroad or was born of immigrant parents. This fact surprised me, but it went some way to explaining the initially incongruous sight of a near-naked black man advertising underwear on Stockholm bus-shelters. Apparently, he was a Swedish boxing champion.

Steve and I jumped into a cab that drove us along the waterfront boulevard of Strandvägen towards the restaurant. It wasn't until we came to pay that we realised our driver was Kris Kringle, a Santa Claus look-alike with a blond beard that hung down into his lap. Inside the restaurant, we were welcomed by a Swedish UNESCO representative named Kerstin who looked at my rubber boots and asked me whether I had just come from the Arctic Circle.

For a conference on multi-culturalism, there was an appropriate array of participants: a Pole and a Romanian now living in Sweden, a Dutchman who worked in an East European institute in Vienna, a Turkish-American woman from Canada, and a senior citizen from the English Midlands whose sole topic of conversation was based on the fact that Coventry City had just won at home. After a sip of specially brewed Christmas beer, and a slug of schnapps, the feast began.

We were faced with a Swedish Christmas smörgåsbord: several large tables groaning under the weight of dozens of dishes. Steve and I looked at each other. 'OK, here goes,' he said.

Despite her snide remarks about my footwear, Kerstin, the woman in charge, took me under her wing and talked me through the eating etiquette. We started with fish: four types of pickled herring, smoked salmon, poached salmon, smoked eel and shrimps. Next came the cold meats: tongue and turkey and beef and brawn and special ham with Cumberland sauce. There were pickled cucumbers, pickled prunes, gluten-free potato salad, Waldorf salad and six types of bread. And this was just for starters.

Kerstin was enjoying herself. She was a large, middle-aged woman, a victim of her own healthy appetite, and more than somewhat talkative. Like most Swedes, her English was excellent, but she came out with some interesting idioms every now and again. I asked her about the reindeer that I had seen for sale in the market. Did Swedes eat many of them, I wondered?

'Yes, well, there are too many, you see,' she explained slightly breathlessly between mouthfuls of beetroot, 'so they have to be culled extensively. We have many elks too, so many we don't know what to do with them. We could water the garden with them.'

'Now we run them over a lot too,' added the woman of Polish origin who sat across the table toying with her food and gazing in awe at Kerstin's ability with knife and fork. 'Because German tourists steal the elk warning signs on the roads.'

I had tapped an interesting topic of conversation. The Romanian exile complained about the roe deer that kept breaking into her garden in suburban Stockholm and eating the roses.

We moved on to the hot dishes. There were meatballs and joints of all kinds, boiled potatoes and mashed, red and white cabbage. I turned the conversation to Europe. Did Sweden feel more a part of Europe now that they had joined the EU, I asked? Kerstin waved a meatball at me with the end of her fork. 'We always have been part of Europe,' she asserted from behind the meatball. She reeled off a series of historical examples to prove her point. 'It is just the ignorance of people in France that there is anything north of Germany; it's a problem in their heads, not our problem.' The meatball disappeared into Kerstin's mouth and was quickly followed by a pile of red cabbage. She reloaded her fork with another meatball.

'A hundred years ago we were the Calcutta of the civilised world – now look at us,' she declared. 'There has been a very rapid move from the countryside to the cities since the 1930s; living standards have rocketed.'

'Is it fair to say that it's an entire country of middle-class people?' I asked, echoing something Steve had suggested earlier in the evening. Kerstin hesitated with half a chicken leg poised at her lips. 'Yes, I think so, but they all vote socialist.' The chicken thigh disappeared and it struck me that I hadn't actually seen her remove the bone. 'There is a saying that Sweden consists of eighty million spruce trees and behind every tenth tree you find a Swede; nowadays you are more likely to find them behind the wheel of a Volvo.'

By the time we got to the pudding course, I had to loosen the belt on my trousers. Kerstin was eager to introduce me to various delicacies laid out on another table and I couldn't resist taking a helping of what another reveller aptly described as 'rice pudding in a whipped cream environment'. 'You need jam with that,' Kerstin instructed, as she helped herself to a handful of jelly babies to go with her cheese. Beside the cheese board was a towering structure a full metre high that looked like a cross between a beehive and a pyramid. 'Swedish spit cake,' said Kerstin. As I was wondering just what it was about Swedish saliva that made it good enough to eat, she explained, 'Made with about a hundred eggs, a tonne of sugar and not much else. It's cooked rotating on a spit.' I was about to cut myself a piece when she added, 'And it tastes like dust.'

When the coffee arrived, I felt fit to burst. I had been forced to decline the cheese course as this would have involved me removing my trousers altogether. As we left the restaurant some of us elected to walk back into the city centre. The pavements were made of solid bumpy ice and piles of yesterday's snow were heaped beside the walkways. Even with my Arctic boots on I made slow progress on the slippery surface as Kerstin strode on ahead. The Romanian woman lagged behind to keep me company and soon began talking about the difficulties she had encountered living in Sweden. They were an odd lot, she thought, not like Central Europeans. 'You asked about them joining the European Union,' she said. 'It was a very strange time. One of the pro-European campaign posters carried the slogan "It's funnier to be in than out".' A keen wind had begun to whip in off the bay. I opened my mouth to express surprise and all that came out was a shiver. Far in front of us Kerstin laughed. Her coat was open and flapping.

When I got back to the flat, Anki was still nowhere to be seen.

Over the next few days the weather got worse. Daytime never really got going as murky snow competed with freezing rain to make my life a misery. The sky was low and grey and people walked with a stoop, as if they were afraid of bumping their heads on it. The ice-bound streets of Stockholm were lined with single gloves, lost and lonely on bus-shelter seats or still on the pavement waiting for a kind passer-by to place them carefully on the nearest wall. And everywhere I went I was confronted by posters of the demure black

Swedish boxing champion modelling underwear, and scantily clad blondes advertising bras with names like 'push-up' and 'uplift' and 'balconette'. Another series showed a young woman who was clearly not in need of artificial bosom-enhancement. She was enticing you to buy late-night swimwear. But with all that snow around there was something not quite right about the idea of love in a cold climate. I found it difficult to resist the urge to offer my ski lift operator's wind-cheater in recompense for their gallant efforts.

I took a day out to visit Uppsala, dominated by Scandinavia's largest cathedral, a red-brick affair, and the region's first university. It was a quiet pocket-sized town on a modest frozen river with lots of students and a good bookshop. Its traffic was well behaved and the streets were lined with unthreshed corn sheaves, traditionally put out for small birds to get their share of Christmas cheer. I had wanted to have a look at Carolus Linnaeus's botanic gardens, but of course they were submerged under about a metre of snow and it struck me as peculiar that such a famous botanist had come from a place where the objects of his interest were totally obscured for several months of the year. I made do with seeing the man's black tombstone in the cathedral and ate lunch in the small indoor market opposite. Swordfish was on special, and it came swimming in a tartare-sauce sea. As in other self-service cafeterias in Sweden, you paid for coffee at the same time as your meal and poured yourself a cup from the machine on the counter when you were ready. The system wouldn't work in the UK because too many people would cheat, but Swedes are very law-abiding people. As I had recently been in Italy, the civic discipline came as a bit of a shock. Moving straight from one end of the Continent to the other made me wonder about European unity. What had a land of dark, anarchic gesticulators got in common with this model society full of undemonstrative blonds? Not much, as far as I could see, other than a common hostility towards Brussels.

As the light was fading, I trudged through the complex of dignified university buildings where, on a snow-clad lawn, they had collected seven rune stones from the Uppsala area. Most of them dated from the Viking era in the eleventh century and were erected in memory of local dignitaries, to help their souls through the fires of purgatory. The writing on the red granite obelisks ran round their borders, entwined with whirling designs like a game of Viking snakes and ladders.

Back in Stockholm, I did a lot of window-shopping and fell in love with every female shop assistant I laid eyes on. Not all were blonde, but as my American friend Steve put it, 'I've never been in a country with such a high proportion of babes.' I ate more meatballs than were good for me and, despite its unfortunate name, I became addicted to a Swedish toffee-filled chocolate bar called 'Plopp'.

Scandinavia seldom featured on the itineraries of the original Grand Tourists, so I had no check-list of places to see. In the eighteenth century Sweden was where iron came from and didn't have much else to recommend it. Charles Theodore Middleton observed that the place had an interesting climate, 'nine months winter, and all the rest are summer', but as I had already discovered, this rather limited the opportunites for seeing things. Travellers in Sweden 200 years ago were also hampered by the size of the country's currency. Swedish money consisted of huge copper coins in those days, 'some as large as a tile, and when a person receives a sum of this money it must be carried home in a cart, wheelbarrow, or sack'. Travelling with plastic made things a lot easier.

Hence, for my modern equivalent of the Grand Tour, I had to rely on my own initiative. I started over on the island of Djurgården where I spent an afternoon exploring the world's first open-air museum, Skansen, an entire hill covered in reconstructed farmsteads, schoolhouses and other pieces of Swedish rural culture brought from all over the country. The Swedes love the outdoors even when it's bloody cold, so it came as no surprise that there was also a more modern complex devoted to educating the young about Swedish forests. Inside the log cabin, junior Aryans could disappear into a talking tree that told you about photosynthesis or climb aboard a gigantic cast-iron ant and pine needle. For the grown-ups, the National Forest Enterprise of Sweden provided multi-lingual booklets on the green revolution quietly taking place within Swedish forestry.

Across the road from the entrance to Skansen was Sweden's archaeological showpiece, an odd-shaped black building put up around a resurrected seventeenth-century warship. The *Vasa* was built when Sweden was a European power to be reckoned with. It was commissioned by King Gustav II Adolf, the 'Lion of the North' who reckoned he could trace his royal lineage back to Noah's grandson. Now shimmering and ethereal in the spotlights, the 50-metre black oak vessel was designed to lead his fleet. It was a queen of ships which, like that other queen of ships the *Titanic*, sank on its maiden voyage. The *Vasa* was launched from its mooring south of Gamla Stan on an August afternoon in 1628. It sailed for a few hundred metres, met its first light breeze, was blown over and sank. The ship stayed at the bottom of Stockholm's harbour for 333 years. It came as a bit of a shock when I studied a wall map of the event to realise that the *Vasa*'s mooring was now used by the Viking Line ferries to Finland. I had booked a passage on one only that morning.

Despite my Arctic gear, the cold made constant café pit stops a necessity, to thaw out any parts of the anatomy affected by long periods wandering outside. Every time I entered a building, a burning sensation would seep through my ears, nose, head and toes before they returned to normal operational temperature. And all that coffee forced me to become familiar with Stockholm's public toilet facilities, an expensive pastime. Even in McDonald's, which is usually good for a free wee if little else, there was a 5-kronor charge for the pleasure.

I spent prolonged lunch times in the Kulturhuset café, alongside tables of Africans and Middle Easterners looking rather sad and out of place as they smoked their cigarettes and watched the world go by. Anthropologists like Steve had a phrase for it: diaspora nostalgia. The academic journals were full of case studies of these guys and the challenges they faced in setting up a new life in Scandinavia. It wasn't just the nine months of winter that bothered them. Somali refugees arriving in neighbouring Finland got a rude shock after their initial delight in spotting a mosque in Helsinki. The place was run by Russian Tartars who hadn't heard about political correctness. They weren't very welcoming of their black Moslem brothers. Faced with such tribulations, it was understandable that some immigrants clung to vestiges of their own culture. Another study I was told about concerned a group of Yugoslav workers whose cultural security blanket included sightings of Serbian vampires on the streets of Stockholm. In the street below the Kulturhuset café, well-wrapped people, most of whom were probably not vampires, went about their business in the lee of a sculpture consisting of giant electric-blue spillikins.

Each evening I would return to Anki's and punch in the combination to the main door of the apartment block, hoping that at last I would meet up with the countess, only to find I had missed her again. I would flick through the TV channels to discover that, as in every other country I'd visited for this book, the late-night film was *Taxi Driver*.

After a few days roving the streets of Stockholm, I realised that certain essential elements of the modern European cityscape were missing. One thing that struck me was that there were no pigeons. Had they all flown south for the winter, or have the Swedes discovered a secret remedy to a problem that plagues every other European capital I have been in? Beggars, tramps, and vagrants were also notable by their absence. Or were they just too well dressed for me to notice them? There were gaggles of idlers outside some of the exits from the central underground station on Klarabergsgatan, but nothing to compare to London or Paris, Lisbon or Milan. One evening I had to make a phone call from a credit card telephone in the central station and I was having trouble getting the machine to accept my piece of plastic. A guy, who looked as close to a bum as any Swede can get, approached and told me to press the language button to get instructions in English. When my card still wouldn't produce the desired results, he asked to look at it, licked his finger and ran it along the card's magnetic strip. 'Sometimes this makes it work,' he said gently. When I swiped the card through successfully, he told me to dial now and put my card away, in case someone grabbed it. I'd thought that this was what he was supposed to do.

There seemed to be little doubt that in many ways the Swedes have got most things sorted. As one book I read on the country suggested, Sweden is about as near to a model state as the twentieth century is likely to see, although the Danes would probably take issue with that. It is a very egalitarian society in which social welfare is high on the list of priorities: I was amazed, for example, when I first learnt that parents are entitled to a year's paid leave from work each time they have a baby. Of course, Swedes pay for it through the nose with high taxes, and in recent years the cost of it all has brought a few cut-backs. Child benefit and unemployment allowances have been reduced, but according to one person I spoke to, the worst aspect of the belt-tightening was that local authorities were having to cut down on the number of open-air ice rinks they supported.

Sweden has employed a number of crafty techniques to create the new Swede for the perfect society. Back in the early 1930s, when eugenics was a trendy little idea in many parts of Europe, the Swedes passed a law on the subject. Sterilisation became mandatory for people with certain hereditary diseases, including insanity. While the Nazis were employing similar purification rituals to the extreme, Sweden expanded their operation in 1941 to include other practitioners of deviant and antisocial behaviour, such as criminals and incurable alcoholics. Around two thousand undesirable Swedes were sterilised every year until the law was abolished in 1971. My image of Sweden as being an open, egalitarian and generally right-on society was tarnished somewhat when I learnt this, but it did help to explain the lack of tramps on the streets and all those identikit blond tennis players.

Eugenics notwithstanding, another of the key achievements that has helped to turn Sweden from the 'Calcutta of the civilised world', as Kerstin put it, to what the country is today, is the campaign against alcohol. When it comes to booze, they don't neuter repeat offenders any more, but the Swedes are still kept on a pretty short leash. The state has a monopoly on the manufacture, importation and sale of the stuff, and if you don't know where they are, the off-licences run by *Systembolaget* are notoriously difficult to find. Part of the reason is that they don't adhere to most foreigners' preconceptions of what an off-licence should look like. Their window displays do not consist of attractively presented assortments of bottles, like in any other country, but of posters informing you of various interesting facts relating to the evils of alcoholic beverages, such as how many people died at the wheel under the influence of alcohol last year, or how many fell into the river. Many of these establishments are protected by the sort of electronic security doors that you would normally associate with a bank and, once you get inside, you find all the demon bottles are kept behind glass. You make a mental note of your choice, take a numbered ticket and wait to be served, but assistants will refuse to help you if they think you don't need it. And these places are not open at weekends.

It wasn't always like this. Back in medieval times, the national obsession with alcohol meant that almost every daily activity was an excuse for a quick drink, or *sup*. People knocked back a *jaktsup* before hunting, a *fiskesup* before fishing, a *körsup* before driving the buggy, a *gångsup* before walking and a *nattsup* before turning in at night. And of course one *fiskesup* often led to another and before you knew it there was no fish for dinner. No matter, because for a long time many Swedes were under the blissful delusion that alcohol was as good for you as bread, since it was made from the same grain. And there wasn't any question as to which tasted better. On several occasions in the mid-eighteenth century the government had to ban citizens from distilling their own spirits because cereal harvests were poor and people tended to use what they had to make booze rather than bread.

No doubt this tendency to hit the bottle coloured Middleton's views on the Swedes. Although they were naturally strong and hardy, he summed them up as 'very inactive, and their mental facilities are exceeding imperfect: they are in general very dull of apprehension'. When sober they were obliging, civil and remarkably hospitable to the few foreigners that turned up in their midst, however, Middleton noted that 'when intoxicated with strong liquors, they are furious and ungovernable'. Whilst they were happy enough to drink beer and wine, the staple Swedish tipple was something called *brännvin*, literally burnt wine, distilled from anything they could lay their hands on. Latterly, however, the term *brännvin* has been confined to vodka. Many of these interesting facts I learnt in a museum that you could probably only find in Sweden. It was the Wine and Spirits Historical Museum, and it traced the country's technical and cultural history of alcoholic beverages. I found it one dark afternoon on the first floor of a converted warehouse at the bottom of a long, slushy, ice-blown street called Dalagatan.

Like most museums I visited in Sweden, the Wine and Spirits Historical Museum was very well kept, slick and had lots of working displays. It was also very poorly illuminated and on a couple of occasions when I nearly tripped over some of the exhibits I was worried that I might be deemed to be under the influence and ejected for drunkenness. Illuminated panels and interactive diagrams showed such things as how the distillation of potatoes works and the movement of modern-day Swedish *Absolut vodka* exports. There was a full-scale 1920s bottling, corking and labelling production line that at the press of a green button rattled into action, to make the sorts of noises you hope you will never hear with a hangover. There was even a seventeenth-century recipe book open at the page for birch sap wine, that informed you that 'it doesn't taste bad in summer when it is hot'.

Apparently, *brännvin* was first made in Scandinavia in the fourteenth century and was linked to the production of gunpowder. Swedish powder-makers soon learnt how to distil wine to make *brännvin* which was used to moisten a mixture of charcoal, saltpetre and sulphur. The concoction was dried and crushed into grains of powder. The result was a potent one.

One indication of how seriously the Swedes took their *brännvin* was to be seen in the uniform of a cavalry officer shown in one exhibit. The belt had the usual rapier and pistol, plus a special holster for his *brännvin* flask. Some distinctively Swedish civilian travel accessories were also on display. They included a hollowed-out walking cane for spiritual refreshment on arduous strolls, and a hip flask disguised as a pair of binoculars. Elsewhere, the scale of the national regard for the hard stuff was indicated by a map showing the distribution of *brännvin* stills in 1756. Sweden could boast no fewer than 180,000 production points, which amounted to one for every ten Swedes.

It is tempting to link the national drink fixation to the climate. As I was by now well aware, Sweden is cold, dark and miserable for half the year. In these conditions I could see the attraction of prolonged inebriation. Academic geography has a term for this: environmental determinism. It's not very politically correct to talk about it these days because Victorians used the idea to argue that Africans were inherently lazy because their climate was so hot, but in the Swedish case perhaps the concept is not so wide of the mark.

The death knell of Sweden's alcoholic age was rung in with the founding of the Temperance Society in 1837. *Brännvin* companies were established, not to produce more of the stuff, but to regulate the scale of production and to curb drunkenness. The first was set up in the Falun copper mine, where it was thought that output might be improved if the miners' habit of drinking to excess could be modified. Propaganda on the evils of drink was zealously produced. One poster in the museum showed a still in the shape of a dragon with its mouth open to be stoked with logs. Drunk and depraved youngsters were laid out across its spiralling tail.

Finland, which was then a province of Sweden, got the same

treatment. A fictitious character was created for a series of 'temperance tales' in imitation of the Finnish national epic poem, the *Kalevala*. The character's name was Turmiolan Tommi; a rough English translation would be Paul of Perdition Place. It was a cautionary tale, tracing the decline of family life. After a major bender in the pub one night, Tommi murdered his wife and spent the rest of his days in prison.

By 1916, ration books had been introduced in Sweden to control the consumption of spirits. In 1922, the Swedes narrowly missed out on prohibition after a national referendum: 51 per cent voted against. But the ration books for spirits were only withdrawn in 1955.

The temperance movement has certainly done a good job. Sweden couldn't have got where it is today without their crusade. And although Swedes do still like a drink, their image abroad is far from that of the bunch of alcoholic revellers of times gone by. You can't really imagine Britt Ekland sharing a bottle of the hard stuff with Björn Borg. Although perhaps sex has replaced the bottle as a national trait, this is largely in the eye of the beholder. After stunning the world with his controlled and emotionless tennis, Björn Borg now has his own line of underwear, but it is just as tedious: no bright colours and boring patterns. Swedes aren't actually obsessed with sex. They are too busy being practical. Thanks to Swedish ingenuity, the world can now enjoy the many benefits of dynamite, the blowtorch, paper clips, spherical ball bearings and string vests.

Many of Sweden's emotional problems were caused by the bottle so the temperance movement took away the bottle. Later, those who still procured their passion in a liquid form were sterilised for their beliefs. The result is an entire race of people with no emotions. Switch on the television in Sweden and all the presenters are dull and humourless. They do try to inject some passion into what they're telling you, but they just can't manage it. They look jolly concerned but their voices are flat and toneless. What had that pro-EU poster said? 'It's funnier to be in than out', and what a bundle of laughs the Swedes are. It's as if the entire nation has had an emotional lobotomy. It's not just outsiders who find them boring. A lot of Swedes can't stand it either, so they top themselves. They've replaced the vodka with villas, Volvos and Valium.

*

Instead of lying blotto, face down in the straw all winter, Swedes now enjoy coffee and buns at the Festival of Light. Around the same time as the temperance movement was sorting out Sweden's alcohol problems, reformers decided to revive some of the nation's more salubrious traditions. One of these is the Festival of Light, or Saint Lucia Day. It is celebrated on 13 December, around the time of the winter solstice. The idea is to rejoice in the fact that the year's shortest day is passing and look forward to the season of daylight. All over Sweden, in homes and in the workplace, schools and factories, offices and hospitals (and on television), a girl dressed as Lucia turns up with an entourage to sing songs. Everyone drinks morning coffee and munches saffron buns while they listen.

Kerstin, the UNESCO woman, invited me to the celebrations at the Ministry of Education. It was the morning after I finally met up with Anki. She was a disappointment. If she was a countess, she certainly didn't look like one. Needless to say, I had been secretly hoping for a female explosive device who would detonate into my wildest sexual fantasy immediately on contact. Not a bit of it. She was blonde, but she was also rather sad and nervous underneath a thatch of fuzzy hair, and she was much too busy playing with her sewing machine to bother with me.

There were a few centimetres of fresh snow on the ground when I left the apartment block at 7.30 a.m. to walk and slide the few hundred metres in the dark to Gärdet underground station. In the central part of town the snow-clearers had already swept the streets clean and spread a fresh layer of grit.

I met Kerstin at the entrance to the ministry offices on Drottning-gatan where I removed my boots to slip on some house shoes. She led me to a conference room where her fellow civil servants were gathering to wait for Lucia. We poured ourselves coffee and piled a plate with saffron buns and gingerbread shapes. The coffee was strong and black; 'We like our coffee to sit up and beg,' remarked Kerstin, and as if to confirm my suspicions, she added, 'To a large extent it has replaced alcohol.'

Kerstin was the antithesis of a Swede. She was a one-woman conversation but fortunately she also had a sense of humour. When I asked her about Saint Lucia she launched into an animated description. Just what this obscure Sicilian saint has to do with

Sweden is not clear, but one account I read suggested that according to legend, Saint Lucia spread warmth and light around her. Kerstin said that this was because she was burnt at the stake.

'It is an old Viking ceremony,' she explained, sipping the strong black alcohol-substitute with a little finger in the air. 'It has survived everything; industrialisation, urbanisation, everything. Lucia arrives wearing candles in her hair dressed in a long white shirt. Her female attendants all carry candles while the boys wear tall hats with stars on their tops. They are called "star boys". The ones who are coming this morning are from a special music school.'

Apparently they had a busy schedule that morning, singing in the Festival of Light in five different Stockholm offices. They were half an hour late when they arrived at the ministry and the sun was threatening to beat them to it. The electric lights were extinguished and a hush fell over the assembly of bureaucrats as the snow-white figures filed in singing the Lucia carol. A wreath of lingonberry foliage held seven candles rather precariously on the lead girl's head. Around her waist, a red sash was tied, to symbolise the blood and suffering of Saint Lucia, Kerstin whispered. She was followed by a procession of teenage girls in their white nightdresses, each carrying their single candles. Bringing up the rear was a collection of adolescent star boys with tapering white cardboard hats. The group assembled in a semi-circle behind Lucia and proceeded to sing a number of songs led by one of the girls who set things going by hitting a tuning fork on her forearm. It seemed to hurt.

They sang for about twenty minutes as outside the sky gradually became a richer blue and for the first time since I had arrived in Stockholm I laid eyes on the sun. There was not a cloud to be seen. The procedure appeared to have worked.

7

Finns Ain't What They Used to Be

The ferry was forty minutes away from Turku and there was just one drunk left in the forward bar. He sat alone at his table, by now oblivious to the double whisky swilling around a pile of rocks in the tumbler at his elbow. He was talking loudly to anyone who would listen, but no one did. Everyone around studiously ignored him. I couldn't understand a word of what he was slurring, but it didn't matter. Pronouncements like his sound the same in any language. He was a slight figure, nearing sixty, who looked as if he had done this before. His face was flat and red, like a squashed tomato; his nose had been broken several times, perhaps by less tolerant victims of his rantings. He had greasy hair that hung down in a mat on the back of his brown nylon waistcoat.

It had been a hard voyage; the drunk had been drinking since we'd left Stockholm ten hours before. I recognised him from the morning breakfast queue. After storing my bag in a locker, I had made my way to the cafeteria on board the MS *Rosella*. Its engines rumbled into life and almost imperceptibly we pulled away from our berth. It was 8 a.m. and I was ready for some food. So were a lot of other passengers, but like the man with the squashed tomato face, most of them were opting for a liquid breakfast. At every window on the port side, elderly couples had taken up position to pop the ring pulls on their cans of Tuborg and Heineken, while over in the smoking section a bald businessman was reading his morning paper over a boiled egg and a glass of beer.

I have often wondered about all those people you see drinking beer in the early hours of the morning at international airport terminals. I had decided that they'd either just arrived from some far-flung destination and their body clocks hadn't caught up with them yet, or that they were members of frequent fliers Alcoholics Anonymous. Now I think that most of them are probably Swedes and Finns.

The squashed tomato had outlasted them all. He had switched to whisky about four hours out of port. I had been braving the icy wind to watch as the ship snaked its narrow passage through the endless succession of rocky islets. Wooden summer houses sat snugly on the spruce-clad outposts and swans foraging for submarine titbits showed us their bottoms as we slipped by.

Finally, we had emerged from Stockholm's archipelago. The ship had begun to roll in the Baltic swell and the wind had picked up. That was the only time I saw the squashed tomato leave the forward bar. We both stood on the icy deck clinging to the railings. I didn't know whether I was blue or green.

After a brief stop at Mariehamn in the Åland islands, the voyage was nearing its end, and the drunk had done his best to drink the ship dry. A middle-aged lady carrying a tray of coffee took a seat behind him and the drunk turned to put his hand on her shoulder and share his thoughts with her. She wasn't interested in conversation so she moved to find another table. The drunk lurched after her and stopped abruptly, swaying on the spot, trying to focus on a leviathan of a woman lumbering across the carpet towards him in a dark green sweatshirt. He shook his head, an action which nearly caused him to lose his balance, and tottered back into his seat as if propelled there by the booming shouts emanating from the mammoth green woman. She looked like a husband-beater and she was telling him what a no-good bum he was. By the look of him, this was something he already knew, and may well have been the reason he'd got drunk in the first place.

The mountainous green woman turned on her heel, a manoeuvre that took several seconds, and wobbled away. The drunk hauled himself out of his seat to totter after her, tripped over a wire from a TV set, and almost fell flat on what was left of his red nose, temporarily interrupting transmission of an ice hockey match.

An announcement over the loudspeaker told us to make ready to disembark and I pulled the ski lift operator's wind-cheater out of my bag.

The snow was thicker on the ground at Turku port than it had been in Stockholm but a flashing red electronic sign informed me that it was 3 °C. There was just a short walk to the railway track where a small group of former ferry passengers assembled to wait for the 20.41 express to Helsinki. Turku, or Åbo as it was formerly known, was the capital of Finland when it was a province of Sweden. Not many Brits ventured this far north in the eighteenth century and the city got short shrift from Charles Theodore Middleton, who described it as the 'wretched capital of a barbarous province'. He quoted another traveller as saying, 'There is not any thing in Åbo which has entertained me in the survey, or can amuse you by the description.' Helsinki, which was to become Finland's capital in 1812, didn't even get a mention.

When the train arrived, I settled myself in a special sub-compartment of a second-class carriage that, according to a small notice on the wall, was reserved primarily for passengers travelling with pets. On the seat beside me there was a tuft of dog hair just to prove it. Within this sub-compartment was a sealed-off zone that I thought was a toilet until further investigation proved it was a hermetically sealed sub-sub-compartment reserved primarily for passengers travelling with cigarettes.

All Scandinavian railway companies appear to have hit on this association between smokers and pets. A similar arrangement had been made in Swedish trains. If you were not in the habit of smoking you could travel with or without animals, but if you wanted to smoke you had to ride in the dog carriage. They were lumping all the antisocial activities together, which seemed rather unfair on the dogs. I suppose it is only a matter of time before some animal welfare group takes the railways to court for encouraging canine passive smoking and then cigarettes will be banned altogether. Conversely, of course, perhaps the arrangements had been made so that the dogs could smoke, although I never saw any evidence to confirm this theory.

I wasn't travelling all the way to Helsinki but to Salo, a small town halfway there with nothing to recommend it other than the fact that it was where I had arranged to meet an acquaintance of my parents named Maija. Maija was a school teacher who lived in a smaller town somewhere north of Salo. I had never met her before and I wasn't quite sure what to expect. My parents were full of her praises, but they had met her in Scotland during the month of June. From what I had read about the Finns, winter did strange things to them. One guidebook I had consulted said simply that you shouldn't go in

129

the winter months. Apart from the dark and the cold, it said, everyone seemed to be drunk, depressed or ready to kill you. For all I knew, Maija might turn from being a perfectly pleasant middle-aged woman in the summer to being an axe murderess in the winter months. I had asked to stay for the weekend. I figured that would be long enough to find out.

She met me on the platform at Salo station dressed in a long padded coat and a woolly hat. From what I could make out she looked normal enough, with a round, smiley face and eyes that had the faintest hint of a slant. We exchanged pleasantries and jumped into her red Opel Kadett which she said was loaded with sandbags to make it more stable on the icy roads. We left Salo and were soon on a straight white road heading north through a continuous forest of sugar-coated Christmas trees that shone in the moonlight. Above us, the sky was clear and full of stars. Directly in front sparkled the Great Bear.

'I hope we don't hit an elk,' said Maija cheerily. 'A deer is bad enough in this car, but if it was an elk we wouldn't stand a chance.' Apparently, it would have been different if she'd been driving an articulated lorry. Maija was concentrating hard to keep to the slightly darker tyre marks where previous vehicles had gone before us. Every now and again the little car gave us just a hint of what would happen if we were to veer too far from these tracks, by gliding slightly sideways. If an elk did appear and we didn't hit it, we would end up in the ditch.

I sat tight and kept a look-out for wayward elks. Actually I would have quite welcomed the sight of a real elk, since my only previous encounter had been with the elk salami on a Stockholm market stall. An average elk is rather bigger than a conventional deer, more the size of a large horse, and must make quite a lot of salamis. Perhaps that is what happens to those that have unfortunate experiences with motor vehicles.

We drove on, only occasionally passing a car coming in the opposite direction. Maija was chattering on about the various types of antlered beast that wander the forests, and seemingly also the highways, of Finland. 'What's the difference between an elk and a moose?' she asked suddenly. I had to admit that I wasn't sure, but alerted her to the potential linguistic confusion with a dessert made of whipped cream. Maija was an English teacher, so she appreciated the danger. In Scotland, the same creature might be misconstrued as a small rodent chased by cats, I told her.

We reached Somero, a small township of about five thousand people, 'Or so they say,' Maija told me. 'I don't believe it.' We passed a few outlying buildings and turned left into her road just before the main street. It certainly didn't look like a place big enough to hold 5000 people, but then it was dark and Maija explained that in fact Somero consisted of several outlying villages, one of which had a reputation for inbreeding. 'And it shows,' she added.

The following morning it was still dark outside and I began to wonder whether I would ever actually see Finland. We ate porridge and drank strong black coffee for breakfast. I was going to spend the day with Maija at school, a *lukio* for sixteen- to eighteen-year-olds, and she speculated on whether they might be serving blood pancakes for lunch. I'm game to try most things once, but I must say that I didn't exactly relish the prospect, least of all while I was eating breakfast.

The sun had finally decided to make an appearance by the time we left for the fifteen-minute walk to school. The sky was still cloudless and now a perfect blue, but a slice of moon floated in one corner as if to remind me not to get too used to the daylight. Now that I could see where I was, there wasn't an awful lot to see. A deep blanket of snow concealed all the details as we trudged across a small field and along a street lined with modern bungalows before reaching the school building.

I spent the day talking to a series of English classes. The Scandinavians put the British to shame when it comes to learning foreign languages. Virtually everyone speaks beautiful English: bus drivers, bank clerks, laundrette operators, shop keepers and bicycle repairmen, just in my experience. I remember being shocked one morning on one of my innumerable visits to Copenhagen when a man in overalls knocked at my apartment door and asked me something incomprehensible. When I told him that I couldn't speak ...sh he repeated his request, in the best Queen's English, for me leave my front door open while he painted the door frame.

Finland is officially bilingual in Finnish and Swedish, because the country has a sizeable Swedish minority, but at school everyone also learns English. Virtually all of Maija's pupils liked English, but weren't terribly keen on Swedish because they couldn't see the point.

131

It's a good job the Finns do all speak English because Finnish is a fiendish language to learn. It isn't anything like the Indo-European languages used in most of Europe. It's Uralic, related to Hungarian and Estonian, and has no fewer than 15 cases for nouns. Finnish verbs have more than 160 conjugations and personal forms, and for some reason they even conjugate the word 'no'. If Finns didn't all speak English it would be an impossible place to visit because nothing sounds even remotely similar to anything I have ever heard. I can scrape by in many European countries where quite a few key words look vaguely similar to their equivalents in some of the tongues that I can manage, but not in Finland. The word for telephone, for example, is *puhelin* and a town is a *kaupunki*. I wouldn't even be able to say, 'I don't understand,' because God knows how you pronounce *'Ei ymmärrän'*.

Their distinctive language exemplifies the Finns as the odd man out in Europe. There aren't many of them and they live right on the edge of the continent. They aren't really part of Western Europe, nor of the East either. They occupy some sort of nebulous middle ground between the two. Throughout my stay in the country I was often struck by this feeling that here was a group of people who, way back when, had wandered over from the Urals or the Volga river and taken root in a corner of Europe that no one else really wanted. Their country was nominally owned by the Swedes for many centuries and then by the Russians, but in both cases only really as a buffer zone between them. Other than its geographical location, Finland didn't have anything that anybody wanted. It is just a lot of forests and lakes.

But forests and lakes have their uses, and one particularly Finnish one is the sauna. You can't visit Finland and not have a sauna, and Maija had arranged that I do it properly: in a log cabin, by a lake, in a forest. On Saturday morning we drove further north, through a typical snow-cloaked Finnish landscape of wide flat fields a isolated red farm buildings with a background of co Maija chatted all the way, to keep herself warm she sai , po out sites of local interest such as the house belonging to a man w collected junk. After an hour or so, we arrived at a farm stead where her sister and brother-in-law lived, just outside a small place called Ypäjä.

Maija's brother-in-law, Jukka, was a jolly farmer-type with bright eyes, a cheeky smile, a bushy moustache and a shock of jet black hair that indicated a dash of gypsy blood somewhere along the line. He was never happier than when he had a little project on the go. When he wasn't running his farm he was buying abandoned farmhouses, doing them up and selling them on to city folk at a handsome profit.

We ate a lavish lunch of farm produce and leaving Maija's sister to bake a cake, four of us jumped into Jukka's Mercedes for the drive to his piece of forest. I sat up front next to Jukka while Maija and a friend of Jukka's, a chap called Matti who worked in a restaurant, sat behind. Jukka was always joking, and his most recent source of amusement was based on the fact that, due to an infection, he had just been circumcised, which had turned him into a Jew. This transformation didn't prevent him from stopping on the way at a supermarket to buy sausages, however. 'Finnish vegetables,' Jukka declared with a broad smile. 'We eat these and drink beer. This is Finnish men's food.'

As we drove, Jukka was anxious that I shouldn't get the wrong impression of Finnish farmers. 'This is a farm vehicle,' he told me, pointing up and behind him to a sort of extension that had been fitted to the roof of the Mercedes; 'with this extra height, that's what it counts as.' It was a tax dodge, and I got the impression that there wasn't a dodge that Jukka hadn't tried. He was as sharp as they come and when I asked him about his farm, he told me that it was now organic, as this form of farming attracted the largest subsidies from the bureaucrats in Brussels. 'None of the others around here have switched to organic yet,' he said waving his huge hand at the window, 'but they'll have to soon.' Since Finland had joined the EU at the beginning of the year, the price of grain had fallen by half and without the subsidies many farms would have gone out of business. Jukka also kept pigs, but the slaughterhouse price of these had also been falling over the past few years. 'In a couple more years, pigs won't be economic either.'

Jukka was an operator and I couldn't see him losing out to Finland's new state of affairs, but the changes that had come with their new status had hit Finnish farmers not just in their pockets. Finland has worked hard to be self-sufficient and her farmers are proud people. They are traditionally important figures in society and have been treated well, enjoying special benefits for being the nation's providers. There is an arrangement with the state, for example, whereby farmers can take a certain number of days' holiday each year and the government pays for someone to come and do their chores for them during that time. They have always laboured hard and enjoyed the fruits of those labours. Now everyone farms to maximise their EU subsidies which a farmer receives irrespective of how hard he works. Their endeavours don't appear to carry any weight, which hurts. For many, what they see as charity is difficult to accept, particularly when they have no option due to the tumbling grain price. Jukka was against the EU, but he had no qualms about making as much as he could out of the misguided subsidies while he was able.

After a long and winding road that Jukka declared had too many bends and must therefore have been a reject road from somewhere more important, we pulled off the tarmac on to a rough track leading into a dense forest laden with snow. The Mercedes growled its way over the humps for a mile or so until we reached Jukka's cabin. We had driven into a picture postcard. The log cabin sat snugly in the knee-deep snow sheltered by towering conifers, their branches drooping like snow-white beards. In front of the cabin, a slope led down to a small lake, frozen hard beneath its winter eiderdown. Reeds were curved in delicate harmony with their gentle sheaths of ice crystals. Above us the sky was wide and blue. The air was fresh and crisp, the light clean and bright and virgin. The whole scene was gift-wrapped in quietness.

Jukka sneezed. There was work to do. The icy lake had to be broken and water carried up the slope to the sauna. The stove had been lit that morning and I put my head inside the little wooden room on one side of the cabin to assess its progress. The invisible heat engulfed me and misted my glasses, but the thermometer on the wall indicated that the temperature was only 30 °C. Still a long way to go, said Jukka, as he pushed another log into the small opening in the metal stove. Maija appeared with a plastic bag containing a bunch of brittle birch twigs, cut and dried earlier in the year. There was a correct time to cut them, she explained. 'When the moon is full,' chuckled Jukka with a glint in his eye.

While we waited for the sauna to warm up I went on a short recce of Jukka's piece of forest. Finnish farms include patches of forest as insurance against a poor harvest or some problem with their livestock. In a bad year, the farmer can fell some trees to make up the shortfall in his income. But the swathes of trees are much more than that. They are havens of nature where you can go and listen to the winds humming through the branches, enjoy a sauna and swim in the lake, pick berries or gather kindling. They are places where you can sip beer and hear the birds singing as you watch the midnight sun slip towards the horizon from your wooden jetty. They are private places for relaxation and introspection, somewhere to go and get as drunk as you like and only risk embarrassment in front of Mother Nature.

Small and perfect cones nestled in splays of soft green needles and thick hairy lichen sprouted from the sweet-smelling branches. Further from the cabin, the trees were taller, their branches beginning above head-height like risqué skirts revealing a little too much of their slender trunks. They covered a south-facing slope and occasional droplets of former snow fell like part-time raindrops to pierce the white cover below or swat my woolly hat as I trudged past. It was three o'clock and the sun was a fiery orb as it sank to the level of the treetops to throw a honeyed light across the forest, making the silence truly golden.

Back at the cabin, beneath the veranda, Matti had just finished constructing a small enclosure, the size and shape of a beehive, with snowballs. He carefully placed a nightlight inside and lit it with his lighter. Inside the cabin, Jukka had a roaring fire going in the large brick hearth. The amenities were basic and friendly, although Maija told me that the place had been cleaned out by robbers twice in the last few years. The malevolent visitors had probably been from their former communist neighbours, desperate for consumer durables. They had come a long way (the border was more than five hours' drive to the east) and had taken everything they could load into a van, even the half-used bars of soap.

Jukka handed me a can of Lapin Kulta, 'the golden beer of Lapland' as it said on the side, and we sat listening to the fire crackle and the hushed tones of Jukka and Matti discussing the price of alcohol. Trips to Russia had become worthwhile in recent times, now that you could bring 16 litres of beer across the border tax free. Some Russian wide boys did regular sorties for profit. Maija broke open the sausages and Jukka skewered one with a stick to hold over the fire.

At last the sauna was ready and Matti led the way into the tiny outer room. Jukka wouldn't be joining us since his doctor had banned him from the sauna for a week. We peeled off our numerous layers of clothing and entered the hot room with nothing but our Lapin Kultas. It was like walking into the tropics.

Matti didn't have much English, but he showed me the procedure by example. We sat on the elevated wooden bench that took up the outer wall and he ladled lake water from a bucket. He poured it over the hot stones that sat on top of the stove, and loud sizzles and hissing produced a dense steam that filled the small wooden space. Beads of sweat were already trickling down my forehead and into my eyes. Above the stove was a small urn with a tap. Matti flipped the tap to fill a bowl with hot water, and he immersed the neatly tied bundle of dried birch twigs in it. He checked the wall thermometer. It was 55 °C, good enough to start with, he said.

We sat there and sweltered. If I remained still, the sultry atmosphere was hot and rather pleasant, but tended to burn when I moved. It wasn't long before my whole body felt moist and it glistened in what was left of the daylight. Sitting in a hot fog, bathed in my own sweat, looking out of the small window at the deep snow felt like a scene from a Stephen King novel.

Matti took up the ladle once more and said we ought to pour some beer on the stones. I tipped some of the Lapin Kulta into the ladle. The new haze of steam came with a rich smell of malt. It was time for the birch twigs.

The mention of birch twigs in the sauna always brings a knowing smile to the face of the ignorant. The British like making suggestive jokes with sexual overtones, and flagellation is as good a topic as most. I was a tad concerned about this bit, but when Matti handed me the bunch I had to have a go. It's supposed to get your circulation going and make you smell nice, which I suppose it did. It also felt surprisingly good; not painful, just enervating. We washed ourselves down from another bowl of lake water and sat for a few minutes before Matti led the way out to stand on the veranda, like primeval swamp beasts with steam billowing off our broiled bodies.

The sun had disappeared, but it had left a strange, clean, almost blue light. The snow-laden trees looked different again. Pinpricks of stars were beginning to appear in the sky above them this time. My skin felt healthy and pure, as if my very pores were breathing. But it wasn't long before the cold got to my extremities. My toes were about to freeze, so I had to return into the sauna to start the procedure a second time. After my third immersion, I thought I ought to go the whole hog and dash straight out into the snow to rub myself down with the stuff. Matti said he wasn't that keen on the idea. Some fanatics did it, he had to admit, but it wasn't for him.

I poured another ladleful on to the hot stones, knowing that if I thought about it for too long I would chicken out. I filled my lungs with steam, and ran outside coughing. This was really stupid behaviour, I thought to myself as I grabbed great handfuls of the white stuff and rubbed it over my body. To my surprise, it felt wonderful. It wasn't cold but just felt good and clean and rather uplifting. I became acutely aware of my skin, and images of pork crackling whisked through my mind. Matti, Jukka and Maija murmured noises of being impressed, laced with undertones of disbelief that I could be so foolish.

The odd never-never land that is Finland has had a pretty rough time of having the Russians as next-door neighbours. One Finn I spoke to told me that someone had once counted the number of wars the two countries have fought against each other. The total reached nearly a hundred, and the Finns have won only two of them. During tsarist times, Finland was ruled by Russia. However, unlike most of the nations that live in the shadow of the Great Bear, Finland actually benefited from Russia's communist revolution in 1917. They became independent. So while the boys in the Kremlin were busy putting together the Union of Soviet Socialist Republics, and, after World War II, cultivating their socialist brothers in Eastern Europe, Finland was the country that got away.

Since independence, relations between the two countries have had their ups and downs, but the Finns have never really come to trust their eastern neighbours. As the old Finnish saying puts it, 'A Russian is a Russian even if you fry him in butter.' It was like living next door to a family that keeps Rottweilers. Throughout the Cold War, Finland practised a form of self-censorship, being careful not to say or do anything that might upset their friendly neighbourhood superpower. Detractors called the country Soviet Finland.

Imagine what they thought, then, when the USSR collapsed. As Maija said, 'We felt very foolish because we had been so afraid.' Now the Finns make jokes about the Russians, but they haven't forgotten.

When conscripts turn up for their military service, exercises are no longer conducted against a non-specified 'enemy from the East'. Commanders can now say who they really mean. Joining the European Union was sold to the Finns as a safety net against Russia. Maija wasn't convinced; she reckoned Finland had to join because the country owed so much money to Western European banks after a severe economic recession in the early 1990s. Others I spoke to suggested that it was an attempt finally to scotch the rumour that Finland feels more akin to her eastern neighbours than to those on the other side. Older Finns still smart when they remember that the Molotov–Ribbentrop pact lumped Finland in with the Soviet Union.

The last time the two countries came to blows was during World War II. Finland lost heavily, having to pay large reparations to the USSR and ceding part of her territory. A big chunk to go was much of the region of Karelia, in the south-east. The Russians took it as a buffer zone around Leningrad in 1939, Finland took it back in 1941 and the Red Army had the final word in 1944. Nearly half a million Karelians had to leave their homes and go to Finland in 1939. Two years later many returned, only to up sticks and flee back to Finland again towards the end of the war.

Maija took me to pay a visit on some Karelian friends of hers who had made a new home near Somero in the 1940s. An entire village had been transplanted. Finns gave the refugees part of their land so that they could start again and the villagers had divided up their new territory according to what they had owned in Karelia. The old lady of the house had skin as white as the driven snow but her frail body was full of life when we pulled up at her farmstead for mid-morning coffee.

Finns are supposed to drink more coffee than anyone else, an average of nine cups a day. Traditionally, you should refuse an offer of coffee three times before saying, 'OK, maybe just half a cup.' Then you drink four or five. We sat down at a table laden with Finnish and Karelian edibles: *pulla* – wheat buns with caraway seeds, star-shaped filo pastry sweets filled with plum jam, and open pastry cases stuffed with rice, eaten hot, spread with a mixture of boiled eggs mashed up with butter. The walls of the large farmhouse kitchen were lined with faded and fuzzy black and white photographs of their home village in Karelia. They were grainy pictures of wooden farmsteads, family groups and the village church with a pointed steeple. The old lady and her husband had built their new farmhouse here in Finland to look like the one they had left behind and would never return to. Her husband had killed himself ten years ago and the old lady was too frail to go back, even if she had wanted to.

We were joined for coffee by the lady's daughter, a language teacher colleague of Maija's, and her two sons, one of whom worked the farm. He was an unassuming forty-year-old who sat as quiet as a mouse while his mother spoke, but warmed up when I asked whether any Karelians had returned. One of their community had risked imprisonment in Siberia when he went on a motorbike to take a secret look in the 1960s, he told me. Many of their homesteads were still there then. 'But many more people have been back since the end of the Soviet Union, to see what remains. Most of the farmhouses have been demolished by the Russians.' When the first Karelians had returned to see their former home village in 1989, they found all the headstones in the graveyard had been removed and their church full of cows.

I noticed a small framed map on the wall alongside the photographs and the farmer son was eager to point out his parents' village near Kamennogorsk. Then he disappeared into another room to return with a more detailed map of the area, telling me the correct Karelian names for the Russian labels printed on the map. I asked whether anyone had been back to reclaim property they had lost and he shook his head. No one wanted to return permanently, he told me.

His mother still remembered the June day in 1944 when she and her husband had fled their home, for the second and final time. The old lady smiled when I wondered whether anyone still bore a grudge against the Russians. She knew the question was for her, but that I felt unable to ask it directly. 'Not any more,' she said gently. The hate she had once felt had evaporated one day in a church hall when she saw a Russian soldier sitting alone playing the piano with tears rolling down his face.

In what was left of the long weekend I spent with Maija we ate up more kilometres in her little red car. We drove to see her brother who lived alone on a farm. He was a kindly, quiet man in his fifties, with eyebrows like bushes overhanging a rock face and fingers like cracked carrots that had just come out of the ground. He sat in his rocking chair and said little before going out to tend to his chickens. Maija took me on a walk through the forest in the eerie late-afternoon light that made the snowfields between the patches of trees glow blue, even though the sun had long since disappeared. A bitter, elemental north wind swept across the wintry scene and Arctic clouds scudded past in the leaden skies. The temperature had dropped considerably but it was minus 12 °C before I saw Maija's nose start to run. I had been getting through tissues at an alarming rate ever since my arrival in Stockholm.

Back in Somero, we slipped into the local church on Sunday night for the Christmas carol service. It was packed full of families wrapped up warm in their winter coats. The interior decor was simple and unadorned and looked as if it had been designed by Habitat. Plain wood was set off here and there by a lick of grey paint, whilst the floorboards were matt brick red. All the carols were sung sitting down and I could mouth the words to some of the familiar tunes. That night we ate fried perch for dinner.

I was sad to have to leave for Helsinki the following morning. It's not often I turn up to spend a weekend with a complete stranger and come away wishing I could stay longer. Mind you, it's not often that I spend all night drinking with a lady old enough to be my mother. But then, Maija was a Finn. I got a lift into the capital along Finnish highway number 1, which links the country's two biggest cities, and is only just being turned into a motorway.

The hotel I checked into was full of Russians who spent their days striking deals on mobile telephones and their nights gambling the profits on the blackjack and red dog tables of the international casino. If the press reports are to be believed, many of these gentlemen are members of Russia's big-time criminal fraternity. The small-time Russian conmen all go to Sweden to commit overt criminal acts. They do these with the sole purpose of putting their feet up in a comfortable prison while waiting for their court case and the free trip home.

There is quite a Russian feel to Helsinki's neo-classical buildings and monolithic parliament building, but the place manages to be a city while still retaining a small town atmosphere. They were selling Christmas trees in the square in front of the presidential palace which is dwarfed by the huge Baltic ferries tied at their moorings opposite. Across the square is the old fish market and out of the side windows the president can look up from his important papers towards the red-brick Orthodox cathedral.

I spent a pleasant couple of days roaming the streets of the EU's northernmost capital. The pavement ice came in a variety of colours – white, black, *café au lait* and exhaust grey – and it became colder still. It also snowed a lot, but the stuff came down in powdery fairy flakes which was rather atmospheric. Helsinki residents had their furs out and were busy doing their Christmas shopping. I put my head inside the Lutheran cathedral, which had been decorated in the same minimalist style as the church at Somero, and spent an afternoon in the National Museum. One morning I trudged up to the Sibelius Park, where they have erected an awful sixties monument in tubular metal to their most famous composer. Fortunately for Sibelius, he has gone to Jesus, and can't complain.

That evening I found myself in a Wild West saloon bar which served beer called Leningrad Cowboy and was decorated with 1950s Soviet Zetor tractors. (I assumed the Zetors were industrial archaeology until I saw a forecourt full of them six months later outside Dublin.) The bar was jam-packed with younger Finns warming up for Christmas. I got talking to a maverick physicist named Mikko whose interests included single malt whiskys and stud poker. He was dressed in a Sherlock Holmes cape and a long college scarf. Mikko surveyed the mock-Soviet setting and smiled. 'Finally, we see that it was a joke,' he declared.

Mikko appeared to approach everything with scientific precision. He told me that I should have some vodka and he ordered two Screwdrivers. 'I always drink it with orange juice,' he said. 'It is very important to maintain the metabolic balance.' Sometime after midnight an elderly man who had been drinking alone got up to leave and fell flat on his back, hit his head with a loud crack and spewed coins all over the wooden floor. No one moved to help him. Mikko observed the drunk as if he was one of his experiments. 'The older generation used alcohol to get drunk because of the poor conditions,' he explained. 'Young Finns don't do this.'

On my last day I picked up a free copy of the glossy *Helsinki Guide* at the post office. It didn't give me much information on shopping and sightseeing and hotels that I hadn't already discovered, but the pamphlet did include a curious double-page spread entitled 'Finland

– what it is not'. The Finnish authorities obviously thought they had an image problem, but the way they had gone about dispelling a few of the myths betrayed a fundamental lack of national self-confidence. Among the ten points the piece made were the following:

1. Finland is not awfully cold all the time, and polar bears do not roam the streets of Helsinki.
2. Finns don't drink as much as the rumours say.
3. Finland is not the country of limitless sex that it is often made out to be.

Highlighting what Finland isn't seemed typically introspective, and the way the points were made was rather aggressive in a passive sort of way. As I sat over my farewell dinner of reindeer steak in the wooden dacha-like Café Kappeli on Pohjoisesplanadi, I considered how the messages might be perked up in their next edition for a British audience. Outside, the snow was still gently falling and the fifty-odd navel-high Christmas trees sitting in front of the café in tubs were delicately sprinkled with Santa dust. The changes I came up with were:

1. Finland is *bloody* cold in winter.
2. The rumours don't give older Finns sufficient credit for their drinking abilities.
3. It's difficult to think about sex when you're dressed like a polar bear.

But making points like this is not the Finnish way.

8

Sex and Drugs and Pampered Rhizomes

I set out for Amsterdam on the first day of spring. To celebrate, they were doling out free plastic cups of champagne on the Eurostar. The Brussels train was far from full. I shared my compartment with a group of geriatric football supporters from Munich who were in high spirits because they had just seen their team thrash Nottingham Forest 5–1 and so end England's last hope of European football glory for another season. The newspapers were full of the usual stories about the strength of the Germans and the demise of the domestic game, and fog still lingered along with the sheep in the fields of Kent.

Although this was only my second journey under the Channel, there was already no doubt in my mind that the tunnel had brought Britain closer to our European cousins. Taking the train to the Continent is less of an occasion than catching an aeroplane or a ship. It is a ten-minute walk from my house in Oxford to the railway station, from where I can take a series of trains that weave their way above and below ground to reach my required European destination. I was even getting blasé about travelling underneath all that water. After finishing my complimentary cup of bubbly, I fell asleep midway through the tunnel and woke to find myself already in Belgium.

I caught my connection to Amsterdam in Brussels and still felt slightly groggy in the commuter-packed carriage as it trundled its way northward. As it comes into central Antwerp the track runs along an elevated section that looks like ancient battlements before disappearing into a dirty Waterloo-style girdered station beside a large warehouse that said it dealt in gold and diamonds. Some minutes later the train left Antwerp heading back in the direction we had arrived from, something that trains are wont to do on occasion, which always panics me momentarily. I checked my schedule and decided that I was on the right train.

We passed into a level landscape full of plush suburban pads and wide flat fields that smelt as if they had been manured only that morning. Gradually the passengers in my carriage had disappeared to their homes. The scenery continued to be wide and flat but the houses became less expensive-looking and without the country smell. Dusk, mist, haze, or whatever it was, began to close in and an old man climbed aboard to begin a ritual with his pipe. By the time we crossed a huge expanse of water with giant barges on it the carriage was full of a rich cherry smell.

I only knew we were in the Netherlands when we passed the Feyernord football stadium and pulled into Rotterdam CS. Between here and Amsterdam was an almost continuous built-up area, punctuated by numerous modern stations, many of which carried the suffix CS. What did CS stand for, I wondered to myself? My Dutch consists of three words, taught to me by a woman I met many years ago in Greece in slightly dubious circumstances. The words are *sproetjes*, *kip* and *tandenborstel*, which mean freckles, chicken and toothbrush. She probably taught me some others, but those are the ones that have stuck in my mind. Hence I was particularly ill equipped to hazard a guess at a Dutch acronym common to many, but not all, railway stations. I racked my brains. Could it be as simple as 'central station'? I flicked through my guidebook and discovered the answer. CS stood for Centraal Station. I felt a sense of self-satisfaction. I like languages like that. Instantaneously, I had nearly doubled my Dutch vocabulary. (During my time in the Netherlands, however, I realised that five words was going to be my personal best. In its written form, Dutch is packed full of vowels, often doubled up to make life more complicated, has Js and Ks in odd places, and an endless supply of impossibly long words. As an Australian newspaper once put it, written Dutch looks like someone sat on a typewriter.)

It was a short walk across a couple of canals from Amsterdam CS to the hotel where I had booked a berth. The place looked as if it specialised in renting rooms by the hour. It required payment up front and only accepted cash. I paid for a room and that's what I got, but only just. The space I occupied for the next five days wasn't really a room but it was too big for a seedling tray and they probably didn't know what else to do with it. It had the basics all right, a bed and a washbasin, but there was no soap, no towels, and the sheets were too narrow for the mattress. After one night, the bed became an impossible jumble of bedclothes, but since no one ever came to remake it I had to make do. When I chanced my arm and asked for a towel, I was presented with a piece of cotton big enough to grow mustard and cress on.

I had a day in Amsterdam before my back-up arrived. A friend, who was a bit of an ex-hippie, was due to arrive the following morning with a group of all-male accomplices for a long weekend of sin. He had kindly suggested that I might like to tag along, or he may have said, 'Shag along,' I couldn't be sure.

I thought I might begin by orientating myself so I left the hotel and began to wander. I had a mission of sorts in that I had to find the hotel where my friend the Hippieman and his mates were staying and the place where we had arranged to meet the following day. At the corner of my cobbled street were a couple of sex shops with fairly graphic displays of their produce, but nothing I couldn't handle. Night had fallen by this time and I continued down a street lined mostly with cafés and restaurants. At the end of the street was a bar fronted by a large plate-glass window bearing the name of a Dutch lager. Standing in the window were two tall men dressed in more or less identical black garb that consisted of a peaked leather cap and sleeveless T-shirt. Both wore small black moustaches. The two clones appeared to be friends since they were locked in a passionate embrace. Either that or they were adversaries in a tongue-sucking competition.

It suddenly struck me that I was preparing to spend a long weekend with a group of male strangers and I didn't know their sexual orientation. I had assumed that they were heterosexuals on a trip to Amsterdam to engage in the innocent activities of taking drugs and eyeing up prostitutes, two pastimes for which Amsterdam is well known. The notion that they might be a gay group with similar intentions had never crossed my mind. As I proceeded past the bar window, I thanked my lucky stars that the offer of a spare bed in one of their rooms had been withdrawn and that I hadn't been able to get another room in their hotel. It could have turned out to be an embarrassing situation.

I continued over a small bridge and through a crowded alleyway. There were guys hanging about who looked like drop-outs, others who looked like pushers. Some whispered their offers of mind-bending substances – hashish, coca, heroin, ecstasy – others just lounged. They were smoking cigarettes and trying to look shifty, something most of them did quite well, although no doubt they were helped by the fact that it was dark. Other than these characters, and the occasional late middle-aged smart man in camel-hair coat and leather gloves obviously en route to conduct some business (I gave them the benefit of the doubt), the crowd was remarkably normal. There were groups of young men, but also small bands of middle-aged couples taking the evening air and mixed groups of teenagers who giggled at the shop window displays.

The canal Oude Zijds Voorburgwal seemed to be where Amsterdam's red light district began. The crowds lingered and cars cruised slowly by, inching their way along the narrow towpaths on both sides of the water that were lined with terraces of towering housefronts. Some of these buildings contained bars and coffee shops and clip joints with names like 'Banana', but many were faced with door-shaped windows on to long thin rooms about the size of my hotel room. Above each window was a red striplight. Behind the windows sat women, usually on tall stools. There were thin ones and fat ones, blonde ones and black ones. Some were silicon-aided, Pamela Anderson look-alikes, others had all the lumps, bumps and curves they were born with, while a few sported paunches. Most of them wore white bras and knickers which glowed a luminous purple colour thanks to well-positioned ultraviolet tubes. It was like looking at kinky psychedelic goldfish.

Some of the women looked very bored, some were combing their hair to pass the time, others were talking to older women who might have been their mothers. Most, however, were making an effort to attract customers. If you caught their eye, they would smile alluringly, or worse still tap on the glass and beckon you to come on in, just as if she was your long-lost friend inviting you for a coffee and a chat. These were real, live, laughing, smiling, hair-combing sex professionals. They were adept at looking as if they wanted it badly and wanted it with you. Now.

As an Englishman, I found it all a bit embarrassing. It was bad enough looking at these female-shaped pieces of meat, but when they saw you were watching and reacted accordingly it was all a bit too much. I didn't know what to do with myself, except to smile timidly and move on. On occasion a man would approach one of the doors, ascertain the price of what was on offer, and disappear through the glass door to have a curtain drawn over the proceedings. It was all very routine and casual, but the ducks quacking in the canal still seemed incongruous by contrast.

Prostitution is legal in the Netherlands. Prostitutes pay income tax and get tax relief on the tools of their trade. This is typical of the pragmatic liberal Dutch attitude to a lot of things. No one has ever managed to get rid of the world's oldest profession, so why bother trying? Better to regulate it instead. There were health considerations to think about, labour conditions, public order, and of course another source of government revenue. Some said the love-ladies were just getting another pimp.

Walking round this open-air sexual shopping mall, looking at the windows full of diverse sexual equipment, and being encouraged to enter the clubs that lent another meaning to the phrase 'family entertainment' was in one sense all very honest and up front. We all do it, they seemed to be saying, so let's have it out in the open. Sex is a service industry, so let's treat it like any other. In another way it was really rather sad and too concentrated to be arousing. Intimacy and privacy were non-existent.

The northern European approach to sex is very practical. In Denmark, I remembered being surprised one evening at the forthright attitude reflected in a slot machine in the toilet of a Copenhagen bar. The machine had three slots, one for a do-it-yourself breathalyser kit, the second for condoms, and the third purveyed a toothbrush. The logic was all very straightforward. Ten kroner was enough to tell you whether you were still capable of performing, another ten bought you the wherewithal for safe sex, and for just 10 kroner more you could avoid the embarrassment of having to borrow a toothbrush the following morning. One of the non-satellite Danish television channels, which broadcasts news, documentaries and game shows during the evening, transmits graphic sex films late at night.

I had a conversation with an Italian in Rome about sex. Of course, he dismissed northern Europeans as being too mechanical. The Italians got more involved, he said, they were much more passionate. In Italy, sex was a form of intimate communication. This is not to say that Italian TV doesn't also broadcast titillating shows, but if the Servicio Erotico on channel 27 in my Milanese hotel room was anything to go by, it wasn't quite as slick as the Danish offerings. It consisted of bored, boss-eyed Italian housewives in home movies featuring feather dusters. They were connected to a phone sex service, and the screen was so full of telephone numbers and advice on the acceptability of various credit cards that you couldn't even see that much of the feather dusters. Every so often, the screen was hijacked by a message that, roughly translated, said: 'Please dial slowly or you'll cause an intense traffic jam on the phone lines.' Then the whole show would disappear to be replaced by an advertisement for fitted kitchens. Before I got bored, I noticed that the entire operation seemed to be run from Dublin of all places. Perhaps it was some nasty Catholic conspiracy.

The Dutch have come a long way since their first home-grown porno movie was produced. It was in the late 1960s and its maker got three years in jail for upsetting the scales of moral turpitude. I learnt this in one of the museums devoted to the subject of sex which are dotted around Amsterdam. The museum was an odd combination of graphic pornography and an almost fairground atmosphere, like a Disneyland version of the Marquis de Sade's memoirs. There you'd be, having passed the array of modern sadomasochistic gear and peekaboo underwear, to peruse an assortment of rude birthday cakes and a display of early twentieth-century corsetry, when your movement would trigger a conspiratorial hiss from an alcove. As you turned, a life-sized plastic mannequin of a red-faced old bloke would leer out to open his soiled mackintosh and flash at you.

I had been a bit hesitant about venturing into the establishment, for fear of it being full of the real dirty raincoat brigade, but the museum's visitors all looked very upright and apparently no different from the crowds I was to see later in the van Gogh museum. There was an oriental section with a display of naughty porcelain, 78-r.p.m. porno records from France, and walking sticks with erotic scenes hidden in their grips which were very popular with bon viveurs in the nineteenth century according to the caption.

A number of historical sex symbols had their own permanent exhibits. Mata Hari, the infamous Dutch courtesan and spy, appeared as a shop window dummy along with a display of her letters, while a life-sized waxwork of Marilyn Monroe had her skirt permanently billowing over a sidewalk grate. Rudolph Valentino got a small alcove all to himself.

Fertility symbols from every age and from all over the world were all carefully labelled and I learnt some remarkable new facts. The Romans invented the word sex, for example, and the Devil is considered to have the coldest penis ever known. The enterprising museum authorities had even obtained the leather-bound diary belonging to a lady member of an eighteenth-century exclusive London establishment known as the Aphrodites. A detailed explanation of its contents revealed that she had documented 4959 amorous contacts over a period of twenty years. They included 439 monks, 119 musicians, 117 footmen, 47 negroes, 12 cousins and 2 uncles.

I passed through the red light district again a couple of days later on my way to meet Hippieman and his friends. There were fewer ladies in the windows but they seemed rather absurd in the daylight. We met up in a coffee shop called the Grasshopper. In Amsterdam there are coffee shops and there are coffee shops. Some are purveyors of coffee, tea and cakes, others specialise in coffee, tea and cannabis. We met in one of the latter variety.

From the outside, it looked just like a thousand other coffee shops you see on street corners anywhere. It was in a tall, square building and there was a sign over the entrance depicting a grasshopper sitting on an Amsterdam street bollard, which all have three Xs on the side. I walked under that and went up three steps, through a glass door and down a dozen more steps. Inside, there were tables and chairs and a bar where you could buy your coffee, and because it was called the Grasshopper the paintwork was green. Music was playing over the hi-fi system and television screens placed at strategic intervals on the walls transmitted MTV music videos.

Over in the corner of the room was a booth that marked this coffee shop out from others all over Europe. Pressing a button set in the side of the booth illuminated a glass screen menu. On sale were perhaps a dozen different varieties of marijuana. They all had exotic names like Sensemilla Purple, Super Afghan and Ketama Gold. There was even a special offer on Super Skunk. Once you had chosen your variety, you made your purchase at the booth window where a young man weighed out the desired amount on a scale which gave an automatic digital readout on the electronic cash register. You paid your money, the man popped your goods into a small plastic envelope and off you went to roll up, breathe in and mellow out. On the bar there were even free rolling papers to get you started.

Hippieman was sitting at one of the tables nursing a cappuccino and looking rather the worse for wear for having climbed out of his bed in England at four o'clock that morning. He wore a slightly anarchic beard and his hair was tied in a neat little ponytail. I was introduced to the group around the table. As it turned out, Hippieman's accomplices weren't hippies at all; they had respectable jobs in things like engineering, computers and finance. They looked like a normal bunch of thirtysomethings who could have been sitting in an English coffee shop except for the fact that they were smoking additives with their tobacco.

During the course of our weekend together, the faces round the table took on personalities. There was a short, round character with a shiny bald head and a black beard who had organised the trip and looked like a Fixerman. Next to him sat Straightman, the tallest in the group. He had a babyface and was clearly less accustomed to smoking dope than the others. Two others both worked in computers, but since I could only cope with one Computerman, I named the other Leathertrouserman because of his desire throughout the weekend to find a shop where he could buy a pair of hip leather leggings.

The remaining member of the group was Burgerman, a small fair-haired guy with a penchant for hamburgers. He would only eat burgers from Burger King, which he said were much tastier than Big Macs. Non-brandname burgers didn't even warrant his consideration. After our first day of wandering, during which the rest of us grazed on pizza slices and hot dogs, Burgerman declared his need for a proper Burger King hamburger. Having been to Amsterdam before, he knew where the only such restaurant was. We trailed along after Burgerman for more than an hour as he led us across town in search of the elusive Burger King outlet. When we finally reached the place, it had closed down. A notice in the window directed us to its new premises, which turned out to be a five-minute stroll from where we had started. We made our way back, and Burgerman bought three burgers to make up for lost time. Clearly an expert in these matters, he sank each one in little more than a single bite.

On that first morning, as we sat making small talk and discussing the ground rules for the weekend, it struck me what a pleasant and innocuous way of breaking the law this was. Smoking cannabis is illegal in the Netherlands, but it's one piece of legislation the police don't bother enforcing. Coffee shops like the Grasshopper are commonplace in many Dutch cities and there are about four hundred of them in Amsterdam alone.

The Dutch have enjoyed smoking cannabis for a long time, certainly since Holland's golden age in the seventeenth century. I'm not sure what happened in between, but the rate of consumption rose significantly in the 1960s when Amsterdam became Europe's most radical capital, renowned for its liberal attitude towards drugs, gays and personal freedom in general. In 1976 the enlightened Dutch authorities began a social experiment. Rather than legalise the stuff, a policy of tolerance was adopted – consumption and small-scale production are not regarded as serious offences and are generally overlooked by the authorities. Likewise the existence of the coffee shops. Interpretation of the official tolerance policy has changed slightly over the years, so that proprietors of the special coffee shops have had to remove the cannabis leaves that used to adorn the windows and signs of their establishments. But what goes on inside is still the same. Instead of displaying the leaf of the plant in question, many of these coffee shops use a thinly disguised code to advertise their business. Rastafarian colour schemes are common, or suggestive names like Easy Times and Mellow Yellow. A few doors up from my hotel was a coffee shop named the Joystick; a few doors beyond that sat the Amsterdam stock exchange.

Drug-taking doesn't feature very prominently in Grand Tourists' accounts of the Low Countries, but in many other respects the Netherlands does not appear to have changed much in 200 years. The English all thought that the Dutch were very clever to put canals in the middle of their towns, and many commented on how clean everywhere was. The Dutch temperament also seems to have changed little. Charles Theodore Middleton observed that the most distinctive aspect of the national character was avarice. A Dutchman I spoke to in a coffee shop laughed when I told him this. 'Yes, everyone still thinks we are mean,' he said. 'I heard a Belgian joke about a Dutchman who wrote to his newspaper: "Dear Sir, if you keep publishing stupid jokes about Dutch meanness, I shall have to stop borrowing your newspaper from my next-door neighbour."' We both laughed, then he added in a more serious tone, 'But this impression is not really correct. Dutch people are just careful with their money.' I wondered why this was and he said that he thought it had a lot to do with Calvinism. 'We are not very religious,' he said, 'but Calvinism provides a sort of moral code that encourages us to be thrifty.' This inbuilt frugal streak is nourished by the designers of modern Dutch banknotes. They come in no-nonsense primary colours that shriek at you every time you try to hand them over. But although they like accumulating the stuff, the Dutch don't flash their wealth about. As Middleton put it, they 'hate arrogance, and cannot bear the affectation of grandeur'.

Back in the twentieth century, no one in the Grasshopper was affecting any grandeur either. In our group, everyone was feeling pretty relaxed and we decided to get some fresh air. We wandered aimlessly. The streets were relatively clean, but the canals were a fetid green. We marvelled at the gabled architecture and then someone noted that none of the narrow canal houses was actually vertical. Their façades looked like slightly wonky cardboard cut-outs. Fixerman said that this was one of the reasons why he liked Amsterdam: it was as if the whole city was on the piss.

All the canal buildings also seemed immensely tall, partly because of their narrowness. They were probably specially designed this way, in an attempt to inject a third dimension to this flat country. One feature of the interior of these buildings, which I had found to my cost over the last couple of days, was their staircases. They were the steepest, narrowest staircases I had ever encountered. I suppose that they too were all part of the effort to accustom the Dutch to what they would surely encounter if and when they ever ventured outside the Netherlands. In other countries, people get this sort of exercise walking up and down hills. As it happened, my hotel room was on the fifth floor and, needless to say, there was no lift. One evening after a long day spent largely in coffee shops it took me a fortnight to climb them.

After some time, we found ourselves towards the end of one of the canals standing outside the entrance to the Hash Marihuana Hemp Museum, and Fixerman suggested we might like to have a look inside. We all trooped in except Straightman who preferred to continue breathing the fresh air outside.

The fact that there should be a Dutch museum dedicated to soft drugs should have come as no surprise. The Netherlands seemed to have a museum for virtually everything. In addition to all the usual candidates for subject matter, the city of Utrecht is host to an insurance museum and a grocery museum, Lisse has one dedicated to bulbs, whilst Amsterdam's many museums include one devoted to piggy banks and another that specialises in instruments of torture. (A macabre fascination took me in to look at the torture museum. It was full of medieval contraptions lovingly preserved and laid out in a series of dimly lit rooms that echoed to the music of Vivaldi.) I had also been informed by a reasonably reliable source that Amsterdam boasted a museum of excrement, but when I enquired at the tourist office nobody had heard of it. This was a shame because I had been looking forward to saying what a shit museum it was.

The face of the young woman behind the desk at the Hash Marihuana Hemp Museum had been decorated with most of the make-up commercially available in Holland and her hair was a shade of purple that nobody ought to wear. She was smoking a joint. Behind her was a small plaque with English writing on it which read as follows: 'NOTICE: This museum is not to advocate cannabis smoking but to educate the public on all the many uses of this amazing plant.' On the counter in front of the purple woman were multi-lingual brochures produced by the Sensi Seed Bank, an organisation specialising in seeds and all the paraphernalia needed for their successful indoor cultivation. Their catalogue contained everything from appropriate light bulbs and pH meters to hydroponic growing systems and special apparatus for measuring air quality. The various seed varieties had write-ups like any other garden centre product line: 'An absolute must for the greenhouse' and 'A versatile plant which performs well under all conditions'.

When they are fully grown, what you do with your plants is up to you. According to information gleaned from the museum, the various parts of the hemp plant have more than fifty thousand different uses. You can eat it, turn it into paper, clothing, rope, fuel, construction materials, the choice is endless. And if you had any left over, you could always *try* smoking it. In this respect, the Sensi Seed Bank products appeared to have an edge. According to the catalogue introduction, their various strains had won numerous prizes in the annual High Times Cannabis Cup awards.

Elsewhere in the Hash Marihuana Hemp Museum, a carefully researched inventory of historical landmarks in society's changing attitudes to the stuff implied that a number of humankind's most notable achievements might not have occurred were it not for this amazing plant. The Scythians invented the scythe after smoking it and Moslems used hemp to start Europe's first paper mill, about three hundred years after Mohammed said that alcohol was off-limits but that cannabis was OK. Columbus wouldn't have reached America without hempen sails, caulking and rigging, and the same material had been used to make the world's first pair of denims. In 1890, Queen Victoria's personal physician recommended the use of cannabis therapies for mental and muscular disorders.

Whilst not actually advocating experimentation with marijuana's psychoactive properties, which were documented by Herodotus in case you didn't know, the museum came pretty close. There were cases of pipes from all over the world and a range of makeshift disposable methods for smoking it: an apple, a soft drinks can, and an old Biro. A sort of social history of delinquency continued, with exhibits from California (a marijuana board game called Pot Luck, air sprays to dispel the smell, and a hi-brew beer nicknamed 'The Wacko One') and a display of common or garden objects used for smuggling marijuana. The latter exhibits did, however, come with a warning that all of these methods were well known to the authorities.

When we left, I had to admit that I had widened my knowledge of the non-psychoactive uses of cannabis. But after a looped video on home-growing, numerous displays on smoking methods and detailed accounts of the expected effects, I was also pretty well versed on the smoking aspects. For some further field research, we made our way towards the second coffee shop of our tour. En route we stopped off at a smokers' retail outlet on a main street. Its windows were full of what looked like high-tech hubble-bubble pipes: glass test-tube affairs designed to enhance the effect of smoking the illegal weed. When we arrived at the Bulldog, there was a large microscope permanently fixed to the dope bar so that you could examine your acquisitions in detail. To my disappointment, however, no one appeared to be making ropes or sails with the stuff.

From a legislative point of view, the Netherlands seemed to be rather confusing. One of the most effective exhibits in the museum had been a mirror with iron bars in front of it. Above the mirror, a caption said 'This Could be You'. Detailed below were statistics from a number of countries on what the museum authorities were pleased to call cannabis 'prisoners of conscience'. The unrivalled Dutch attitude towards soft drugs, frowned upon needless to say by all their EU neighbours, was brought home to me some weeks later when I sat in a hotel room in Luxembourg watching a CNN documentary about marijuana. The programme makers had interviewed the Dutch health minister who explained the official line. The woman looked like your mum. When asked whether she had tried cannabis herself, she said that she had. She had rolled a joint with her husband and they had both had a smoke. Neither of them had enjoyed it, she said.

The interview sat in stark contrast to another with an elderly US citizen who had been prosecuted for growing the stuff for his aged wife, a multiple sclerosis sufferer. The man's sad story was interspersed with footage quoting numerous medical doctors who prescribed cannabis for patients suffering from painful illnesses. The FBI had subpoenaed the elderly man's partner to testify against him. She became so distraught at the prospect that she committed suicide. The FBI still managed to arrange for the now single man to spend some time in jail for the offence and had confiscated his house. As far as the man could remember, he had never broken the law before. He hadn't even received a parking ticket.

The long weekend passed off well. We spent a lot of time in and around the red light district sampling the ambience of numerous coffee shops. We shot a lot of pool and when we got bored with that we fed money into the Cyber Cycle machines in the amusement arcades. Then someone would lead us past the illuminated windows in search of something to eat, and when we left the red lights Straightman observed how strange it was to see restaurant windows full of people who were fully clothed. We ate Argentine steaks and Dutch pancakes and Burgerman made regular sorties to the king of the fast-food outlets.

Amsterdam was a good city to wander in and we did a lot of walking. Straightman commented on the irony of coming to Amsterdam and finding that your feet ended up throbbing more than any other part of the anatomy. Whilst cars appeared to be a rarity in Amsterdam, compared to all the other European capitals I had visited so far, the usual dangers encountered in crossing roads were more than made up for by legions of sit-up-and-beg bicycles and fast-moving trams that crackled on their overhead wires. The city authorities' attempts to provide free bikes that could be ridden and left for the next person to use have failed – Amsterdam's Take-a-bike scheme collapsed because someone took them all – but pedal-power remains a popular form of transport. For seven grown men reduced to child-like status thanks to the power of the weed, bicycles represented a formidable danger.

We hung out in bars until the small hours. Each bar had its regulars with skin the colour of men who only go out at night, and at least two TV screens, one of which had a permanently fuzzy picture. The picture on the other was usually either too bright or too dark. If they weren't showing music videos, it was a compilation of great sporting calamities. We had conversations and made comments that amused us. One evening when trying to decide when we should have dinner, I looked at the digital wall clock which said 19.45 and announced that we had more than fifty years to decide. It seemed funny at the time. As Hippieman was heard to say, it felt as if we had entered a different time zone. It started at a different hour and went in varying directions at different speeds. It was twelve noon and he had just emerged after a morning smoke and an unsuccessful attempt to sort out a basic group fiscal policy. He didn't know how far gone he was until he tried doing a simple task. He was leaning on a police van in the midday drizzle. He said the van felt very comfortable. Later, he even claimed to be walking with a slur.

The soft drug culture was all around us, although most of the participants seemed to be foreigners. There was a fellow Englishman who worked in my hotel who always looked at the list when I asked for my key and said, 'Mr Middleton, yeah?'

'That's right,' I would reply and he would counter, 'Sorry, I won't ask next time. I've got a pretty shit memory and unfortunately I'm in the wrong place to get it back.' But at least he looked at the list.

Our group activities seemed to occur without much planning but with remarkably few mishaps. Although everyone was content to vegetate in bars and coffee shops for long periods, all concerned were also keen to see some of the less disreputable sights. The tram system was mastered and everyone successfully rendezvoused at the Rijksmuseum, Amsterdam's answer to the Louvre, a huge pile on three levels with ecclesiastical overtones in its arched stained-glass windows. We split up to peruse the cavernous galleries full of the usual Dutch subject matter. There were pictures of wooden boats with gabled houses and windmills in the background, winter scenes with men in outrageous collars skating on the ice, and still-life leftovers from yesterday's dinner or fowl slung over a table before the preparations for tonight's feast. My favourite was a small dark number entitled *Still Life with Asparagus*. Many of the portraits depicted slightly surreal men and women whose heads appeared to be floating on seas of frothy white ruffles.

The Dutch Masters flourished in the seventeenth century, when the Netherlands was at her zenith, after she had wriggled out of the clutches of the Habsburgs. Rembrandt, Hals and Vermeer were on hand to paint it all as an empire was built, the great cartographers (Mercator, Ortelius, Blaeu) charted the new territories, and the Dutch East India Company raked in the cash. This was when the Netherlands included the countries we know as Belgium and Luxembourg, but the whole lot was dominated by the province of Holland, the bit that some still confuse with the entire country today.

During this period, the Dutch led Europe, but although they were painting in their country's golden age, the Dutch Masters produced a lot of dark paintings. Blacks sucked away the light into the canvases, or at least this is how it seemed. Rembrandt's finest work was given its well-known abbreviated name, *The Night Watch*, long after he painted it, but when they cleaned it 300 years later the painting turned out to be a daytime scene. It was hung on the top floor at the end of a long gallery studded with freshly cut flowers on majestic pedestals. Like most of the other famous Western European paintings I had seen, it was surrounded by tour groups so that when you sat on the seats opposite the huge canvas you couldn't see a damn thing.

The painting depicts a group of volunteer civic guards hanging around with their weaponry and flag, ready for action. If something similar was commissioned today, it would be a team photo of the local Neighbourhood Watch. The militia members all chipped in and the more they paid the closer they were to the front. The head honcho must have written a large cheque because he was treated in a special way. He stood in the foreground resplendent in a pale lemon-yellow dandy's outfit discussing tactics. He looked overexposed, as if a flash bulb had gone off at an unexpected moment.

Like the *Mona Lisa*, *The Night Watch* has been the subject of deliberate vandalism in the time before it became recognised as a sacrosanct cultural item. In the eighteenth century someone wanted to hang it between two doors in the town hall. The painting was too big, so they chopped a piece off from one side and three militiamen were lost for ever.

Having seen the artistic offerings in the Rijksmuseum, I wanted to compare the nineteenth-century Dutch Master, Mister van Gogh. He has his own museum in unfortunate concrete a short walk away. Unusually for a major world artist, virtually all of van Gogh's work remains in his native country, and most of it is to be found in this purpose-built complex. The paintings are displayed in chronological order, and his earliest efforts have the same dark Dutch trademark as many of those up the road. Vincent started out as an evangelist and he worked in the Belgian mining region of Borinage. When he first began painting he produced pictures of sturdy peasant women and burly miners that look as if they have been painted using the heavy green-brown earth the workers toil with. Then van Gogh moved to Paris, threw out his dingy palette and discovered colour. Everyone knows the results, and seeing them in the flesh was no disappointment. It was also the first time I had really noticed duck-egg blue skies in a picture. For decades I had unconsciously assumed that the colour had some kind of military significance because it was always what I painted the bottom of my Airfix World War II model aeroplanes with.

The resplendent blossom and flowers in van Gogh's later canvases reminded me that I couldn't really come to the Netherlands and not check out a few tulips. I had thought I'd timed my visit well, because for a couple of spring months each year the country opens up the world's largest garden at a place called Keukenhof. I left Hippieman and friends to buy their leather trousers and other souvenirs and boarded a train to Leiden.

After a couple of journeys through the Netherlands you realise just how overwhelmingly flat the place really is. This is because most of it should be underwater. It used to be a bog or a lake or even part of the seabed; but today more than half the country is a drainage works. For wetland enthusiasts the Netherlands is a major crime against ecology; for the Dutch it's a triumph of man over marsh. Most of their major cities are below sea level. Those parts of the countryside that aren't built upon are either covered in glasshouses or plastic sheeting or are left open as low, flat, manicured fields split into a vast grid by drainage canals. The fields are wide and neat, covered in fresh green grass or carefully furrowed earth like huge slabs of chocolate that had just been grated. There are no fences or hedges, just narrow drainage canals. It comes as some surprise in such an intensively managed environment to see ducks, or the occasional pair of swans, standing alone in a green expanse, pecking at the grass.

The Dutch ability to control nature is exemplified in the bulb business, perhaps the most awesomely efficient horticultural industry anywhere. Reclaimed sand dunes with a bit of peat and a dash of clay are great for growing bulbs in, and every year the Dutch grow more than eight billion of the things. Then they dig them up and sell them. Most go abroad, and a lot come to the UK, because the British buy more bulbs per person than anyone else. But the Dutch hang on to six million bulbs to plant in the Keukenhof, along with 6.5 tonnes of grass seed and a lot of love and attention. Keukenhof means kitchen garden, and it's some kitchen garden.

Or at least I think it is. Although spring had sprung, it had been a cold winter in Europe, and when I turned up at the biggest bulb show on earth there wasn't much to be seen. A few clumps of crocuses were still extant beneath the bushes, but otherwise Keukenhof was mostly earth. But what lovingly groomed earth. I strolled the network of tarmac paths that weave through the manicured park. A single line of turfs bordered the paths, some of the turfs expertly trimmed to make way for a tree root. Next came the perfectly tilled soil, now sprouting delicate grass blades. The centrepieces were islands of freshly turned peat beds studded with succulent green shoots, each with a small dark green notice stating the species and a larger wooden board naming the section's designer. It was a sanctuary for pampered rhizomes. If someone had told me that they have twenty-four-hour weed patrols, or that an alarm sounds as soon as a slug ventures on to the scene, it would have sounded perfectly normal. They probably even comb the grass when it gets to a certain height.

The weather had taken a turn for the worse and the odd snowflake appeared from the heavens, so I made my way to one of the garden's greenhouses. It was full of greenhouse guys and gals doing a bit of arranging and pushing large trolleys laden with blooms, the tools of their trade (a pair of scissors and a mobile phone) sticking out of their back pockets. Immediately I got an idea of what Keukenhof must look like when all the bulbs are out: I was hit right between the eyes by a riot of blooming tulips. The atmosphere beneath the glass was warm and slightly damp and heady with the scent of cut freesias that were being boxed in the centre of the complex. A deep breath through the nose was enough to send you into orbit in a way that the gaseous envelope in an Amsterdam coffee shop never could.

It was a phenomenal display of tulip design, each variety with an appropriate name. I suppose flower breeders must have long and serious meetings to hammer out new names, in the same way that paint manufacturers do. But unlike paint manufacturers, the tulip growers seemed to have got it about right. Most of the names were appropriately descriptive and conjured up the right sort of mood. The blooms in one plot were a damson mousse colour with a white edge called Ballade. Ballerina had bright orange spikes, Merry Christmas was a sumptuous red, Arabian Mystery a deep dark purple that hinted at black. A few varieties were still awaiting inspiration, their name tags bearing a coded number, but then I came across the delinquent section. Whatever possessed someone to call a tulip Attila, or Zombie? Were these names the result of a flower breeders' meeting in a coffee shop, or was someone trying to make a rebellious statement here? If it was the latter, why not go the whole hog? What's wrong with names like Paper Bag, or Bank Vault, or Chopped Mongoose?

Nonetheless, the scene was a magnificent assault on the senses and the glasshouse was full of admirers. Groups of youngsters were snapping photographs of their friends in front of the enchanting displays and elderly couples stood gazing with broad grins on their faces. This was nice to observe, but I didn't want to stand too close to the old ladies because their perfumes were coarse in comparison with the heady aroma of the freesias. It was only when I noticed the faint Muzak and the automatic bank teller at one end inside the glasshouse that the experience dimmed somewhat.

Before leaving the Keukenhof, I bought some bulbs at a stall outside the greenhouse. I chose some unusual purple specimens for myself and for my parents a white flower that looked similar to an iris in the photograph on the front of the packet. To my surprise, the packets gave a total lack of guidance for planting: nothing about when, how deep, how far apart, what sort of soil, or anything. 'There are no instructions,' I said to the lady behind the wooden table that served as the counter. She looked at me as if I was a simpleton: 'You plant them in the earth,' she said, 'and then they grow.'

'Oh, right. Pretty straightforward then.'

'Very easy,' she said kindly.

Not wanting to leave the woman with the impression that I was a complete idiot, I told her that I was only asking because the soil in my garden had an unusually high pH. I've no idea whether this is true, but I thought it sounded impressive.

'These will grow anywhere,' she assured me as she rummaged around in her box for some change. 'Dutch bulbs are the best, we export them everywhere.'

Riding on the bus back to Leiden, we passed several fields planted with purple and yellow crocuses and I read something about bulbs that made me sit up. It was thirty years too late, but I had found a brilliant answer to a childhood trauma which, if I had known it at the time, might have got me off a very serious charge of ecological vandalism. Apparently, the magnificently colourful displays provided by the bulb fields are not designed for the observer, but are just a stage in the process of bulb cultivation. When the plants reach full bloom, someone comes along and beheads them all. This is so that the bulb absorbs the stem as sustenance for future flowering. When I was about three or four, I remember enlisting the help of my best friend to behead all the tulips in my parents' back garden. We carefully collected the heads and carried them into the kitchen to present triumphantly to my mother. Expecting great praise for this thoughtful act of generosity, we were aghast when all we received was an extremely severe reprimand. If I had only known what I know today, I could have argued that, in the long run, our actions were actually beneficial to my mum's precious tulips. As it was, I carry the mental scars of a week's disapprobation to this day.

The tulip is not native to the Netherlands. The first bulb was imported from Turkey where the tulip is the national flower. Even the name is from the Turkish, a variation on the word *dulban*, which means turban. Another Dutch national symbol, the windmill, is also an import. The first windmills were built in the Middle East and the concept was probably brought to Western Europe by the crusaders. But, as they have the tulip, the Dutch have embraced the windmill and used it so widely that the two have become almost synonymous.

Windmills were used to grind corn and to drain the polders, but they are not quite as common a sight in the Dutch landscape as in times past. Just a hundred years ago there were about ten thousand windmills in the Netherlands. Nine hundred surrounded Amsterdam in a protective ring to prevent the city from flooding. Then the steam engine was invented and most became obsolete. Leiden's remaining windmill is now a museum, although the red-brick structure still dominates the skyline as the town's only high-rise building.

It was the first thing that struck me after I'd extricated myself from the building site that was Leiden station. Everywhere I went in the Netherlands they were busy building things. Everything looked new (well, except the old buildings, but they were lovingly preserved). The only other EU country I had visited that came even close to this level of new development was Finland. There too, all the buildings looked as if they had just been built. The only difference was that in Finland there weren't so many old structures. Most of them had been made of wood, which has a tendency to burn down.

Leiden seemed like a pleasant little place with the usual canals. It also had red-brick pavements and red tarmac on the roads. The town has an eclectic variety of claims to fame. It is the birthplace of Rembrandt, whose father ran a windmill, and is the site of the country's oldest university and botanical gardens. The university was set up after Leiden proved to be the only town to withstand the Spanish siege of 1574, though a third of its inhabitants starved to death before the Spaniards gave up. A few decades later, the Pilgrim Fathers hung out there for eleven years before setting sail on the *Mayflower* to pastures new. Today, there are bicycles everywhere and a phenomenal number of restaurants. I chose a Surinamese one for my final Dutch dinner where the meal was served on a pancake and they produced a mean green jungle cocktail to wash it down with. The next morning I bought a ticket for Belgium, learning in the process that Dutch Railways is the only rail company in the EU that doesn't accept credit cards. We passed a huge greenhouse full of old caravans outside Rotterdam and for the first time on Dutch public transport I heard a mobile phone ringing.

9

They Eat Horses, Don't They?

As we were pulling into Antwerp I saw a lorry with an escalator on its back crawling along in the morning traffic. It was an odd sight, a moving staircase that wasn't moving the way you expect. It was an appropriate sign of things to come. Belgium turned out to be an odd place.

The few indicators I had about the country already pointed that way. All I remembered about Belgium from my school geography lessons was that it was divided between two tribes, the Flemings and the Walloons. Just the names were usually good for a laugh. I also had it on good authority that Belgium had established the world's first museum of underwear. And how many other countries are run by a prime minister who keeps chickens and joins his favourite football team in the bath to celebrate them winning the league?

Yet in Britain we hardly ever get any news about Belgium. There are endless stories about the Eurocrats in Brussels, of course, but real Belgian news? Nothing. This might go some way to explain why it is that we think Belgians are humourless and boring. I don't think they are, it's just that we don't know anything about them. This even extends to the fact that the best-known Belgians are all fictional: Tintin, Hercule Poirot and Maigret. Seemingly, the only interesting or remarkable real-life Belgian was René Magritte, and he was certainly an oddball. After this visit, my first to Belgium, I decided that Belgians are a bit bizarre. They are also quiet and unassuming and really rather ugly.

One of their best-kept secrets is their food. Everyone has heard of Belgian chocolate, but how many people know that Belgium has more three-star Michelin restaurants per head than France? Nobody, because the Belgians don't brag about it the way the French do. They want to keep it all to themselves.

I first learnt the importance of food to the Belgians from a trainee shipping lawyer named Konrad. Konrad was at law school in Oxford with my girlfriend, and shortly after she started the course she began to arrive home with amazing stories concerning the size of this Belgian's lunches. Apparently, Konrad owned the largest Tupperware lunchbox in the world. It was more like a picnic hamper, and each day Lorraine would regale me with stories concerning the contents of Konrad's midday meal which he devoured as if it was the last meal he would be eating for many days. It wasn't. As time went by, it also became clear that lunch was by no means Konrad's main meal of the day. He simply ate a great deal more than the average person. He started the morning with a significant breakfast, squeezed in a snack at around eleven, devoured the by now infamous lunch at midday, tucked away a bowl of soup at about five, consumed a large dinner at nine, and always ate a midnight snack before he went to bed. Konrad revealed later that all he ever had to eat at school was Nutella. He had obviously never quite got over it and was making up for lost lunches.

Despite his world-class eating skills, Konrad was not fat. He was lean and fresh-faced and almost permanently flustered. He was also prone to accidents and bouts of forgetfulness, which might have explained why he had never learnt how to tie a tie. He always got someone else to do it for him. All the shirts in his wardrobe were primed so that he could just pull them on over his head and tighten at the neck.

The full seriousness with which Konrad took his food was only revealed when he came round to my house to cook dinner one evening. He arrived to begin the preparations before 6 p.m. We were due to eat at about eight, but we didn't start until ten. We were still eating long after midnight.

While Konrad was preparing the feast, he gave me a brief run-down on things to see and do in Belgium. I should only bother with the cities, he told me, since Belgian countryside is ugly and full of motorways. I should go to Brussels and Antwerp and Bruges, and if there was any time left, his own town of Ghent was well worth a visit.

Konrad's comments on the Belgian countryside echoed in my thoughts as my train chugged towards Antwerp. In places it looked like Eastern Europe: grotty, dishevelled and strewn with aerial wires to run the trains on. We seemed to cross a motorway on average every five minutes. One of Belgium's claims to late twentieth-century fame is that when it is lit up at night, the national motorway network is one of the few manmade landmarks that astronauts can recognise from space.

We arrived at Antwerp's central station. On my way to Amsterdam, when my train had pulled in and out of here, all I had seen were the filthy girders and windows that hadn't been cleaned for a hundred years. This time I saw the rest of it. The grand foyer had been recently spruced up and it was magnificent. The interior detail and the half-rose window at the front made it look more like a nineteenth-century cathedral than a railway station.

Much of the rest of Antwerp was impressive too. The main drag that led away from the station and the skull-capped diamond merchants on Pelikaanstraat was as classy a wide and tree-lined boulevard as any in Paris. Baroque edifices sprang up from nowhere and cobbled side streets revealed row upon row of trendy little bars and eating places. From the raised esplanade on the bank of the River Scheldt the medieval Steen Castle looked forbidding. Although now a maritime museum, over the centuries it has seen many a mangled body dispatched through the stone trapdoor in its lowest dungeon to be taken away on the tide. Across the road, the sixteenth-century meat market looked like a red and white *millefeuilles* garnished with five pentagonal towers.

On the other side of the old meat market sat the Grote Markt, the ancient marketplace hemmed in on all sides by the towering façades of the professional guilds, all supporting multitudes of golden icons of cherubs and eagles and archers and many-masted ships. Towering above it all was the main tower of the lop-sided cathedral, a bizarre construction with a pointy cupola that made it look as if some of its builders thought they were constructing a mosque.

After ogling all this lot for a day, I felt hungry. In fact I felt very hungry, hungry enough to eat a horse, and of course in this part of the world I could do just that. I found a restaurant called De Peerdestal with a picture on its sign of a cute little horsy poking its nose out from its stall to look at you with that wide-eyed innocence that only horses can manage. Too little too late, I thought to myself, as I pushed open the door.

Inside, De Peerdestal was cavernous, but the first thing I encountered was the bar, a solid wooden affair with a barman behind it. He was an odd-looking character in his late twenties, with a shaven head and shaggy eyebrows. Other than the eyebrows, a moustache and dark eyes dominated his face. It wasn't that the man didn't have a nose, mouth and all the other customary facial features, just that there didn't seem to be much room for them after the facial hair and eyes. The eyebrows were heavy and black and the moustache a neat little counterbalancing strip. His eyes had a haunted, nervous look and were dark around the edges. He was straight out of a Tintin cartoon strip. He looked as if he'd escaped from the Belgian paratroops regiment and was expecting to be recaptured at any time. He took one look at me and disappeared. I didn't see him go, he just vanished. One moment he was there, the next moment he was gone.

There have been occasions, when faced with this sort of welcome, in which I have turned and left the restaurant, but it was so cold outside that I thought I would stick it out. Besides, I'd never eaten horse before. I gave their selection of aged malt whiskys the once over as I stood there wondering what to do.

My eyes moved to the area above the bar. A child's rocking horse, now removed from its rocker, had been tilted through ninety degrees to look as if it was riding an ancient iron tricycle. Over on the far wall hung a number of etchings that depicted horses engaged in more conventional activities, like racing and carrying pompous individuals on their backs. Overall, there was a wattle and daub stable atmosphere to the place. A range of horse-drawn agricultural implements hung on the other walls and a large, stuffed bird of prey looked over the proceedings with its wings spread.

The barman reappeared still looking shocked and mentally unstable. I asked him for a table and he gestured in a direction without looking at me. Seconds later a menu appeared in front of me, although I didn't see the man put it there.

I thought I'd avoid the eel in green sauce starter and go straight for the fillet of horse with fried mushrooms and a home-made béarnaise sauce. Although I was famished, I was wary of the size of Belgian dinners since Konrad considered that most British restaurants served only children's portions. Besides, if I was still hungry, I could always have two puddings.

When I looked up from the menu, something else had appeared on the table. It was a spoon on a plate. On the spoon was a vaguely orange commodity with a slice of cucumber on top. I raised my head further. The barman was nowhere to be seen. I couldn't decide whether the spoon had just been absent-mindedly left on my table or whether it was actually meant for me. Surreptitiously I looked round the restaurant for clues. Diners at the other tables were deep in conversation or busy tucking into their equine steaks. I picked up the spoon and inspected its contents. The orange modge looked deliberate, so I cast another quick glance around the restaurant to make sure no one was looking and put the spoon into my mouth. The modge tasted of salmon. It was very good.

The horse arrived in the same way that everything else arrived: seamlessly and without any apparent movement on behalf of the barman. The fillet was topped with cress and a wide shaving of carrot. It looked like beef, smelt more or less like beef, and had a slightly gamy aftertaste. Cutting it was like the proverbial knife through butter. After eating it, I only had room enough for coffee which was served with a small bowl full of chocolate Easter eggs. Having paid my bill, I exited De Peerdestal to a beaming smile of relief from the nervous barman. Perhaps he was waiting to join a witness protection scheme.

One of the central reasons for establishing the European Union was to put a stop to that age-old European pastime of killing each other. We Europeans have been responsible for the Seven Years' War, the Thirty Years' War, the Hundred Years' War and two world wars, to name but a few, and as it happens, significant parts of many of these wars have been fought in Belgium. This is because several nations have found it more convenient to use Belgian battleground facilities rather than wreck their own countries. Enterprising local business-men even established an armaments industry in Liège to keep the visiting armies supplied. Among the better-known Belgian battles is the one held at Waterloo, near Brussels, which finally ended Napoleon's European rampage. Belgium also came in handy during World War I when Flanders was turned into a mudbath for trench warfare. Given Belgium's pre-eminence as an arena for armed conflict, where better to set up the new capital of a united friendly Europe?

Yet Belgium isn't really a country at all. It was created by foreigners in the early nineteenth century as a buffer against France. Although there have been people called Belgians since before Julius Caesar conquered them in 52 BC, they have only recently had their own country. Throughout much of history the place has been more like Italy, a bunch of city states. Many Belgians still have a greater allegiance to their regions and cities than to the country as a whole. When I asked Konrad whether he felt more Belgian or European, he looked puzzled for a moment and then said he didn't feel anything. When prompted, he said that he was from Ghent.

Most of the area we know as Belgium today was ruled by the dukes of Burgundy in the fifteenth century before being taken over by the Habsburgs. Napoleon took it back into the French fold in 1797, but it was taken away from him and repackaged with its northern neighbour to be marketed as the United Kingdom of the Netherlands in 1815. The Belgians finally got tired of all this foreign influence and had a revolt, eventually being recognised as an independent entity in 1831. The idea of a monarchy appealed, but they had no royal family. So they imported a king from Germany.

There's no escaping the impression that Belgium still looks like a scissors and paste job. In Flanders, the flat northern half of the country, they all speak Flemish which is virtually the same as Dutch, whilst the hilly southern half is suspiciously like France. Although the people there are known as Walloons, most of them speak French. The issue is confused by a small pocket of German-speakers in the far east and the fact that Brussels, although predominantly a French-speaking city, is in Flanders, but the basic Fleming–Walloon linguistic divide sums up the whole country. I consulted Konrad on this issue but my timing was poor. He said that it was much too serious a topic to deal with over the mashed potatoes. In simple terms, the situation can be summed up thus: they hate each other.

In recent times, this mutual hostility that has characterised Belgium ever since independence was calmed by the introduction of separate regional governments. Everything in Flanders had to be in Flemish and everything in Wallonia in French. Things got ridiculous. Both sides wanted the country's oldest university, a bilingual institution at Louvain, close to the linguistic border. So they chopped it in half. The Flemings were allowed to stay in the old part, which they had always called Leuven, and a modern French equivalent, Louvain la Neuve, was built a few kilometres down the road for the Walloons. Even the library was split in two. If you want to consult an old encyclopaedia at Leuven, you'll only find every other volume there. If, after consulting volume A–B, you want to look something up in volume C–D, you have to drive 25 kilometres to do it. Such divisions still run deep. Several people advised me strongly against speaking French in Flanders and against trying to speak Flemish in Wallonia. 'What would happen if I did?' I asked. 'They'll castrate you,' I was told. That seemed a good enough reason.

As the country's capital, Brussels plays piggy in the middle. The city is officially bilingual and the sensitivity of the language issue is clear for all to see. Brussels runs a TV station, and when they show foreign films there are two sets of sub-titles. All the metro stations have their names up in both French and Flemish, but the authorities must have had a long and animated discussion over which should come first. The result was a compromise. As the train pulls into one of the central stations, you look out at a sign that reads 'Bourse Beurs', quickly followed by the next that says 'Beurs Bourse'.

So despite Brussels' inability to impose unity on its own country, it was chosen as the setting for the capital of a project designed to bring unity at a higher level. Although the machinery of the European Union is actually fairly spread out, most people think of Brussels as its capital. This is because Brussels is home to the European Commission, the bureaucratic heart of the Union, the institution most people think of as being the most important body in the whole EU.

In some ways it is, in others it's not. The Commission was established by the Treaty of Rome to think up draft legislation for the new Europe and to make sure that countries are implementing it. If they don't, the Commission can take them to the European Court of Justice in Luxembourg. The Commission has a president who sometimes likes to think of himself as the President of Europe. He's not; like most civil servants, he and the other top dogs in the Commission – the Commissioners – are not elected. There is a strict nationality quota and individuals are appointed by their national governments. Some see the European Commission as a retirement club for failed politicians who have been rejected by the electorates in their own countries. They get shipped over to Brussels, earn lots of money, pay hardly any taxes, and do very nicely thank you. There is a legendary story of a visitor to the Commission who asked how many people worked there and was told, 'About twenty per cent.' If it has no other faults, the European Commission certainly has a PR problem.

In truth, however, it is not the Commission that makes most of the important decisions about European rules. The last word in new EU legislation is taken by a body called the Council of Ministers. To some, the Council of Ministers appears to be a shadowy institution, because it doesn't exist in permanent session, although it does have a permanent secretariat and special ambassadors in Brussels. Its members are simply the ministers from the fifteen countries with responsibility for whatever it is that is on the agenda that week. If it's a question about pollution control, all the environment ministers turn out to talk about it and make a decision, or not. When a farming problem raises its head, as it did when I was in Brussels in the form of the beef crisis, these people are replaced by their colleagues from the ministries of agriculture. Although it is usually the Commission that gets bad publicity whenever an apparently stupid new rule emanates from the European Union, this is a bit unfair. All the ideas on new regulations and directives put forward by the Commission have to be agreed upon by the Council. Old Brussels hacks have a phrase for it: 'The Commission proposes, the Council disposes.'

If the Commission gets a hard time in the press, it does at least wield some considerable powers. The other EU institution that is based partly in Brussels, the European Parliament, doesn't have much at all. When most people hear the word 'parliament', they assume, not unreasonably, that this must be where the real power lies. Like Britain's Westminster, this must be the place where elected Euro MPs, or MEPs, properly debate the issues and make the decisions. Not really. For a start, MEPs were only directly elected for the first time in 1979, twenty-two years after the whole thing was set up. Prior to that, MEPs were national MPs seconded to do a bit of European duty. Even now that they are directly elected, they still don't really have much sway. The European Parliament was originally established to play an advisory and supervisory role. It tells the Commission how much money it can spend and has recently become a bit more involved in making legislation, but there is still a long way to go before it can be regarded as a proper European parliament according to what most people would understand by the term. The simple fact that it has two permanent homes, one in

Brussels, the other in Strasbourg, rather undermines its efforts to be taken seriously. So long as its members have to run back and forth between the two cities every month, most of their time is going to be spent packing their bags and wishing they hadn't forgotten that crucial bundle of documents.

I can't remember whether or not I voted in the last European elections, but before I left for Brussels, I looked up the name of my Euro MP and wrote him a letter. Could I come and have a look round the place, I wondered? His assistant contacted me and we made a date.

There were the usual flags and security at the entrance to the European Parliament and once I had negotiated those I was faced with a sea of black marble floors and white moulded walls bearing coded signs that indicated 0.026–0.028 was this way and 0.104–0.121 that way. A variety of men and women looked bored and/or aggressive in glass booths. I approached one of them and told a beefy woman in red that I had come to look around the Parliament and I needed a pass. Judging by the look she gave me, she thought I was the last remaining carrier of smallpox. 'Have you been invited?' she snapped, edging her chair back from the window. I said I had.

'By who?' she replied ungrammatically and without any attempt to conceal her disbelief. I had toyed with the idea of wearing a tie for my visit but decided against it because I don't like wearing ties. But there are times when such an item can smooth the way, and this was probably one of them.

'My MEP,' I told her.

'You're in the wrong building,' she said dismissively, 'go across the road,' as if she was talking to a particularly recalcitrant child. I thought about letting her have the 'If it wasn't for people like me you wouldn't have a job' routine, but decided that she had heard it all before. She might actually have been rather grateful if there weren't people like me, since that way she could get a more fulfilling job. I retired gracefully to a sit-down zone to await my MEP's personal assistant who had said he would meet me here. In due course, a young man in a suit appeared, introduced himself and led me back to the woman in red to get me a pass. I gave her my sarcastic smile, followed by a sneer when I received the pass, and considered the honours about equal.

The assistant was accompanied by two other constituents from

Hampshire who had also come to look around the Parliament. They were introduced as Miss Randall and Miss Hopcraft, which made them sound like a firm of private detectives. They looked more like elderly bastions of the Newbury Women's Institute. Miss Randall wore a red hat and gloves, a sensible tweed skirt and walked with a stick, which might have just been for effect. Miss Hopcraft was dressed in a dark suit and deck shoes and wore too much face powder. They were old friends, having worked as nurses together during the war.

Like proper English county types, they were both instantly friendly and jolly in a slightly condescending way. They also asked beautifully direct and simple questions and gave you their unexpurgated opinions. Their knowledge of the EU was not encyclopaedic. On entering a lift, the MEP's assistant warmed us up with some basic statistics. There were 626 members of the European Parliament, he told us. Ninety-nine of these were German, eighty-seven each from France and ... 'Any Swiss?' chirped Miss Randall before he could get through his mental list. The young man answered very politely that Switzerland was not in the EU, though I could tell what he was thinking. 'Yes, they've always been very wise, haven't they?' Miss Randall responded airily.

The MEP's assistant was a clean-cut young American whose name was Wes. Mid-way through our tour, I asked him how he came to be working in the European Parliament. 'Oh, that was the first thing we asked him,' said Miss Hopcraft immediately, 'we know all about Whiz. He has a girlfriend in Harrogate, or is it Halifax? He's from Washington.' 'North Carolina,' corrected Wes gently, 'I used to work in Washington.'

'Of course you did,' said Miss Hopcraft as if she had only been testing his story. Randall and Hopcraft knew the story, but I had to wait until later before I would hear it.

We were in a committee meeting room, faced by banks of desks backed by glass booths normally occupied by interpreters. Wes was doing his best to explain the basic procedures that a parliamentary committee follows.

'Where does the boss sit?' asked Miss Hopcraft.

'Can the others sit anywhere they like?' asked Miss Randall waving her stick over the proceedings.

'Do they bring their secretaries with them?' from Miss Hopcraft

173

again. Whiz was supremely patient, and managed to get through a basic outline of the ways in which the Parliament operates to murmurs of 'Fascinating,' and 'Goodness, I see,' from the Newbury private eyes.

There were four basic ways in which the MEPs got involved in the making of European Union legislation, Whiz explained. The standard, so-called 'co-operation' procedure involved the Commission drawing up a proposal, a committee of MEPs chewing it over in a room like this one, followed by a vote on it by all MEPs in a plenary session of the full Parliament. This would all be reported back to the Commission which would then take the Parliament's views on board and submit a revised proposal to them for a second reading.

'And do they finally come to a decision?' asked Miss Randall.

Whiz smiled, but Miss Hopcraft's brow had furrowed beneath the layers of face powder. 'It wouldn't be any good in a war, would it?' she declared.

We moved out of the committee meeting room, took a couple of lifts and walked some long corridors, heading towards a new building called the Espace Léopold, custom-built for the Parliament. Somewhere down below it, MEPs had their very own new railway station, Whiz informed us. Randall and Hopcraft were slightly bewildered by the endless corridors. 'Are you given a map when you arrive?' enquired Miss Randall. 'It's very complicated.'

We were proceeding along a wide underground corridor which linked the building we had started in with the new Léopold construction. The corridor was lined with sculpture. 'They've even got modern art here,' observed Miss Hopcraft acutely.

'Are you making a note of those ghastly things?' Miss Randall asked me as she waved her stick at the offending objects.

While we waited for another lift to take us up to the new Parliament chamber, I asked Miss Hopcraft what she thought of European unity.

'A lot of people think it's a waste of money, you know,' declared Miss Randall before her associate could answer.

Miss Hopcraft was more measured in her response. 'The common market was a good idea,' she declared, 'but I don't think we want to get too involved. We're not an island for nothing,' she continued as Whiz pushed the lift button again. 'It's protected us through so many wars. When Hitler wanted to invade it was only the Channel

174

that saved us.' From somewhere in the dark recesses of my mind I heard the strains of 'The White Cliffs of Dover'.

I closed my eyes to fight off the stirrings of the little Englander inside me and saw a stream of lemmings cascading over the chalk cliff face. 'But we're not enemies any more,' I replied, 'that's the point of the EU.' Miss Hopcraft looked at me with a kind smile on her face and was about to answer when the lift arrived and we all held back as Miss Randall manoeuvred her way in, whacking a junior bureaucrat on the shin with her stick as she did so.

Up above, the new Parliament debating chamber was large enough to host a game of football. Curved lines of orange desks and their black chairs were splayed out in a semi-circular arrangement beneath a white ceiling with more lights than a planetarium. We took a well-earned rest in the public gallery as Whiz identified the national flags of all the EU member states in the chamber down below. MEPs sat in political groupings irrespective of their nationality, he told us. The socialists were the largest group (murmurs of disapproval from Randall and Hopcraft) and they sat on the left. This wasn't the Parliament's only chamber, Whiz explained, they had another one in Strasbourg. Randall and Hopcraft looked puzzled. 'Once a month we all pack up and move to France,' he said.

'Why?' asked Miss Randall.

It wasn't the sort of question that Whiz could easily deal with. 'The Parliament has one-week plenary sessions every month at Strasbourg,' he said. 'Committees meet in Brussels because it's closer to the Commission.' The why question was left hanging. 'Wouldn't it be easier to do everything in one place?' Miss Randall enquired. Whiz had to agree that it would be, but he thought the French would never concede to giving up the monthly trek to Strasbourg, which of course they saw as a monthly trek to Brussels. Indeed, the French were so peeved at the obvious desire by the majority of MEPs to move to Brussels permanently that they had twisted a few arms and started building *another* new parliament building in Strasbourg. The Espace Léopold was Europe's largest building project; the Strasbourg version was a snip at half a billion pounds. Randall and Hopcraft shook their heads in unison. Here was clear evidence of the barmy way of doing things in Europe, and I had to agree with them. If he had the choice, Whiz would rather everything happened in Strasbourg, he told us. It was more central and the food was better.

He said that all they ever seemed to serve in the canteen here was boiled cabbage, which surprised me given my experience so far of Belgian cuisine. 'But there you go,' he said as if it wasn't really his problem, 'it's run by the Belgians.' It sounded more like a dismissal based on ignorance than one founded in culinary awareness.

The final stage of our visit was a brief rendezvous with our MEP who appeared as if by magic from out of a mêlée of Buddhist monks as we sat waiting in a coffee area. The monks were part of a delegation that accompanied the film star Richard Gere who was shortly due to address the membership about the human rights situation in Tibet, so Whiz said with a slight sneer. My MEP reminded me of my dentist. He was a tall man with grey hair, a ruddy complexion and a double chin that was still under construction. He was jolly and spoke as if he had something awkward in his mouth. It may have been a small plum.

He had just come from an emergency meeting about cows. A couple of days previously the British government had announced that there might be a link between a particularly nasty disease that turns your brain into a sponge and a similar ailment called BSE that affects cows. No one really seemed to know what was going on, but the fault apparently lay in the fact that we had been making cows eat bits of sheep that we couldn't think of anything else to do with. It struck me that we got what we deserved. Everyone knows that cows are meant to eat grass.

Nevertheless, the European beef market had understandably been thrown into turmoil. Since everyone who hadn't already got a serious brain disorder didn't really feel like contracting one, no one wanted to buy the stuff. The Commission had banned the export of British beef to other EU countries. It looked like the beginnings of a major crisis and our MEP's committee had been drawing up a resolution on the situation. They had produced a first draft, he told us, which was mostly in German, with a few French phrases thrown in for good measure. This was how most first drafts were written. I suppose that on such occasions he would have to exchange his plum for a frankfurter.

After a few pleasantries, our MEP disappeared back into the Buddhist monks and Whiz led me and the Newbury contingent down to the foyer. We all bade our farewells and I left Miss Hopcraft to help Miss Randall get her stick caught in the swing doors.

I walked away from the European Parliament building past a line of derelict houses and a disused church. They say that if you see a nice old building in Brussels you had better make the most of it, because next time you come it will have been demolished to make way for a new office block. Behind me sat the futuristic architectural complex of the new Espace Léopold building. I turned to take a final look and the bright sunshine glinted off the glass dome as if it was winking at me. As an old friend who works for a British newspaper put it, 'Never in the history of parliaments have so many parliamentarians, with such little power, had such a big building.'

My mind turned to Strasbourg. Make that two big buildings.

I suppose you know you've reached a certain level of distinction when your logo seems worth a merchandising venture. Down in the centre of Brussels several shops specialised in all manner of blue things adorned with the twelve yellow EU stars. You could buy an EU keyring to carry your keys on, and some EU braces to keep your trousers up, an EU umbrella to keep the rain off and an EU towel in case you forgot it. EU boxing gloves were available for those serious international incidents, and a variety of cuddly EU toys of indeterminate sex were on sale to comfort the loser.

The T-shirt manufacturers had risen to the challenge of characterising fifteen national stereotypes for whatever activity their customers chose to portray on their chests. 'The perfect European should be ...' sober as the Irish, humble as a Spaniard, cooking like a Brit, talkative as a Finn, humorous as a German, and so on. The Italians were portrayed as being out of control, the French terrible at driving. Beyond these, the jokes got weaker. The Greeks were portrayed as disorganised and the Portuguese as technical idiots. The Belgian cartoon indicated that Belgians are all bureaucrats who are permanently on holiday.

A less salubrious version encouraged you to 'Do it like a European' with fifteen couples having sex in supposedly nationalistic ways. The Germans were strung up wearing militaristic costumes, the British positioned alongside Big Ben, while the Portuguese were depicted doing something unmentionable while thinking about anchovies. Another T-shirt had a slightly more profound message behind the humour: it showed an EU Ark with suitcases bearing national flags lined up ready to be carried on board. The slogan was 'Destination Europe'.

The happy little band of friendly countries has grown somewhat since the day in March 1957 when six states signed the Treaty of Rome to create a European Economic Community. If you want to trace things back further, one of the roots of this enterprise lay here in Belgium, when it created an economic union with its neighbours the Netherlands and Luxembourg in 1948. As the European venture grew, and more countries signed up, its identity was transformed. From the EEC, it became the EC, and now the EU. As each new country joined, more stars were added to the logo, but they stopped when they got to twelve. This must have been very handy for the designers of the EU watch.

Although Belgium is one of the original members, most Belgians I spoke to didn't really take much notice of the EU. The way they saw it, this was just the latest in a long succession of bureaucracies imposed on them by outsiders. Their prolonged history of foreign domination has taught most Belgians to keep their heads down and get on with things like tax-dodging, which seemed to be a national pastime. Most of those who did have an opinion were ambivalent about the whole thing. Some were quite proud to be the new capital of Europe. Others just complained about the wholesale destruction of parts of Brussels for new EU offices and the effect the overpaid Eurocrats had on the capital's rents and property prices. Many EU officials preferred to remove the EUR symbol from their car number-plates for fear that the resentment could result in vandalism.

The inhabitants of Brussels traditionally have an irreverent streak which is immortalised in the city's symbolic hall-mark: the statue of the Manneken-Pis. In London tourists flock to see the statue of Eros shooting arrows over Piccadilly Circus, while visitors to Copenhagen head for the Little Mermaid gazing demurely out over the Øresund strait. Go to Brussels and all you get is a small boy pissing on a street corner.

The bronze statuette was located down an insignificant side street lined with shops selling chocolate, lace and tacky souvenirs. It was on a corner next to a bureau de change. The naked boy stood with his hand on one hip urinating into a semi-circular bath big enough for him to drown in. This unusual little piece was in the same disappointment league as the Little Mermaid. It was only when I read the official notice attached to the railings in front of the figure that my interest was awakened. The notice listed a series of dates indicating when the said Manneken-Pis would be passing water in costume.

Unlikely though it may sound, the statuette is like a municipal Action Man. This curly-haired street urchin has a wardrobe consisting of more than five hundred different outfits. You can see some of them on display in a specially dedicated room in the Museum of the City of Brussels. The room is lined with glass cases full of reproductions of Monsieur Pis dressed as soldier, sportsman, gourmet, carnival lover and general man(*neken*) of the world. Among the lovingly detailed costumes on display when I visited were that of a bee-keeper, a frogman, an anaesthetist at the University of Turin and an Argentinian gaucho. Outside on the streets, Manneken-Pis appeared as all sorts of tourist knick-knacks. He was a gift for the cork-screw manufacturers. The most popular postcard of the little fellow was, I suppose, inevitable. He was dressed in a blue tunic studded with those tell-tale yellow stars. The caption read 'Veni Vidi Peepee'.

The whole costume business was as odd as anything Belgium could offer. Since the Manneken-Pis was such an important public figure, it seemed unlikely that any one person was charged with deciding what the little man should wear on particular days. City bureaucrats must meet in a regular committee to do the job. They probably have animated discussions on the subject. Should Manneken-Pis wear his frogman gear on Fridays? Will they offend their ethnic minorities if they dress him as Lawrence of Arabia during Ramadan? The more I thought about it, the more bizarre it became. Do Brussels' residents make special pilgrimages to see him in his latest outfit? Are there Belgian equivalents of trainspotters who can claim to have seen Manneken-Pis in every costume? One evening I met a Belgian academic who claimed that Magritte hadn't agreed with being labelled a surrealist because Belgium was really like that. I was beginning to think that he was right.

It should come as no surprise to learn then that Brussels had an underwear museum. I say 'had' because to my disappointment I learnt that it was closed down two years previously. The woman in the tourist information office was apologetic. Not enough people were interested in knickers, she said. I bought a city guide in English and flicked through it to find some alternatives. I noted that when the guide lapsed into the vernacular, it was French rather than Flemish, hence Grand'Place rather than Grote Markt. This probably meant that it had been produced by a Brussels French mafia, but since I didn't understand Flemish, it was fine by me. I just made sure I held the book below my navel whenever I asked someone the way.

Most of the really interesting museums appeared to be temporarily out of action. Visits to the Belgian endive museum were by appointment only and the place was only open in winter. The lift museum would not be opening until 1997. I did a double-take on page 67. The entry read 'Brussels' Little Museum of Breeding-Cage and Feeding-Through'. 'What's this one?' I asked the woman. She looked at where my finger was pointing and shrugged. Just then her telephone rang. I consulted the entry again; the museum was only open on the first Saturday in each month, so I never found out what it was.

I started with the brewery museum. It was just a few doors away across the cobbles in the Grand'Place, itself an open-air museum because it was like stepping back into the Middle Ages. 'The great square or market place is one of the most noble in Europe,' Charles Theodore Middleton declared in the late eighteenth century. It still was. Nowhere on my travels through the Continent did I see a more impressive one, although the Marienplatz in Munich came close. The brewery museum was located in the cellar of the old brewers' guild building, next door to the former headquarters of the butchers' guild, a building with a life-sized white swan above the door. Le Cygne, as the house is known, was where Karl Marx sat down with Friedrich Engels in 1847 to write the *Communist Manifesto*. Karl and Friedrich would turn in their graves if they could see it today. It's a very up-market restaurant where a starter of Iranian caviar will set you back seventy pounds.

Although the Belgians are justly renowned for their beer, it's not really the sort of thing that makes for a great museum. It's better to drink the stuff, and since it was nearly lunch time I retired to a bar on the Grand'Place called Le Roi d'Espagne. It was in another ancient building, with an Italian baroque façade, formerly the HQ of the bakers' guild. Inside, sitting at a sturdy wooden table, I could imagine Middleton writing about Brussels hostelries: 'The inns, or eating houses here, are equal to any in the world: a stranger may dine any time between twelve and three, on seven or eight dishes of meat, for less than a shilling English. The wines are also very good and cheap.' It seemed that the only thing to have changed were the prices.

Hanging from the ceiling of Le Roi d'Espagne was a collection of elderly string marionettes dressed in military uniforms and around each light bulb there was an assortment of inflated bladders the colour of old Sellotape. Beside the central creaking staircase was an entire stuffed horse. A short write-up in the menu said the atmosphere was Brueghelian. I was getting used to this.

After lunch I made my way to the comic-strip museum. A grand old Art Nouveau warehouse had been converted for the purpose. Brussels was a curate's egg type of city: overall rather ugly but good in parts. Some of the good parts were spectacular, the rest was just shabby concrete. The warehouse was designed by Victor Horta, the father of Art Nouveau. The man was such a great architectural influence that they made him a baron. Then they pulled down most of his best buildings to make way for more shabby concrete.

The comic-strip warehouse was worth saving. It was full of ornate metalwork, with a large expanse of glass roof. Being Belgian, Victor Horta put an enormous lamppost in the middle of it. The bit that most interested me was the section devoted to the work of Georges Rémi, a native of Brussels who is better known as Hergé, the creator of Tintin. I went through a Tintin phase when I was young and still have all the books lined up on a shelf in my parents' house. I spent a half-hour reminiscing while wandering round the original cartoon paintings.

Being in a Tintin sort of mood, I boarded an underground train and travelled on Line 1A out to the north-western corner of the city because this is where, in 1958, they created the Atomium. Have you ever tried to imagine what an iron crystal atom looks like when magnified 165 billion times? Forget it. It's been done before. It's the sort of structure that Professor Calculus would have dreamt up in his spare time, and the Belgians have gone and built it. It's a huge, silver-coloured molecule that towers 102 metres high and looks very 1950s. Since it is Brussels' answer to the Eiffel Tower, the Atomium has to be on anyone's list for a modern-day Grand Tour of Belgium. Once you've seen it, you could make your own scale model, perhaps only magnified one billion times, by taking nine tennis balls and joining them together with toilet rolls and wrapping the whole thing in silver foil.

Considering the fact that the entire structure is built out of metal, it struck me that the Atomium must be made up of quite a few life-sized iron crystal atoms. I tried to work out whether there would be 165 billion of them, but I've never been very good at that sort of thing. Nevertheless, not having been inside an iron crystal atom before, I paid my 200 francs and prepared to enjoy myself. There is a lift that ascends the central loo roll between the bottom and top tennis balls, and according to the propaganda it's the fastest lift in Europe. For those who like to collect such statistics, it moves at 5 metres a second. Inside you get to know what it's like to be a potato wrapped in tinfoil ready for baking.

From the top of this pile of atoms, there is of course a view. All of Brussels was laid out in the distance and I walked around inside the uppermost tennis ball to take it all in. Annotated diagrams helped the viewer to appreciate what they were looking at. As I perused one of these diagrams, my heart sank. A label pointed towards something called Mini-Europe. I strained my eyes, but couldn't really tell what I was looking at, so I splashed out a few more francs on one of the resident telescopes. What I saw was horrifying.

Down below, at the foot of the Atomium, was what looked like a fenced-off theme park full of models. There was a miniature Arc de Triomphe and an Eiffel Tower, Big Ben, an Acropolis, a Leaning Tower of Pisa ... My God, *everything* was there. What I was looking at may have been just a few more billion atoms, but they happened to be in the shapes of all the major European cultural monuments that I had spent the best part of a year travelling to look at. Here I was, nearing the end of a bloody expensive tour through Europe to see this stuff, while it was all here in Belgium all the time. I felt stupid, then angry, then deflated, then stupid again before the money ran out. I took the series of moving staircases that descended through the angled loo rolls down the Atomium and emerged into bright sunshine to find Mini-Europe.

The entrance was inside a complex called Bruparck, something the tourist literature referred to as a 'four-star leisure paradise'. It had a large cinema complex, a water funpark, shops selling nothing you would ever want to buy and the usual string of plastic-looking fast-food joints, which aren't fast at all in Belgium (Quick in Brussels is the only such place I've ever been in where they put your grub on to cook when you order it; 'medium-pace-food' is a more accurate description). When I eventually found the entrance to Mini-Europe, it was still shut for the winter.

That night, I lay on my bed wondering whether I had been a complete fool in undertaking this mission. Of course, seeing all those monuments in the flesh was much more authentic than simply spending an afternoon wandering around Mini-Europe, but the experience had shaken me a bit. The string of reactions I had received from my friends on hearing that I was writing a book about the European Union kept whizzing through my mind. After penning travelogues on Mongolia and Mozambique, here I was writing about fourteen European countries, and none of them even began with M.

'Europe? That's a bit tame,' said one. '*Fourteen* countries?' from another. 'Do you have to do them all? Even the boring ones?' A third one was more prescriptive. 'Ignore Germany altogether,' he told me, 'pretend it's not there.'

After lying awake half the night thinking about the book, I spent the other half dreaming about the same subject. In my dream, Manneken-Pis was dressed as Tintin and was standing on top of a home-made loo-roll-and-tennis-ball Atomium pissing in the middle of the new European Parliament debating chamber. His trusty dog Snowy was eating a banana, an activity which Tintin told him was now illegal due to new EU rules on curved bananas. Snowy then stood on his hind legs and sang a Portuguese pop song that I remembered hearing some years ago in Mozambique. In English, the refrain is 'Squashed bananas don't make you rich.' When I woke up the following morning, I realised it was time to visit the European Commission.

In truth I had been trying to set up a meeting with someone at the Commission for some time. I had got hold of the name of a man in the Information, Communication, Culture, Audiovisual Information and Communication Strategy division, thankfully known to the cognoscenti as Directorate General X, or better still, DG Ten. I had faxed Mr Armstrong to ask for an interview a week before leaving for the Netherlands. OK, this was a relatively short time for him to respond, but I thought it would be an interesting test of their system. I wasn't really surprised that I hadn't received a reply before leaving England.

When I first arrived in Brussels, I rang Mr Armstrong's office. His secretary answered. He wasn't in the office right now, she told me, but he had replied to my fax. I explained that I hadn't been there to receive it. 'Oh dear,' she said.

'What did the fax say?' I asked her. 'I don't know,' she replied. Mr Armstrong typed a lot of these things himself apparently, and he hadn't kept a copy. She suggested I call back.

I rang home instead and got a colleague to read out the fax. It wasn't from Mr Armstrong at all, but from someone called Henk Beereboom. The message said that Henk was busy that month and suggested I contact someone in London. I thought it would be better to pretend I had never received the message.

The day I spent doing a few Brussels museums was punctuated with regular attempts to contact Mr Armstrong by telephone. By an uncanny twist of fate, I always got through just as he had stepped out of the office. When would Mr Armstrong be back? I asked. It was hard to say, came the reply. For a directorate concerned with information and communication they weren't doing too well. I began to think that it would be easier to contact the dead than the men from DG Ten.

Finally, I asked his secretary whether I might be able to make an appointment. She agreed. I was given 11.30 on a Friday morning.

Meanwhile, I got an inkling as to why setting up a meeting had proved difficult. One evening in a brasserie I met a consultant to the Commission who told me that everyone in the Commission was scared stiff of journalists because they kept writing critical stories about the organisation. 'But I'm not a journalist,' I protested.

'They are scared stiff of journalists,' my new acquaintance told me. The brasserie appeared to have an echo.

'But I'm not a journalist,' I heard myself saying again. Definitely an echo.

The brasserie was an Art Nouveau establishment with plum-coloured decor and ornate chandeliers. The table-tops were marble and the waiters all wore long white aprons with black waistcoats. You could be forgiven for thinking that you had stepped through a time warp and regressed a hundred years, until we ordered and the waiter pulled out what looked like a TV remote control from beneath his apron. He pointed it at the wall and punched in our order codes for *gigot d'agneau*. '... scared stiff of journalists,' I heard again. A double echo, that was interesting.

I asked the man what he did for the Commission. He told me that he worked for some kind of programme set up to liaise with journalists.

Friday morning came and this time I put on my tie for the meeting with Mr Armstrong. I decided to walk to the Commission building off the rue de la Loi. My hotel was in the north of the city, a steep hike up the hill from the Gare du Nord which was surrounded by glass skyscrapers like square goldfish bowls. It was an immigrant quarter where you were more likely to hear Arabic being spoken than French and every evening the local menfolk could be seen playing cards in the cafés. The local take-away assembled the world's largest kebabs, made with juicy *merguez* sausages, and served with chips and mayonnaise on top. The grocery shops sold fresh almonds still in their green velvet cases and there was a lot of phlegm on the pavements. The area looked like Peckham on a bad day but it had a friendly sense of community.

I made my way along a series of run-down streets heading southeast. I wanted to sweep past the Berlaymont building, the original home of the Commission that had been abandoned when they found it was full of asbestos. It was a star-shaped construction, maybe ten storeys high. They probably designed it in the star shape because of the EU symbol, but the symbolism struck me as doubly appropriate given the Commission's role as a sort of Lone Ranger of Europe. While they are busy extracting the 3000 tonnes of asbestos, they have wrapped the whole building in gleaming white, you-can't-touch-me clean canvas. It looked surreal, as if it was the latest open-air installation by Christo Jaracheff, the artist who wrapped up the Berlin Reichstag and built a fabric fence along the Pacific coast of the USA.

Some people might think it a good idea if Jaracheff had wrapped the Berlaymont in canvas, with the Eurocrats still inside. *And* the asbestos. I have to say that the thought crossed my mind after I had been in Mr Armstrong's office for an hour. It was an ordinary office with beige-coloured walls which were hung with maps and two posters advertising art exhibitions, one of work by Mondrian, the other by Cézanne. There were two desks. One was submerged in papers, the other, rather larger, was obviously for meetings like this one. Beside the computer terminal on the main desk was an anglepoise lamp and a bottle of Contrex water. The chair was facing the door as if its occupant had just leapt up and left. Over in one corner was a metal cupboard, the doors of which hung open to reveal another half-dozen bottles of Contrex standing by. As an office it was fine, but for me it had one drawback. Mr Armstrong wasn't in it.

His secretary was apologetic but not overly concerned. He had been out at a meeting, but hadn't returned. I could have worked that out for myself. She let me wait with the Contrex bottles and I browsed most of the publications on his side table while I did so, but resisted the temptation to read his correspondence. After an hour, I gave up and departed.

If I had left it at that, my job would have been much easier. I had wanted to quiz Mr Armstrong about so-called Euromyths, apocryphal stories regularly carried in the British press about the nonsense world of the barmy Brussels bureaucrats and the stupid rules they were making us all obey. I could have written a mystical little piece about it, centred around my inability to meet the man charged with dispelling these myths. Mr Armstrong himself, it seemed, was a Euromyth.

But stupidly, I made one last effort to meet the man and succeeded. To make matters worse, he turned out to be a nice bloke.

It didn't seem likely that I would say anything complimentary about him when I left his office, after my hour's wait, to brave the bitter wind that whipped along the shabby concrete highway of the rue de la Loi. I hurried past the Parc de Bruxelles and ducked into the cathedral when the rain started. Even here, the Euro-images followed me. Halfway up the nave on the right-hand side, the spectacular brown wooden pulpit was a mass of figures and foliage like a child's tree house. It depicted Adam and Eve being driven out of paradise and the redemption with Mary and her sibling holding a rather large cross. Mary's halo was made up of small stars, just like the EU symbol, only there were thirteen of them.

I ate lunch and caught a tram that thought it was a metro, because it went underground, south to the Gare du Midi to check the times of trains to Luxembourg. A couple of hours after leaving his office, I put through a final telephone call to Mr Armstrong. When the man himself answered I nearly fell over.

Some time later I found myself retracing my steps through the wind and the rain along the depressing rue de la Loi. The building where Mr Armstrong and his office were located was a nasty square prefab concrete job and there was a nasty modern sculpture on the corner of the street to go with it. I exchanged my passport for a pass at the entrance, took the lift up to the eighth floor and walked the final one. Mr Armstrong was not what I'd expected.

With a name like Armstrong, he should have looked British, but he didn't. Italian would have been my guess. He was a tall man with short, black, slightly kinky hair that was thinking about going grey. His suit was a grey double-breasted pinstripe, his shirt blue check and his tie was red. He cut a loose, relaxed figure but he looked tired and his hands were shaking slightly. I sat at his meetings desk and he waved a long arm at the window where the spring showers had turned into a flurry of snowflakes. Mr Armstrong spoke slowly in English, choosing his words carefully. 'Someone I was just with, who had a sense of humour, said this is the start of the Belgian summer.'

I told him what I had come to see him for: all those stories about Brussels banning prawn-cocktail flavoured crisps and abnormally bent cucumbers, declaring asymmetrical Christmas trees illegal and planning to standardise coffins. Mr Armstrong smiled. Most of these stories were appropriately called Euromyths. The Commission had produced glossy booklets documenting many of the worst examples and explaining them away. Some were totally untrue, others a result of muddles and misunderstandings. Some arose out of the overzealous national implementation of new rules, while just occasionally such reports contained more than a few grains of truth. Most were underpinned by that old hack's adage: 'Never let the facts get in the way of a good story.' Was Euromythology a particularly British phenomenon? I asked.

Yes, he said, the British press appeared to have the most fertile imagination in this regard. I wondered why he thought this was. He paused and then quoted someone else's ideas. A British academic had traced it all back to Mrs Thatcher and her press secretary Bernard

Ingham, 'who harnessed the popular press to take political issues through the backyard', Mr Armstrong suggested. The fashion of Brussels-bashing suited many things at the same time, he thought, reflecting the general resistance of the British public to continental Europe.

There were certain stories that caused concern elsewhere in Europe. The Spanish became very agitated when they thought the Commission was going to outlaw the tilde – the squiggly accent over the N in España. In Denmark there was an outcry over threats to their favourite apple, whilst the risk of losing some of their cheese threw the French into turmoil. The Germans were particularly interested in a report suggesting that Eurocrats earned higher salaries than German politicians. One story that surfaced periodically in Italy concerned a supposed plan to paint all their taxis white.

These stories reflected people's ferocity towards attempts to harmonise everything for a truly common market to work properly. A lot of the rules were made in the 1970s. 'We have piled up a lot of nonsense and bad legislation,' Mr Armstrong reflected with surprising candour, 'but that was a very long time ago. Before the UK joined the Community.'

It seemed to me that the bureaucrats in Brussels always chose their words very carefully. Things had to be 'harmonised' because that sounded calming and serene, rather than 'standardised', which smacked of automatons and authoritarianism. It was the thought of losing the little differences and national quirks that upset people, especially when they couldn't see a good reason for it. Nobody likes being told what to do, and the fact that these rules appeared to be emanating from what many perceived as a foreign body just added to the inherent suspicion many feel for bureaucrats.

But it wasn't just the British people who had this reputation for regarding Brussels with suspicion. The British government too, despite being essentially in favour of the EU concept, was regarded by many as an awkward squad of feet-draggers. One explanation put to me by a British diplomat for our apparent truculence towards many new dictates was that when Britain signed up for something she took it seriously. We weren't going to agree to measures if we couldn't implement them. By contrast, the Greeces and Portugals of this world just said 'yes' and took no further notice. Mr Armstrong obviously thought there was truth in that. 'Britain has a reputation for good bureaucracy,' he added with a definite sound of approval.

The idea of drawing up standard rules for everything must have delighted the Brussels brigade. It must have been a bureaucrats' dream project, and for the entire European Union, such a large canvas for their picture of a perfect continent. Poor publicity had given the Commission's Eurocrats the image of regulatory zealots, hard-line missionaries with a warrant for Euro-success. It was Franz Kafka meets Alice in Wonderland in the world's biggest law factory. Their reputation for arrogance didn't help, and although their ideas had to be passed by elected politicians from member states, the Commission's powers did not sit comfortably with the fact that they were not elected by anyone. Mr Armstrong shrugged dismissively at this point. 'There's nothing we can do about that,' he said. Yes you can, I thought to myself. You could change the rules.

But trying to 'harmonise' everything had proved to be an impossible task. Mr Armstrong seemed crest-fallen when he said that. The emphasis now was on mutual recognition of each other's products and ways of doing things. Hence, according to the Commission, carrots were considered to be fruit. But only when talking about jam. Why? Because everyone knows that jam is made with fruit, but the Portuguese make jam with carrots. This logic may seem reasonable to the labyrinthine mind of a Eurocrat, but to everyone else it just makes them look like morons. The more I considered the matter, the firmer was my conclusion that if we continued like this the so-called 'western civilised world' was destined to disappear up its own bottom. And the only thing left would be billions of pieces of paper with stupid rules written on them.

But I didn't think I could burden Mr Armstrong with my theories on bureaucracy's inbuilt self-destruct mechanism. Instead, I wondered aloud whether resistance to the whole EU idea wasn't at least partly due to growing pains. European unity through consensus, rather than by force of arms, was still a new idea in the wider scheme of things. Mr Armstrong seemed to think there might be some truth in that. Whilst certain observers were suggesting that the end of the nation state was nigh, some of the older nation states found the idea hard to swallow. The Euro-engineers were either before their time, or the whole thing was a pipe dream.

Mr Armstrong was convinced that with Europe in decline, and with countries like the USA already starting to turn their backs on us, the time had come to stand up and take it seriously. 'Otherwise we'll be left behind,' he said soberly. Since the fall of the Berlin Wall the geopolitical reality of Europe had changed, he said. The Franco-German axis was where it was all happening, and in carefully chosen words he intimated that anyone not joining in risked becoming marginalised.

What beautifully basic geographical facts lay at the heart of the matter, I thought to myself. Apart from anything else, it seemed to me that there were a number of fundamental reasons behind the United Kingdom's general reticence towards the EU. One was this element of *realpolitikal* obligation towards joining two of our long-term arch-rivals (France and Germany). Second was the fact that we weren't in it from the beginning (if we had been, we would have made sure the rules were more to our liking). Third came our political system, essentially designed to produce winners and losers, so that government by consensus struck us as rather a foreign idea. Last, there was our own geographical reality as an island. That cold sea full of herrings made us a bit different, so we thought.

Mr Armstrong didn't agree with the island argument, but at that moment we were interrupted by one of his colleagues who came in to bid us farewell. She was going to Israel for Easter. Henceforth, the Commission's Euromythology Rapid Reply Service was closed for business. I had missed my chance. My father, someone who can certainly be described as a Eurosceptic, had armed me with a question to test the system. He had read that Luxembourg, the country with the highest living standard of any EU country, was a net recipient of EU funds and he wanted to know why.

Our meeting was coming to an end. Mr Armstrong lamented the fact that everyone seemed to treat the Commission as a scapegoat. By so doing, we were all in danger of delivering a fatal blow to the whole enterprise, he thought. And that, of course, was just what many of the EU's critics were hoping to do.

As I battled my way through the elements on the rue de le Loi for the last time, something Miss Hopcraft had said in the Espace Léopold came to mind: 'The common market was a good idea, but I don't think we want to get too involved.' I had sympathy with this. The common market was a good idea, but you could have too much of a good thing. At heart I was too much of a nationalist to envisage losing the pound, or voting for a proper president of Europe. And having visited more than half the EU member states, I still couldn't quite believe that many of them would really agree to a sort of United States of Europe.

But if full political and economic integration did go ahead, and Britain didn't join in, what then? Without a serious influence in Europe, surely we would just be relegated to the position of a has-been. We'd be back where we'd started: a small island in a cold sea full of herrings. And we'd even have to fight for the herrings.

10

Where Reptiles Fear to Tread

It was snowing again the morning I left Brussels. The Belgian summer was really getting into its stride. As my train pulled out of Brussels Midi, millions of tiny flakelets drew a veil over the proceedings and for the next twenty minutes we travelled through a gossamer mist. Then all of a sudden the snow had gone, revealing dark ploughed fields that looked as if they had been sprinkled with icing sugar. The sun shone brightly enough to generate wisps of steam on the bank of a wooded stream. Droplets of water on branches and twigs sparkled like a thousand Antwerp diamonds.

After Namur, where the platform signs were only in French, the snow got serious again. The flakes swirled as thick as fog, but they were hardly falling so much as hesitating, as if they weren't sure about the idea of landing on Belgium. As we passed through Ciney, I checked my map. Somewhere off to the right was the small town of Dinant, birthplace of Adolphe Sax, who invented the saxophone. The wind got up to give us a full-scale blizzard. Then the snow dispersed again and we got driving rain instead. The conductor couldn't understand it. As she clipped my ticket she exclaimed, 'Snow, sun, rain: bizarre, huh?'

I was glad for the diverse weather conditions. I had only a handful of short chapters left in the novel I was reading, so I forced myself to stop after each one to take in some more view. By this time we were in Luxembourg, not the country but the Belgian province of the same name that is actually bigger than the country itself. Trees were getting together to make forests, an unusual sight after my time up north in Flanders, and hills started sprouting to tell me we were entering the Ardennes. The railway track had been forced through numerous cuttings in hard grey rock faces, and we trundled along sweet little valleys with neat green carpets on their pocket-sized floodplains. Contrary to what Konrad had led me to believe, this was actually rather pretty Belgian countryside, and there wasn't a motorway in sight. Then it struck me that this was Wallonia, so as far as Konrad was concerned it probably didn't count.

The snow came down again after Arlon and we must have crossed the border between Luxembourg the province and Luxembourg the Grand Duchy. Without warning we pulled up at Luxembourg City's central station and I got out.

I found a hotel with a vacancy on the rue Joseph Junck. Most of the streets in Luxembourg City gave a one-line biography of their namesakes at the bottom of their plaques and I learnt that Joseph Junck had been a philanthropist. His benevolence towards human-kind had been expressed in modern Luxembourg with a small string of strip joints, several bars, a sex shop and the Hotel Zurich. For some reason I had not been expecting a Grand Duchy to have a seedy side.

In my room, I perused a couple of pieces of literature I had picked up at the railway station, eager to get a handle on some local cultural events. A small *What's on in Luxembourg* pamphlet informed me that I had missed out on the regular Thursday Scrabble session but that I could still make the 1996 European Dog Championships taking place that weekend at the Foires Internationales exhibition halls. Some 7500 dogs were expected to take part. The lead story in the English-language weekly magazine *Luxembourg News* was inevitably on BSE, but there wasn't much of a story because Luxembourg had never recorded a case of the disease. When I got to the listings page, I was disappointed to note that I wouldn't be around for an unusual event in the town of Echternach. Apparently the place had been overrun by tortoises in recent months and local lettuce growers were anticipating a disastrous crop. To combat the plague, a tortoise round-up had been organised. Participants were invited to meet outside the town hall where they would be issued with tortoise-catching equipment consisting of special gloves and lobster baskets. They would be rewarded with free beer for tortoises captured. On the same day in Luxembourg City, a man named Jacques Bintz would be lecturing in German on Vulkanismus at the Bonnevoie Cultural Centre. I had no idea what Vulkanismus was, but I had a feeling that Luxembourg was going to be a pretty wild place.

I left my room and ventured out to have a look at the capital of the EU's smallest country. The avenue de la Gare was just a shopping street, albeit peppered with more banks than would be usual in any other European city. It ended with a bridge over an abyss, a gash in the landscape about 100 metres deep that looked like the biggest moat in the world. Way down at its bottom a pathetic little river trickled in a concrete bed. A keen wind whipped up from the ravine to deliver a biting cold that sliced straight through my jacket and into the bone zone.

On the other side of the bridge was the centre of town, or the old town, I wasn't quite sure which, but it was another part of town anyway. The snow began again, large flakes this time, and the Saturday shoppers got their umbrellas out. Despite being the wealthiest country in the EU, Luxembourg didn't look much better off at first sight. The people didn't seem to be better dressed and the shops not much smarter than any I had seen in Brussels. I even saw an old man with one arm and a badly swollen leg, sitting on a piece of cardboard, playing a recorder for donations. I hadn't seen any buskers or beggars in Belgium.

It was 2.30 and I was too cold to continue my recce so I ducked into a brasserie to eat a late lunch. It wasn't a particularly distinctive sort of place, with posters of London theatre shows on the walls but curiously no publicity for Jacques Bintz's lecture on Vulkanismus at the Bonnevoie Cultural Centre. I ordered knuckle of pork. This was my first mistake in Luxembourg. Some moments later I was presented with a large, round, white dinner plate, the central feature of which was a joint slightly smaller than my head. It sat on a bed of sauerkraut sprinkled with a few juniper berries and was accompanied by a large bowl of potatoes supporting a modge of apple sauce. It looked like my food ration for a week.

For someone trained from an early age always to clear my plate, this presented me with a not inconsiderable problem, exacerbated by the fact that the pork looked pink, succulent and was falling off the bone. Gallantly I set to. It was delicious, but by the time I had eaten an adequate sufficiency, as my cousin Richard always says, I had barely made an impression on the plate in front of me. I forged on, mentally kicking myself for not packing a second stomach.

The pork melted in the mouth and the sauerkraut was dripping in juices. I'm not a great fan of pig meat, but this was spectacularly good. Nevertheless, by the time I felt fit to burst I was less than a miserable halfway through. I had to admit defeat.

I found some solace in the fact that the woman at the table in front of me, a shopper who had also sought refuge from the cold for a bowl of soup, complained vociferously when the waitress brought her a tureen that the woman claimed would have fed her family of five. The waitress responded rather defensively that such portions were customary in this establishment. As it turned out, the woman was on a day trip from France. As another piece of tourist literature I read sometime later accurately pointed out, Luxembourg gastronomy has been defined as a happy marriage of French quality and German abundance. What puzzled me, however, was the total absence of fat people in Luxembourg. Perhaps they needed all the food to fuel their daily clamberings up and down the deep ravine.

The fact that there is still a Grand Duchy of Luxembourg at all is a tribute to the place. West-central Europe used to be honeycombed with independent duchies, but Luxembourg is the only one to have survived. It has had its ups and downs, of course, and at times it has been touch and go whether the place would survive as an independent entity.

Luxembourg's written history dates back more than a thousand years. In 963, Count Sigefroid of the Ardennes, founder of the first Luxembourg dynasty, had a castle built on a rocky promontory, so laying the foundation for the modern capital. Luxembourg did all right for itself for a few hundred years and in the fourteenth century four members of the House of Luxembourg took turns at being Holy Roman Emperor. One of them elevated Luxembourg's status to that of a duchy. Soon after began a period when the strategic attraction of fortress Luxembourg resulted in a long succession of bloody battles to conquer it. The Burgundians, Spanish, French, Austrians and the Prussians all had a go at ruling the place which became known as the 'Gibraltar of the North', except during the time of Napoleon when it was listed as a French forestry department. At the Congress of Vienna in 1815, Luxembourg was made a Grand Duchy and given to the King of the Netherlands. Belgium took more than half its territory when it went solo in 1830, which left what we see today, a country smaller than Lancashire with a population which would get lost in the Paris Métro. Nearly a third of its residents and half of its workforce are foreigners.

During the 400 years that Luxembourg was controlled by various groups of strangers, Count Sigefroid's original castle was embellished somewhat. Three fortified rings with twenty-four forts and sixteen other major defence works were put up, as well as a unique network of underground tunnels 23 kilometres long known as 'casemates'. The lump of rock that made Luxembourg so strategically important over the centuries was riddled with tunnels like a Swiss cheese. They housed all the necessary services for a city under siege: workshops, kitchens, bakeries and slaughterhouses, as well as providing shelter for thousands of soldiers and their horses. Although many of the city's fortifications were dismantled after Luxembourg became officially neutral in the mid-nineteenth century, they couldn't blow up the casemates because half the city would have collapsed with them. As it turned out, they still came in handy during the two world wars when the Germans didn't take any notice of the country's neutrality. They provided shelter for the city's population in case of air raids and shelling.

Today, the casemates and the historic old town are perhaps Luxembourg's main tourist attraction, and in 1994 UNESCO designated them a World Heritage Site. There was a fair number of tourists doing the rounds when I visited the next morning, after a restless night digesting my knuckle of pork. I approached the casemates from the direction of the Grand Ducal Palace which had been recently cleaned so that its spires and turrets cut a pristine silhouette against the blue sky. A solitary soldier marched up and down in front of it pretending not to appear interested in having his picture taken with a group of lissom female Italian tourists.

The entrance to the casemates was in a tastefully restored part of the rocky promontory known as the Bock, Luxembourg's Acropolis, site of Count Sigefroid's castle. Small plaques informed the visitor of key snippets of Luxembourg's history and one of those round north-east-south-west stones had been set at a vantage point telling you what you were looking at and how far away from home you were while you did so (1916 kilometres from Athens, 478 kilometres from London, 6411 kilometres from Washington, etc.). Another piece of public information at the gateway advised against a visit if you suffered from claustrophobia, which made it unlikely that any Luxembourgers would ever enter unless under the imminent threat of a siege.

Out of the sun, the cold cut through to the quick as it can only inside a damp piece of rock, but apart from a horrific spiral staircase that made me feel as if I was descending into the very bowels of the earth, the warren of stone passages was not particularly claustrophobic. Indeed some of the main tunnels were wide enough to drive a team of horses through. Hollowed-out rooms provided superb views from the cliff face out across the valley and I didn't feel too sorry for the eighty-two-year-old Field Marshal de Bender who had to spend a couple of years in this labyrinth during a siege in the 1790s. He enjoyed a separate bedroom, study and antechamber. I suspect his men were less well accommodated.

One of the buildings of note to be seen from the parapets above the casemates was the house belonging to a man named Robert Schuman, and since Schuman is revered as one of the key originators of the post-war dream of a united Europe, I wanted to get a closer look at the place. I made my way down from the Bock along the Montée de Clausen to the sound of crows shouting from their nests at the top of a line of tall ivy-clad trees. Schuman's house was of a classical design in an off-white almond colour with a standard slate roof and a small turret on the right-hand side. It was nestled at the bottom of a precipitous cliff face. High above it sat the modern buildings of Robert Schuman's legacy: Luxembourg's European Centre which includes all the institutions of the European Union that are firmly based in the Grand Duchy. These include the European Court of Justice, the European Investment Bank, the General Secretariat of the European Parliament, and the European Court of Auditors.

Robert Schuman was a true European. He was brought up in Luxembourg, served in the German army in World War I, and later became prime minister of France. These experiences helped to convince him of the need to settle the enmity between France and Germany once and for all. It was during his period as French foreign minister that he came up with his plan to do this by creating a higher authority, initially over the essentials of war: coal and steel. His Schuman Plan, which led to the formation of the European Coal and Steel Community in 1952, was the first step in the creation of the EU, and hence Schuman became known as the 'father of Europe'. He has a whole roundabout named after him in the centre of Brussels. And rightly so. You can say what you like about the European Union, but transforming two mortal enemies into best mates is some achievement.

It should come as no great surprise that Luxembourg has featured fairly prominently in the progress towards European integration from its outset, both because of Schuman and because of the country's position sandwiched between two of Europe's great powers. Instead of becoming a car park for the Frankfurt park and ride, Luxembourg has done pretty well out of it all. As one national I spoke to put it, Luxembourgers have the most positive attitude to the EU that I would be likely to come across. 'Because we stand to make the most out of it,' he said candidly. 'It is the only way we get any attention, through such wider platforms.'

Somehow it doesn't seem right that there should still be Grand Duchies in late twentieth-century Europe, so perhaps becoming part of a larger whole is the only way forward. In many ways Luxembourg is not cut out to be a modern state. She's just too small. I didn't feel as if I was in a whole country; it was more like being in a city with a bit of hinterland. And even the city was really only big enough to be a town. Admittedly Luxembourg has most of the accoutrements of a contemporary country, but many are difficult to take seriously. They have their own money, for example, but it is of equal value to the Belgian franc and you can use Belgian currency anywhere. Visitors are, however, advised to change all their Luxembourg money before they leave the country, because Luxembourg francs are not accepted in Belgium. The country also has a national football team, but when it won a game in February 1995 Luxembourgers celebrated in the streets because it was their first victory for fifteen years.

The half-serious currency, the fact that most of the people who live there were foreigners, the common use of French and German in everyday activities (despite the fact that they have their own Luxembourgish language), all added up to the perception that Luxembourg was not a terribly distinctive place. Back in the eighteenth century, Middleton didn't think it was either: he gave it a single page in his *Complete System of Geography*. In fact, any modern-day Grand Tourist short of a bit of time should seriously consider missing out Luxembourg altogether. And since the country has already lost much of its national character simply because of its dimensions, the gains to be had from any greater amalgamation with its European cousins would readily outweigh any further erosion of national integrity.

But at the same time there was no doubt that Luxembourg had

found its niche in the modern world and did, therefore, display some distinctive features. Luxembourgers are very good with money, for example, most of it other people's. Where London has pubs, Brussels has chocolate shops, and Vienna has coffee houses, Luxembourg has banks. Banks love it there. At the last count, Luxembourg was home to 222 of them, along with 900 investment funds. That's more banks and investment funds than in any other city in the world.

I learnt these facts from a banker, so they must be true. He was sitting at the table next to mine in another restaurant. It was Sunday evening and he was wearing casual gear: a coloured tie with his suit. He was in his early thirties and he looked as if he'd never had a good time in his life. When I first started talking to him he pretended not to hear, and then looked terrified when I made my comment again, as if this might be a prelude to assault. All I'd said was, 'The asparagus is good,' which seemed like a safe opener since the restaurant specialised in asparagus. They even had a special asparagus menu. But you're not supposed to talk to people at other tables in restaurants in northern Europe. I don't usually, but I hadn't talked to anyone for a couple of days so I thought I'd live a little and chat to a Luxembourger.

'Yes,' he said carefully in answer to my comment and then he returned his attention to his plate. He was eating his spears with his knife and fork and had clearly been ruffled when he saw I was eating mine with my fingers. I wasn't going to give up, so I asked him whether he was from around here.

'Yes,' he replied again, 'I am from Luxembourg.'

'Oh good,' I said, perhaps with too much glee, 'I've been looking forward to meeting a Luxembourger.' This was a lie, but it didn't matter because he didn't answer. Instead he concentrated harder on cutting his spears into ever smaller pieces.

'What do you do?' I continued. He couldn't not answer that one. He put down his cutlery, puffed himself up, and declared that he was an investment banker.

'Interesting work,' I lied again just to keep the conversation going. He nodded, with a satisfied smile on his face. I asked him how many banks there were in Luxembourg and he gave me the information with a look that suggested that if I wanted to know more I'd have to pay for it. He asked me if I was on holiday. I replied that I was working. He gave me a puzzled look, as if nobody could be working if they weren't wearing a tie. But he was opening up; he asked me what line of business. 'I'm a writer.'

'A journalist,' he declared with a dismissive sneer.

'No, I write books.' The banker popped a fat piece of white asparagus into his mouth and nodded in a patronising way, as if I'd said I was a toilet cleaner or a dog catcher, not really the sort of person a banker should be fraternising with. I asked him where most of his clients came from.

'Oh, I can't tell you that,' he said pompously. 'We in the banking world have a code of client confidentiality.' And with that comment he motioned to the waiter who was hovering in the background and asked in French for his bill. I changed tack and enquired whether any of the banks in Luxembourg are ever robbed. Startled and offended, he said, 'No,' and pulled out his wallet. I thought for a moment he was going to hand it over and plead for mercy, but he just riffled through his credit cards. I wasn't getting very far. Just before he got up to leave, having only eaten half of his spears, I asked whether he thought a single European currency would really happen in 1999.

'Of course,' he replied, as if this childish question aptly reflected my sorry ignorance of all things financial. He gave me a slight bow of the head to say goodbye and turned to leave, probably to go and do something much more intellectually stimulating, like combing the fringe of his carpet. I deliberately slurped my last piece of asparagus in reply.

The following morning, while walking round the city, I got an inkling as to why my banker friend had been suspicious of my saying I was working in his country. Even the gardeners all wore business shirts and ties. The whole of Luxembourg City was supremely neat. Ever public park, garden and flowerbed was lovingly tended and the streets were clean, safe and orderly. I looked hard, but I didn't see a single item of litter in Luxembourg, not even around the main post office where the city's youth hung out being bored on a Saturday afternoon, or near the railway station where a small band of drunks could be seen on a Sunday morning. As in Stockholm, there didn't appear to be any pigeons either; perhaps they simply don't bother to infest really prosperous countries.

And although many residents owned dogs, another aspect of note was that their excrement wasn't a feature of the city's pavements.

Luxembourg seemed to have found a workable solution to a problem that plagues all other French-speaking European cities. In Paris and Brussels the local authorities' attempts to combat the dog shit problem amounted to pavement silhouettes of small dogs with arrows directing their bottoms to the gutter. In Paris all these pictures are of dachshunds, so other breeds think it doesn't apply to them and crap in the middle of the pavement. In Brussels, the pictures are of cartoon dogs. Real dogs just enjoy looking at them while they relieve themselves in the centre of the thoroughfare. Dotted around the streets at strategic intervals in Luxembourg are brown slot machines designed to appeal to their conscientious owners. They purvey do-it-yourself pooper scoopers. Beneath a slogan that advises Luxembourgers to keep their streets as they should be is a graphic showing you how to clean up after your canine accomplice. Dog owners even have to pay ten francs for the pleasure, but it works.

Despite these positive features, however, there were still some undesirable aspects of life as a modern state that even a Grand Duchy couldn't avoid. Another article in my copy of *Luxembourg News* revealed the alarming fact that the country's prison population has almost doubled over the last twenty years. The number of reprobates languishing in Luxembourg's jails has reached record levels, 470 people, though seemingly none of them are bank robbers.

Although Luxembourg was well organised and everything worked, good organisation doesn't necessarily equate with efficiency. This became clear when I visited the post office to purchase some stamps. Like most post offices, this one contained a row of numbered counters, totalling twelve in all. Four of these were open for business, but only one of them (counter number 3) sold postage stamps. There was a queue of nine people at this counter while all the others were quiet. Unfortunately for those of us in the stamp queue, the woman at its head looked as if she was mailing early for Christmas. She had a trolley beside her piled high with curiously shaped parcels. Law-abiding Luxembourgers would enter the building carrying a single letter, take one look at the nine-person queue and approach one of the other three operational counters to ask for a quick stamp. The response was inflexible. Counters 1, 2 and 3 were for stamps. They would have to join the queue. I waited for twenty-five minutes before I was served.

In one sense, however, I was not too distressed at having to wait so long in the post office. I had looked at the capital's old city and followed the two walking itineraries suggested by the national tourist office. I had been into the Musée National, an impressive building with a beautifully displayed collection and probably the only national museum in Europe where you don't have to pay an entrance fee, but now I was running out of things to do. I was determined not to get involved in the 1996 European Dog Championships and it was still several days before Jacques Bintz would be lecturing on Vulkanismus at the Bonnevoie Cultural Centre.

As I was walking aimlessly on the avenue de la Liberté, the outline of a fluorescent yellow cobra caught my eye on a public display of information. The poster advertised an exhibition of living reptiles that was '*Exceptionnel*' and was currently showing in the place du Glacis. I consulted my street map. Like everywhere in Luxembourg City, place du Glacis was within walking distance, so I walked there.

It was a large car park on the northern edge of town. Over on the far side was a sizeable marquee in front of several lorry trailers that belonged to Pierre Durand's travelling exhibition of living reptiles. According to the writing on the side of the trailers, this was '*une importante collection*'. I paid the entrance fee and went in. Just inside the tent I was met by a man in a brown tweed jacket. He had large bulbous eyes that were half-closed and carried a glazed expression. If this was Pierre Durand he had been spending too much time with his reptilian charges, I thought to myself, because he looked as if he might be a reptile himself. He tore my ticket in half and tried to sell me a programme.

Inside, the marquee was warm and muggy after the still-sharp temperatures outside. It was like those marquees that people hire for smart weddings, with ornate chandeliers, but instead of wedding guests it was full of temperature-controlled glass display cases. Inside the display cases was an impressive variety of plastic vegetation, no doubt designed to highlight the assortment of snakes, crocodiles, geckos and lizards that the cases also contained. Like the imitation foliage, most of the live reptiles struck distinctly inanimate poses, as if they too were really rather bored with being in Luxembourg.

Two baby boa constrictors were curled up asleep in their water bowl whilst a Central African forest cobra had recently shed its skin and was recuperating after the effort beneath a piece of log. A pyramid viper was on the move, but when he encountered the small screwed-up face of a junior Luxembourger on the other side of the glass he promptly stopped slithering and fell asleep. Most of the crocs were even less animate than their limbless relatives. They slumbered in a variety of uncomfortable-looking poses, in or out of their water, completely motionless. They didn't even blink. A caiman was lucky enough to have been issued with its own radiator, just like the ones you have in your living room, and he was stretched out beside it looking extremely fed up with his hanging plastic ivy as if this was not what he had been expecting when he left South America. Elsewhere, the most active member of the whole reptilian party was a two-metre-long Nile crocodile which was trying to wedge his head into a square corner of a tank the size of a small bathtub. He looked pissed off and bordering on the psychotic. Otherwise, the only specimens which looked less than soporific were the giant tortoises which occupied the largest and the only open corral in the centre of the marquee. They were eating lettuce. All in all, Pierre Durand's travelling exhibition just made me feel sorry for the reptiles, so I returned to my hotel to clean the fluff out of my tummy button.

On my final morning in Luxembourg I decided to get my hair cut. I have to admit that I had been deliberately putting off this event in anticipation of little else happening to write about in Luxembourg. On first consideration, a hairdresser may not seem the most likely place to find excitement, but then I was in Luxembourg, and besides some of my previous encounters with foreign barbers had proved to be interesting experiences. Some years back I had a haircut in Mexico City that turned into a bloodbath. The barber accidentally snipped my earlobe which bled excessively. I had never seen so much blood and it was all mine. I held a large towel to the side of my head while the man snipped away at what he was supposed to have been cutting all along, apologising profusely the while. The mishap put him off his stroke and the haircut was so bad that a week later, when my ear was well healed, I had to find another barber to get a decent cut.

On another occasion, in Muscat in the Middle East this time, I walked into a barber shop in the souk and sat down to wait while the hairdresser dealt with another customer. After I had been sitting there for some minutes, the barber began talking to the other man who was waiting on the plastic couch beside me. Their conversation was in Arabic and I had no idea what they were saying, but the barber sounded encouraging while the man beside me looked slightly reticent. His demeanour was appropriately wild, as if he usually cut his hair with the large curled knife on his belt, and he kept throwing thoughtful glances in my direction. After a while, the wild man stood up and motioned me to a second chair. I looked at the barber who smiled cheerfully and also gestured towards the empty seat. I had a notion that something might not be quite right, but I took my place. It only dawned on me towards the end of the procedure, after the man cutting my locks had shown a singular lack of aptitude with the pair of scissors, that the barber had offered to cut my assailant's hair for free if he agreed to have a go at doing mine while he waited. I clearly didn't understand what was going on and I wouldn't be able to complain since I didn't speak the language, so what had he got to lose? It was easily the worst haircut I have ever had.

Unfortunately I didn't appear to have picked a good day for a haircut in Luxembourg City. The unisex Salon Anton on rue Joseph Junck was shut on Monday mornings and Salon Biver, a gentlemen's establishment, was closed all day. Eventually I found one that was open, indicated by a pair of red neon scissors above an inconspicuous entrance next to a bank. I descended the stairs and entered a gleaming world of white tiles and chrome.

A young woman took my jacket and asked me to wait on one of the black metal stools. A tall, thin young man who wore a white polo neck beneath a breezy cheesecloth shirt and a large amount of gold jewellery on his wrists came to attend to me. I hadn't got an appointment, so the white will-o'-the-wisp consulted Pascal, who obviously ruled the roost. Pascal was busy with a customer, but he turned to give me the once over. He was dressed in black to go with the stools and his complexion matched the white wall tiles. His outfit was set off at the waist by a silver cowboy belt, and he wore a blond goatee beard and a small earring. Pascal looked as if he could do with a haircut himself. He smiled at me delicately and said something in German which obviously meant that I had passed muster. His white assistant led me away to have my hair washed.

When I returned, Pascal issued some abrupt instructions for the man he had just finished and turned to me. I asked him if he spoke English and he shook his head. Since I don't speak any German, or Luxembourgish, I told him in English anyway. It was pretty straightforward: I wanted a haircut. Pascal set to and in no time at all he had moved on to his next customer to be replaced by his white assistant. To my surprise, the white waif produced a cut-throat razor from a small bowl on the counter, flicked it open, and inspected the blade. It has been some years now since British hairdressers have given up on the cut-throat razor, ostensibly because of the threat of transmitting AIDS via the blade. But like BSE, Luxembourg had probably never recorded a case of AIDS. After my neck had been scraped, I was finished off with a huge soft brush. To the jangle of gold bracelets, any nasty little snippets of hair that might still be lurking around the collar line were swept away. The whole episode had taken less than twenty minutes and the haircut was excellent.

Slightly disappointed, I made my way to the railway station where the drunks that had been hanging around the main entrance the previous day were nowhere to be seen. With an hour to kill, I bought a cup of coffee in the cafeteria. The place was done out in a super-polished red granite and Easter decorations hung from the ceiling. There were cardboard cut-outs of barrow-loads of flowers and paper Chinese lanterns in the shapes of eggs in nasty bright purples, pinks and yellows. A notice behind the cash register said *'Pas de pique-nique S.V.P.'* The woman in front of it wore a paper tiara on her head.

As I sat at my table, a tall man with a red face and glasses, dressed in a trench coat and tweed hat, came in through the automatic glass doors. He walked around the cafeteria once and left, letting in another rush of cold air as he did so. As in Belgium, everywhere in Luxembourg seemed to be equipped with glass doors that whooshed open and shut automatically. After the man in the tweed hat had left, I wondered how it was that these automatic doors often seemed to have greasy hand marks on them.

A black man stood up from his seat and tripped over a Ford car bumper that was wrapped in strong plastic on the floor behind his chair. He recovered himself, picked up the bumper and manoeuvred his car accessory through the automatic doors.

The people sitting at the other tables were doing the usual things to pass the time before their trains departed: spinning out coffees, reading newspapers, filling in crossword puzzles and eating an early lunch. Behind me, a bar area was thinly populated with Portuguese construction workers, distinguished by their soft Russian-sounding lilts. They were drinking their lunch. None of these activities appealed, so I thought I would try to sum up the EU's smallest and most prosperous country. Luxembourg was France without the dog's muck, Belgium without the chocolate shops and Germany without the Turks. They had Portuguese people instead. It was time for me to make my way to platform 3B for the 12.10 to Liège.

The train soared across Luxembourg City's deep ravines as if in flight and we proceeded in a northerly direction following the valley of the River Alzette. Most of it was unremarkable pastureland. As we passed an electricity relay station, the conductor with a neat little pigtail poking out from under his cap clipped my ticket. As the train slowed down to stop at Mersch I saw a schoolboy smoking a cigarette beneath a bridge. There were grain silos on one side of the station and a BMW showroom on the other.

I sat on seat number 26 in a second-class non-smoking compartment. The seat was made of blue plastic, the floor was grey, the walls were white down the sides of the carriage and bright orange at the end. Small browny-yellow curtains in a material like sacking hung at the windows. It wasn't a pleasant combination of colours.

We passed through a tunnel before a place called Colmar-Berg, and there was a cemetery sandwiched between the railway line and the main road coming into Ettelbruck, where a man who breathed very loudly boarded the train and sat behind me. Ettelbruck seemed to be a fair-sized place with rail connections to other places. The hills that had been building up for the past twenty minutes got larger and started closing in on the railway line, and the catkins were out on the riverbank. The train's pace was unhurried though not very smooth and I found it difficult to make notes. I decided to record the number of tunnels instead, since this only required a straightforward mark in my notebook. In all, we passed through seven tunnels between Ettelbruck and Kantenbach. At least I think we did. I may have lost count in all the excitement.

We were travelling through more forest than previously. Most of the trees were grey and without leaves, save for the odd golden-brown splash from the occasional beech. The other leaves I saw were also grey and lying on the steep valley slopes. There were lots more tunnels before Wilwerwiltz but by this time I had stopped counting.

Clervaux seemed like a really significant town. It had a football pitch and there was snow on the ground at the end of neat little gardens. The man with the loud breath got off. There was more snow further on, in the lee of the trees on the eastern side of the valley which was quite wide again now. We progressed through two small places whose names translated to Five Fountains and Three Virgins. I thought there might be a joke in that, but I was past that stage. Then we were in somewhere called Gouvy which wasn't on my map of Luxembourg so I assumed that it must be Belgium. Gouvy also had lots of tracks, which made it unlikely that we were still in Luxembourg. In little more than an hour, I had travelled almost the entire length of the country. I went straight to the toilet. I'd been bursting for the last ten minutes but had been saving it in case I missed anything.

11

Land of the Trojan Dog

I hadn't wanted to go. Just thinking about Greece made me tired. All those ruins and monuments and gods and museums full of artefacts and inconsequential pieces of pot. I wasn't one of those people who can distinguish a Greek god from its Roman equivalent at twenty paces, and to be frank, I've never wanted to. They were all the same to me. I was a child of the twentieth century and I resisted any attempt to imbue me with a classical education. As far as I was concerned, Apollo was a type of space rocket, Nike was a sportswear manufacturer, Athena was where students used to buy their posters and Pluto was a cartoon dog. If the truth be told, I was rather scared of all that ancient history because I felt I ought to be interested in it but I wasn't.

When I landed at Athens Ellinikon International Airport it was like arriving in the Third World. Customs and immigration men smoked cigarettes and wore their ties at half-mast, whilst the building itself was drab and dusty. The toilets were smelly and the plumbing didn't appear to have progressed much in the last 2000 years. The cubicles came with warnings against squatting on the rim of the bowl but no instructions on what to do with your loo paper. Disposing of your bum swipes in a bin is a complete anathema to people brought up to drop them into the dark recess below their rear. You stop and wonder what they're saving them for. Then you find yourself peering tentatively into someone else's discarded excrement certificates, just to make sure that this is where you should be jettisoning your own. And of course most foreign visitors can't quite bring themselves to do it, so like almost everywhere else in Greece, the public toilets in Athens international airport are all permanently overflowing.

Beyond the casual customs check in the blue EU channel, gangs of tour reps stood patiently waiting with their contact signs held aloft, some specially printed with company logos, others just scribbled names on old bits of cardboard. Over at the Greek National Tourist Organisation booth they gave me a street map of Athens and I wandered out to join the taxi queue. The man in front of me said he was from Crete and was going home after completing his M. Phil. in something to do with systems at Southampton University. He asked me where I was staying and I told him the unlikely name of the Hotel Austria. He had no idea where it was and neither had I.

The driver of my yellow taxi confessed to knowing, however. He said it with a nice big smile and promptly switched off his meter. Friendly though the grey-haired gentleman appeared, I wasn't falling for that one. 'Aren't you using the meter?' I asked innocently.

'Yes, of course,' he came back, flicking the switch again to reilluminate the digits, 'it's automatic.' Then he switched it off again, perhaps to save energy, I thought to myself. 'Why do you ask?' the driver enquired amiably. 'Did someone not use it last time?' I couldn't think of an appropriate wisecrack, so I let that one pass, but I dug into my bag to find the guidebook I had brought with me and looked up the going rate for a taxi ride to the centre of town.

We swept into Athens and the kind-hearted taxi driver did his best to avoid pulling up at the traffic lights next to a huge oil tanker that was belching black smoke into the Athenian air. I was just thinking what a drab and characterless city it seemed to be when the driver pointed through the windscreen towards the Acropolis, which had just appeared above the skyline of medium-rise apartment blocks. The first sight of this large lump of limestone, with its fortress walls and delicate columns, is as memorable as the first glimpse of the Eiffel Tower in Paris or the Colosseum in Rome. It sat there, majestic and timeless above the hustle and bustle of its modern counterpart. We've all seen the pictures, but they can't compare to the real thing. It sent a shiver down my spine.

A few minutes later, the taxi pulled up outside the Hotel Austria. The driver flicked the button on his meter and four little green digits appeared on its display. They were a nine, an eight, a five and a zero, in that order. Momentarily I was confused. My book had suggested anything between 1500 and 2500 drachma for a ride like this one. I laughed. 'What's that in?' I asked pointing at the meter. 'Italian lira? Somali shillings, perhaps?' The driver screwed his head round to look at me with his best unworldly gape. 'What's wrong?' he asked. 'Too much?'

I felt like saying that I always liked to pay ten times the legal price because it made my tax returns easier, but I sensed that sarcasm would be lost on him. 'You know it's too much,' I told the man.

At first he didn't react, but, obviously well versed in these encounters, he opted for Gullible Tourist Plan B from the Greek taxi drivers' guide to ripping off your customers. 'OK, up to you,' he said, and he got out of the taxi with a long look on his face to open my door and make me feel as if *I* was ripping *him* off.

I pulled two crisp, new 1000-drachma notes from my top pocket and handed them to him. He didn't seem dissatisfied. 'Maybe there is a problem with the meter,' he suggested.

The only Greek words I remembered from my previous visit to the country many years before were *kalimera*, which means good morning, and *malacca*, which if my memory serves me correctly means wanker. Put them together and I had a complete phrase, but I hadn't been expecting to use it so soon after my arrival.

The Hotel Austria was just a marble's throw from the Acropolis, perched on the side of Filopapou hill to the south. The only Austrian thing about it was the triangular slab of Happy Cow cheese they served along with the cotton-wool bread and Greek jam at breakfast. My room was on the fourth floor and it had a small balcony with a white plastic chair. From here I could survey the higgledy-piggledy concrete boxes that pass for houses in Athens. It was July and it felt good to be in a part of Europe that was hot after the bone-chilling winter in Scandinavia and the Benelux countries. I left the french window permanently open and slept beneath a single sheet. On my first night I was kept awake by a thumping headache and the sounds of a cat dying a very slow and agonising death. It got so bad that I even left my room in search of the strangled shrieks, but to no avail. The second night it was indigestion that thwarted my slumber and the cat was dying again, which made me think it was a baby screaming all along. But after being so bored in Luxembourg I was almost glad to be kept awake. At least something was happening here.

Greece was never a part of the traditional eighteenth-century Grand Tour because the place was overrun with Turks at the time and thus hardly counted as Europe at all. The country had been part of the Ottoman Empire since the mid-1400s. As Charles Theodore Middleton put it in his *Complete System of Geography*, Greece was 'under the unnatural tyranny of barbarians' and the once-great metropolis of Athens had become a 'despicable place'. Although Greece spawned the civilisations of most of her Western European neighbours, she missed out on much of their common history after the fall of the Romans and the Byzantine Empire. Charlemagne, the rise and fall of Burgundy and the Bourbon–Habsburg rivalry, all happened far away beyond the Balkans. Then they got the Turks for nearly four hundred years and they're still pretty bitter about it.

You come across caustic references to sadistic sultans and their pugnacious pashas all over the place in Greece. On my first morning, I walked into the old Plaka district that nestles around the foot of the Acropolis and stumbled on one in the city's cathedral. I knew it was the cathedral because standing in front of it was an American couple telling their video camera as much. They held it at arm's length, pointing towards them so that they could talk to it. 'This is the cathedral,' the young man told his machine. 'It's beautiful inside but they did kick us out because we were wearing shorts.' Since I wasn't wearing short trousers, I ventured in. From the outside, the chunky nineteenth-century building looked like a Gotham City theatre, complete with a jazzy golden mosaic above the entrance and stage curtains at the doors. But in its dark interior the small building became a splendid church full of icons and ornate chandeliers. On the left side of the nave hung a painting of Saint Philothei of Athens that people crossed themselves in front of and then kissed. Next to this painting was a casket with a glass window in its top. Through it you could see her sacred relics. A note on the wall above the casket told how Saint Philothei had been tortured for her devotion to Orthodoxy in 1589 'during the dark and long years of slavery of the Greek nation'.

Punch-ups with her Moslem neighbours from Asia have punctu-ated Greek history ever since Greece gained independence from Turkey in 1832, after a twelve-year struggle. They had a little war right at the end of the nineteenth century, Greece clawed back bits of what she considered to be Greek territory from the old enemy in the Balkan wars, and was given some more prime cuts of European Turkey as a reward for joining World War I on the right side. The visions of a new greater Greece were spoilt, however, when they overstepped the mark in trying to snatch some chunks of Asia Minor. Atatürk became Bashagreek. The defeat ended with a brutal exchange of population in the 1920s, designed to eliminate the Greek excuse for her territorial claims. Most of the million or so Greeks kicked out of Turkey took up residence in Athens or its port of Piraeus, hence the profusion of white boxes with little architectural merit.

With them, these bedraggled refugees brought new nuances to reinforce the Middle Eastern flavours that centuries of Turkish rule had left behind. In Athens you can savour them in the crowded bazaar between Omonia and Monastiraki Squares and in the haunting sounds of *rembetika*, an urban blues music rooted in the sufferings of the dispossessed Asian Greeks. The history of Moslem incursions into either end of Europe has left contrasting legacies. In Spain, the most enduring reminder of their Islamic past is the splendid Moorish architecture; in Greece it is the doner kebab.

I had wanted to sample some *rembetika*, but I learnt that with appropriate Greek perversity almost all the *rembetika* clubs in Athens close down for the summer. I had to make do with a few snatches in the Museum of Greek Musical Instruments instead. I like music, but I am by no means an expert and I found it rather off-putting when I first entered the converted nineteenth-century Plaka mansion to see signs to chordophones this way and idiophones that way. I needn't have been, because you didn't need to know what an idiophone was to appreciate the glass cases full of bells and rattles and terracotta trumpets. There was even a case containing a string of worry-beads and a couple of small ouzo glasses, with a series of photographs beside it showing you how to make music by rubbing the one against the other. Attached to each case was a set of headphones so that you could listen to examples of the music made as you perused the appropriate case. Upstairs in the chordophone section was a bewildering array of mandolins, bouzoukis and lutes, and pear-shaped fiddles called *liras*. The samples of *rembetika*, backed by these stringed instruments, were hypnotic and melancholy ballads seasoned with an essence of the East.

The Museum of Greek Musical Instruments was just the right size, not too small, but more importantly, not too big. My next stop was too large, but then its subject matter demanded it should be because this was the Museum of War. With a few thousand years of history behind it, Greece has been the scene of a fair number of armed conflicts and most of them were remembered in some form or other in this museum. It was located in another square concrete box of a building custom-built beyond the Plaka's narrow streets on a wide thoroughfare that swept eastward from the national parliament. Outside on its forecourt was a display of retired fighter aeroplanes and artillery pieces. They were presided over by a couple of squaddies, in regulation fatigues and moustaches, whose job it was to keep enthusiastic boys a respectable distance from their grown-up military toys.

Inside, row upon row of sabres and pistols, machine guns and ancient bronze helmets, campaign maps and busts of revolutionary heroes stretched as far as the eye could see. Fortunately for me, most of the explanatory notes were only in Greek, so I didn't feel guilty for not dwelling on all of them. Among the more unusual exhibits was a small compartmentalised tray dating from World War II. Each compartment contained a bullet case and a sample of soil. The label said the soil was blood-stained and had been taken from a firing range after Nazi executions. An even more bizarre presentation commemorated Leonidas Petropoulakis, described as a freedom fighter from Mani, whose life was saved by his briefcase. The briefcase, which I have to say looked more like a handbag, was there with knife cuts slashed across it. The caption did not say why Mr Petropoulakis was carrying his briefcase at the time.

Although Athens is full of much more ancient artefacts, the Museum of War is a relic from an era in the recent past, less than thirty years ago, when Greece was ruled by a military junta. It is odd to note that the country generally agreed to be the fountainhead of Western civilisation, the birthplace of democracy and so on, has a modern history more like a Latin American banana republic than a respectable member of the European Union.

Back in the 1830s, when independent nation states were all the rage, the big boys in Europe decided that what the new Greece needed was a monarchy, and just as in Belgium they found a spare German prince to fill the vacancy. But the idea never really caught on. A few decades later, he was replaced with a Danish one, and subsequent kings of Greece popped in and out of favour until they gave up on the concept altogether in 1974. In the meantime, the Greeks had sampled republicanism, tried a right-wing dictatorship, allowed the communists to spark a civil war, and served an eight-year stretch under the colonels. Having tried virtually every option, they plumped for a republic again and joined the EU as such in 1981.

As a member of the EU, Greece is a bit of an odd man out. It's the only country which doesn't share a border with another member state for a start. On any map of the community, there is a neat pile of countries and then a splash of dots down in the bottom right-hand corner which is Greece. And of course Greece is the only country that uses a different alphabet to all the rest. This makes for that nice feeling of being properly abroad when you first see Greek signposts, a feeling that you just don't get in places where the Roman alphabet is used, whether you can understand what they say or not.

In other ways too, Greece seemed to be behind when compared to its more northerly European cousins. They're still selling Nana Mouskouri tapes, motorcyclists don't wear helmets and the streets of Athens are not lined with recycling bins. They are patrolled by skinny cats and vicious dogs instead. The cats all had mange, and most of their canine rivals looked as if they had something unpleasant inside, like rabies for example. In most of the other countries I had visited for this book, I had enjoyed the ease with which I could draw cash in local currency from hole-in-the-wall banking machines. But not in Greece. Travelling with plastic money is not nearly as commonplace as it is elsewhere in Europe. Greeks prefer the feel of cash, and large numbers of their banknotes are held together with grotty strips of Sellotape to prove it.

And then there was their attitude to smoking. Greece even lags behind Spain in the cigarette-bashing stakes: they are the heaviest smokers in the world. Campaigns against tobacco are still in their infancy. When the government declared 1995 to be anti-smoking year, consumption rose by 3 per cent. When I visited Greece the Olympic Games were just starting in Atlanta and the headlines were dominated by a story concerning the Greek basketball team. One of their number had nearly got them all arrested for a quick fag in the toilet during the transatlantic flight on the strictly tobacco-free Delta Airlines. Newspaper cartoonists had a field day. Players were depicted lighting up with the Olympic flame beside a basketball net drawn as an ashtray. The slogan read 'Basketball is hazardous to your smoking'.

The start of the Atlanta Olympics, the hundredth anniversary of their resurrection, brought mixed feelings to the Greeks. They were, of course, proud that this fundamentally Greek institution was still alive and well and enthralling audiences across the world. And their own team was doing pretty well in the weightlifting. But at the same time, they were a bit pissed off that all their competitors had to travel to the USA to celebrate the centennial modern Olympiad. Athens got the 1896 games and they still have the stadium, built on the site of a fourth-century BC counterpart. The arena is simplicity itself, with forty-seven tiers of clean, smooth white marble seating: a monument to the fact that modern Greek architects can still design classically elegant structures when they want to. But there was a fat chance of them hosting this one. Marble is too hard for the average twentieth-century bottom, and there's no room for the TV cameras and commentary boxes, let alone the hamburger and kebab stands.

I decided to go and walk round the Acropolis on a Sunday because it was supposed to be free. Naturally enough, several thousand other tourists had the same idea and the Greek authorities had given up on the free Sunday entry anyway. As I stood in the snaking queue, waiting to pay 2000 drachma for the pleasure of walking round a ruin, I cursed Thomas Cook for starting the whole mass tourism thing. Cook took over from where the Grand Tour had left off thanks to the Napoleonic wars, which made the Continent a dangerous place for roving British aristocracy. The Grand Tour never really recovered. The coming of the railway brought mass transit for those lower down on the social ladder and Cook's Great Circular Tour of Europe was the precursor to today's tourist millions. Jolly good thing too, of course. I'm all in favour of as many people as possible getting out of their own countries to see what life is like elsewhere. I just wish they wouldn't all come on the day I want to see it.

On the way up to the rock, a large notice made all visitors aware of Law 5351 that prohibits a wide range of inappropriate activities on ancient Greek monuments, such as singing and making loud noises. Up on top, the venerable bits of architecture that hadn't been reduced to rubble were cordoned off from the masses and were patrolled by a small army of whistle-blowing attendants. There was a light breeze up here in the upper city and occasional gusts were enough to blow small clouds of limestone dust into the eyes of the spectators. Where the modern authorities had not put down gravel to stroll on, the rocks had been worn smooth by the tramp of feet. This looked very pretty but was a pig to walk on for the assorted representatives of the leisure industry leading motley collections of attendant humanity round the piles of ancient building blocks.

I swung from group to group, like a tourist Tarzan, listening to snippets of spiel.

'You can find monuments and temples all over the world and Europe. Some are very decorated. Some even look like birthday cakes they're so decorated. But none is as elegant and beautiful as the Parthenon.'

'... perfect harmony and balance.'

'Fifteen hundred years later, in the Renaissance, there were many great craftsmen, artists and sculptors and many beautiful buildings were built. But none will ever beat the perfection of the Parthenon.'

'... forty-six columns in total, all in the Doric style.'

'... an optical illusion. None of the columns is straight up. There isn't a single straight line in the temple.'

The Parthenon had a crane in the middle, the Erechtheum was partially covered by a tarpaulin and there was scaffolding everywhere. As one awe-struck observer put it, 'They're putting it back together again. Look at all the stuff they've got to rebuild littered around. Columns and everything.' He was right. All about us, the seemingly innocuous carved boulders that together made the Acropolis look like a disaster area were in fact all carefully documented and numbered. It was an antediluvian jigsaw puzzle of precious stones awaiting reconstitution as memorials to another age. In a modern-day version of the labours of Hercules, the Greek authorities were carefully reconstructing their classical heritage.

Or at least that's what they want you to think. But while they've been carefully rebuilding some parts, they've been just as carefully dismantling others. Tour guides gnashed their teeth as they spat the words 'Lord Eljin' and pointed to where he wrenched one of those six maiden-shaped pillars from the Erechtheum. Then, in muted voices, they pointed out that the other five caryatids had been ripped out by the Greek authorities. Why? Because the originals were all rotting in the cocktail of atmospheric pollutants they call the *nefos*.

This most recent restoration of the Acropolis (part-financed by the

216

EU, of course) has been going on for twenty years, but it's unlikely to be completed before 2036 because of delays, lack of funds and bureaucratic red tape. Around the time they started, the authorities became aware of a new threat to their architectural treasures: that delightful yellow fog with which modern Athenians have shrouded their priceless monuments.

The *nefos* began to obscure the clear blue summer skies of Athens in the 1970s. The photochemical pollution got steadily worse during the 1980s and Athens gained the dubious distinction of the most polluted city in Western Europe. The politicians promised that a solution could be found in months, but although the Greeks invented politics, their politicians don't seem to be much better than anyone else's. The problem is still getting worse.

It's not entirely fair to lay the blame squarely at the feet of the politicians. Part of the problem is that Athenians seem to have lost their sense of civic duty. Local authorities started to combat the *nefos* in 1982 by introducing a scheme to reduce the number of private cars in the city centre. Vehicles with licence plates ending in an even number were only allowed access on even-numbered dates while odd-numbered dates were reserved for cars with odd-numbered licence plates. It didn't work. Many Athenians promptly went out and treated themselves to a second vehicle, with a licence plate allowing them in on the days when their first car was banned. These second cars tended to be of the older and more polluting kind, so things got worse. A year later, the authorities changed the rules. This time, cars with plates ending in zero to four got access one day, those ending in five to nine the next. The change in the rules came with a warning that the regulations would be modified again if people went out and bought yet another car.

In 1985, the authorities assessed the situation. The new regulations seemed to have worked. There were 22 per cent fewer private cars in the city centre. But strangely enough, the pollution didn't seem to be much better. People were catching taxis instead, whose numbers had increased by 26 per cent.

The authorities decided to include taxis in the ban but the taxi drivers went on strike, deliberately staging traffic jams until their exemption was restored. The authorities tried inspecting vehicle exhausts but with limited success. If drivers failed the test at one station they could usually find another that would pass them. The authorities even experimented with a complete traffic ban, but couldn't quite bring themselves to make it permanent. Meanwhile, Athens is busy expanding its metro system, but no significant improvement in air quality is expected before well into the next century.

Experts reckon that the Parthenon has suffered as much damage from pollution in the last twenty years as in the previous 2000. It's not just the monuments that suffer. On really bad *nefos* days, hundreds of Greater Athens residents are admitted to hospital with heart and respiratory complaints. More than a hundred premature deaths are attributed to poor air quality every year. The only good thing you can say about the *nefos* is that it must cut down on the number of skin cancer patients.

I saw what was left of the five caryatids in the Acropolis Museum along with numerous other lucky statues and busts with just their noses missing. Less fortunate examples lacked limbs and heads. I inched my way through the packed museum behind a group of North American teenagers who were discussing the pros and cons of perspiration. One girl was upset that she wasn't sweating because she had read that it was a good way of getting rid of body toxins. There were outstanding sculptures of strapping lads doing Olympian feats and everyday reliefs of guys dressed in robes pointing in important directions and discussing the price of slaves. Old pieces of pot were thankfully conspicuous by their absence, but this was more than made up for by the collection in the museum of the Agora, down at the foot of the Acropolis.

Ruins are all very well, but they do tend to get tedious after a while. In the ancient marketplace, however, they have faithfully reconstructed a two-storey arcade from the second century BC to house the small museum. The clean and simple elegance of the procession of columns gave a real taste of what ancient Greece was all about, and some of the artefacts on show were a cut above the ubiquitous broken pots, statues and busts. There was a potty from the sixth century BC, with a hole for the child's legs so that it couldn't escape, complete with a black and white photograph of an unhappy modern Athenian kid in position and obviously not enjoying the opportunity to imitate his ancestors.

Next came a *kleroterion*, a 2000-year-old lottery machine for electing local officials. It was a large slab of marble with slots for the candidates' name tags and a little hole that was filled with black and white balls to generate winners and losers. It was then that I realised what I found depressing about all those artefacts. The ancient Greeks had done it all before and the rest of the so-called civilised world doesn't appear to have made much headway since. Plato invented academic study and raised all the philosophical questions that still tax humankind. Doctors the world over still pay tribute to Hippocrates every time they take his oath. Nobody has written better fables than Aesop, better epics than Homer, or better tragedies than Sophocles. Every modern European citizen can cite the story behind 'Eureka' and has some idea why we run the marathon. From Achilles' heel to Zeus's thunderbolt, things ancient and Greek continue to influence our every supposedly modern turn. They had seen it all before. They had been there and done it 2000 years ago. And what progress have the rest of us made since then? We invented the T-shirt.

As if I hadn't seen enough ruins, I went to Delphi for the day with Chat Tours. We sped out of the *nefos* in an air-conditioned bus heading north, through a parched landscape of balding hills and ochre road cuttings. This was retsina and turpentine country, our guide explained, the main products derived from the plantations of pine trees that greened the otherwise pallid scene. The rolling hills promised bigger things in the distance as we turned west into cotton country, endless fields of knee-high bushes succoured by industrial sprinklers that spat their waters through the morning heat. The blazing sunshine supplied a dash of rainbow to the agricultural setting as it caught the jets of spray.

The man on the microphone kept up a steady flow of information in English and French on places of interest we passed. Over to the right was Marathon, scene of the battle and that epic but fateful run with the news. Here was Thebes, once a notable city state, now an insignificant agricultural town where ragged bands of gypsies arrived each year to help with the harvest. Classical references and mythical stories were neatly spliced with more contemporary information. One moment we were passing the spot where Oedipus was supposed to have killed his father ('But of course,' our guide told us in what turned out to be his favourite phrase, 'nothing can be seen today'), and a bit further on was where they were mining bauxite.

When we weren't passing anything of interest, the guide filled in with background material. Did we know that there were 150 million olive trees in Greece, and that some of them lived to be 3000 years old? Did we also know that Greece is a very mountainous country? He laboured that point. We may think of Switzerland when we hear about mountains, he warned, but we had been misled, because Greece is the third most mountainous country in Europe, after Norway and Albania. And talking of Europe, did we know that the ancient Greeks invented that too? I groaned inwardly. Our continent was named after a mythical goddess called Europa whose beauty inspired celestial superstar Zeus to dress up as a white bull and carry her off to Crete. Just why her name was subsequently applied to a continent was not exactly clear.

'And what about the roadside shrines you have no doubt noticed?' continued our fountain of factual knowledge. They were a modern Greek custom, he informed us, put up by the survivors of road accidents. 'You'll see lots of them,' he said cheerfully and apparently oblivious to the fact that we were speeding along in a motor vehicle, 'because there are lots of accidents in Greece.'

We forged on, after a brief coffee stop at Levadia's Friendly Shop, into some more serious mountains and the guide started his Delphi commentary. The complex was devoted to the god Apollo and was set on the craggy slopes of Mount Parnassus. The famous oracle was a virgin who played the futures market from the comfort of a drug-induced stupor. She took up position next to a fissure in the rocks and sniffed sulphurous fumes while chewing laurel leaves. When she got really high, she came out with an ambiguous statement to hedge her bets. The sulphurous fissure was in the Temple of Apollo, our guide told us, 'But of course,' he added inevitably, 'nothing can be seen today.' After a few more 'But of course, nothing can be seen today's, I began to wonder just what we would be seeing today. Stupid of me really. The answer was obvious: more ruins.

After that I thought I'd see some islands. I booked myself on to a vessel called the *John P*, a curious name for a ship. It was like a minor cruise liner with shops, two bars, a bank, a cafeteria and a forward lounge with a temporary exhibition of horrible oil paintings for sale. It had two resident photographers who were intent on snapping pictures of anything that moved and quite a lot that didn't, which covered most of the passengers lounging on deck in the sunshine. There were three Saronic Gulf islands on our itinerary, and thankfully none of them came with a guided tour attached.

Aegina was our first port of call. The main town was kitted out with the standard tourist cafés and shops. Roadside stalls were selling honey and pistachio nuts and chunks of stuff covered in white powder which, inevitably I suppose, was labelled Greek Delight. There were cute little Moke Jeeps for hire, with 'No problem' painted on the side, and polite notices outside the waterfront church forbidding entry to nudists. But sandwiched between the knick-knack emporia were real butchers' shops selling skinned rabbits with their furry tails and feet still on, and a line of pick-ups selling soil-clad vegetables from their backs. Most of the boats in the harbour were honest fishing vessels covered in piles of netting and small, round floats that looked like strings of brown onions.

The water was so deep at Poros that the *John P* could tie up on the main street, dwarfing the T-shirt shop and the bureau de change opposite. The location was impressive. Just a few hundred metres away sat the Peloponnesian mainland and small boats constantly plied back and forth across the sparkling blue strait. There was more of a feeling of what you expect from a Greek island: tourism and tavernas and plenty of yachts, most of them with fat brown men at their helms.

In the hour before reaching Hydra, they squeezed in a buffet lunch. I joined the queue behind a French family who looked as if they had just tossed up for a good dinner and lost. They had. We all edged forward from plate to plate hoping that the next would look more appetising than the last, but it didn't. I was issued with a pile of grated cabbage that looked and tasted as if it had just come through a paper shredder, and a dollop of Russian salad submerged in mayonnaise that dated from the October Revolution. A ration of processed ham was followed by a slice of processed cheese and a small cheese pastry that tasted like dust and formed a small indigestible wodge in the mouth after the first nibble. The only things they couldn't mess up were the olives (three each) and the fresh peaches (one per person).

I followed the bewildered French family to a table where we were descended upon by an army of butch waitresses who looked like weightlifters in drag. They demanded to know what we intended to drink with our lunch, and to add insult to injury, they charged us extra for it. The French contingent touched very little of their meal, but to my disgust I found myself eating the lot. The Gallic family looked on, awe-struck by such blatant proof of the British indifference to all things culinary. I put it down to the sea air.

We called in at Hydra and I could see why the jet set have taken to the place. The terracotta-tiled roofs of the main town clung to the steep hillside that enclosed the harbour along with the prickly pears and the fig trees. Day-trippers and the odd backpacker mixed it with a few members of high society who weren't hidden away in their own elegant mansions elsewhere on the island. On the terraces, young Greek playboys languished with their lissom playmates while their older equivalents had become past masters at making each second seem like an hour. Perhaps the women spent their time arranging their abundant gold jewellery and dying their hair unlikely shades of blond. Whilst the younger ones could pass themselves off as sexy sirens, the older ones only succeeded in looking like mutton dressed up as money.

On the voyage back to Athens, I was perched up on deck reading a book when a young Japanese woman approached and asked very politely whether the seat next to mine was occupied. She sat down and we exchanged a bit of conversation. She had just finished a two-year stint working for the Japanese equivalent of Voluntary Services Overseas in Kenya, and was taking a meandering route home. After several African cities, this was her last stop before Tokyo. It was her first visit to Europe other than an overnight stop in a hotel near Heathrow. Why had she chosen Greece, I wondered. 'Because it is a mysterious country,' she replied, 'full of gods.'

That evening I was back in the streets of the Plaka. Summer visitors were milling past the pavement restaurants to look at the menus and the tourist emporiums to check out the sponges and T-shirts. The kiss-me-quick brigade was giggling at the postcards of Greek pottery scenes which look quaint and authentic from a distance and on closer examination reveal their depiction of explicit sex scenes.

As in other parts of Mediterranean Europe, the usual nationalities were augmented by a sprinkling of Russians, now not as noticeable as they were a few years ago because many of them have invested in some Western clothes. But their arrival on the tourist scene was

222

confirmed by the presence of *Pravda* on the news-stands alongside the usual international assortment of papers. In hotels all across southern Europe too, fire regulations and day-trip brochures had been translated into Russian. Here the Russians may even have had an edge over other nationalities since the Cyrillic alphabet shares many letters with Greek.

I sat down at a table in a square, ordered a beer and watched the world go by, much of it consisting of young women with handbags designed as tiny rucksacks to be worn on their backs. They must have been very useful for keeping paper clips in. Freelance entrepreneurs were working the tables trying to earn a crust. A fat man with a shock of hair that had gone grey down the middle was touring the couples like a badger with a violin. Hot on his heels was another gentleman carrying a Polaroid camera, followed by a gypsy girl with an armful of red roses.

A middle-aged guy who had been hovering nearby asked me the time in Greek and I showed him my watch. Being British, I was immediately suspicious when he claimed to have thought I was a local and then asked to sit down while he waited for someone who was half an hour late to meet him. What did I think of Athens, he asked me, and I told him it was lucky to have the Acropolis. He agreed.

'Athens is just a city,' he said with a dismissive wave of the hand, 'nothing more.' He was from Crete, he said, 'a very beautiful island', but he worked in Saudi Arabia. He surprised me when, after a couple more looks around, he said good evening and left.

A young guy wearing dungarees was doing the tables now, selling small square coloured boxes that he claimed could be used as a multi-purpose present. He must have strained every muscle in his head thinking of that one.

I finished my beer, paid up and went on a wander. I stopped at a stall for a snack. I like doner kebabs. Done well, they are more real than a hot dog and more honest than a hamburger. Eating at least one kebab is as much a part of the late twentieth-century Grand Tour as visiting the Atomium in Brussels or taking a sauna in Finland. In Greece they call them pittas and they are filled from *gyros*, those slowly turning hunks of meat that don't resemble any animal I've ever seen and to me have worryingly canine undertones. Presiding over each one is a man with a cigarette dangling from his lip who sweats profusely and looks as if he has something heavy weighing on his conscience. But the product he serves is juicy, satisfying and bursting with exotic flavours. It's just that they ought to come clean and call it a Trojan Dog.

Within five minutes, I had been asked the time and 'mistaken' for a Greek again. This time it was a scam. I was asked whether I was interested in some beautiful girls. Beautiful girls did interest me, I told him, but not the ones he was peddling. And compared to the Dutch, I felt like saying, you guys are a long way behind the times when it comes to selling sex. Less than 100 metres down the road it happened again. This guy was more measured in his approach. He introduced himself as Pavlos and said he was in the clothing business, based in Cyprus. He had slightly bloodshot eyes set in a gaunt face framed by straggly black hair. A black moustache had grown down to cover his pointy chin. He looked like a direct descendent of the King of Diamonds.

The two of us ambled along exchanging pleasantries. Pavlos was a designer, he told me, but he was doing a sales trip because the usual salesman was on his honeymoon in Spain. It was a long time since he'd been in Athens and this part of town had quietened down a lot. All the clubs had gone and now there was just this string of tourist shops and restaurants.

I thought perhaps Pavlos was legitimate. Why bother with this story if all he wanted was to sell me something? When he suggested we go for a drink, I agreed. Pavlos didn't like the look of all these tourist joints, but he said he knew a place near his hotel, which wasn't far. I still harboured my suspicions, but what the hell, I thought to myself.

We sauntered down a long, ill-lit main street, Pavlos chatting away about this and that as the evening traffic shot past and pumped noxious gases at us. 'Too many cars,' mused Pavlos, 'too much pollution.' He didn't strike me as an environmentalist but he seemed quite passionate when he said it. 'In Cyprus I ride a bicycle,' he added. I hadn't seen anyone riding a bike in Athens and I said so. 'No, I wouldn't like to ride a bicycle here,' he replied, 'too dangerous.'

We were passing one of the metro construction sites that were all over the place in Athens. A huge crane, surrounded by a selection of wooden and metal fencing, rose up towards a sickle-shaped moon.

On the fencing was a blue metal plaque indicating the involvement of Greece's friends in the European Union. 'You want to know what I'd do if I was prime minister?' asked Pavlos, I assumed rhetorically. 'I'd do two things. First I would ban cars, then I would make cigarettes two hundred dollars a pack.' I nodded. 'Cigarettes are bad for you,' he declared as if this might be information I had not encountered before. 'People don't work as hard when they smoke, and look at the hospital bills. Think of the savings you would make.' He sounded suspiciously like an ex-smoker to me.

'You wouldn't be very popular, everyone smokes in Greece.'

'I know. I used to smoke,' he told me. 'I gave up a year ago. Now I feel much better.' He waved his hand at a line of stationary traffic in front of a red light. 'Make them all ride bicycles,' he declared.

We crossed the road and there on the corner in front of us was a large pink neon sign indicating the presence of a strip club. Pavlos hailed the man at the door beneath the pink sign. 'This is it,' he announced. I was disappointed and I declined Pavlos's invitation to enter. I was considering the fact that I only had 2000 drachma in my pocket, and working on the premise that it is easier to walk into places like this than to walk out. Besides, I had already done sex in Amsterdam. 'OK,' said Pavlos unperturbed, 'nice talking to you.' And he disappeared into the night club.

As I retraced my steps back towards the Hotel Austria, past the drivers who should have been riding bicycles, I reflected on what friendly people the Greeks were. But then I'd been following a tourist trail, so I suppose they would be. I had certainly come across many of the stereotypes we in Britain commonly associate with the country, but what with all the ruins and islands I realised that I'd missed out on the Greece behind the postcards. Careless, that. I was on a rat run of a side street leading up to my hotel when I stopped outside an open-fronted greasy spoon that I'd passed many times that week. It was always populated by old men having their dinner or enjoying a smoke and a drink. They didn't look as if they would be interested in their tourist visitors, so I stepped into the café and sat down.

The decor was red and white and rudimentary. A giant salad spoon and fork hung on either side of a wall clock that had been given away many years ago by a drinks company, and the lampshades must have looked dated in the 1960s. An antiquated television set mounted on a bracket was broadcasting Olympic weightlifting from

Atlanta. Opposite the TV, the wall was taken up by a metal spit affair with a few solitary cooked sausages hanging on it and adjacent to this was a bar stocked mainly with an assortment of different-sized glasses. From behind the bar, a terrible hag with a cigarette drooping cartoon-like from her lower lip asked me in English what I wanted. I turned to face her and asked what she had to eat. She moved across to the spit, pushed the grey-haired man in front of it out of my line of view, and pointed at the sorry sausages. As an afterthought, she said, 'Chicken,' and pointed to an unidentifiable chunk of charred meat dangling next to them on the spit. I plumped for the sausages. 'Salad?' she asked. I had no idea how much this was going to cost, so I pulled out my two banknotes to show her and said, 'I only have a couple of thousand drachma, is it enough?'

The man in front of the spit took his eyes off the weightlifting and said, 'That's more than I've got.' He spoke in Greek, but there was no doubt about what he said. I could afford both.

Everyone was concentrating on the weightlifting, in which a Greek contestant was seemingly neck-and-neck with a citizen of one of the former Soviet republics. As I tucked into my sausages, a man wearing a waistcoat walked in carrying a plastic bag full of fat tomatoes and sat down at my table. He placed the tomatoes on the chair beside him, nodded at me and asked for something from the man in charge of the spit. He chose the chicken.

Behind my dining partner, an elderly gent alone at his table got up to help himself from a bottle of retsina on the bar. He carefully filled a small orange plastic jug which he took back to his table. From the jug he poured a large measure into his chipped glass. The hag shuffled over with the chicken for the man sat opposite me. The minutes passed. We all ate in almost total silence, transfixed by the heavyweights on the TV screen. The only sounds were the cars honking their horns on the street outside and the squeak of sausage skins on my teeth.

I had no idea whether the man in the waistcoat could speak English, but after a few smiles, I asked him if he thought the Greek would win. 'Oh yes,' he said confidently, and in English, 'the gold medal. This is a recording. Greece is very good at weights.' As if in confirmation, the picture changed to show the medal ceremony and then moved on to some talking heads in the studio. The man had finished his chicken by this time and he asked me where I was from and what I was doing in Athens. I told him and he nodded as he sucked his teeth.

'On the whole the European Union is good for Greece,' he told me immediately, 'because we are a poor country.' He looked up and said something to the man in charge of the spit who nodded in agreement and made a comment in Greek. 'He says, "Unless you make feta." We have been fighting against Brussels to protect our feta cheese,' he added in explanation. I had read something on the subject in the paper a few days before. The man was making ready to leave. Remembering the stuffy banker I had conversed with in Luxembourg, I asked him about the euro: would Greeks mind losing the drachma if Europe got a single currency? He smiled with his plastic bag of tomatoes in his hand. 'We must say "evro",' he replied, '"uro" means another thing.' And he bade me farewell.

When I got back to the Hotel Austria, I asked the man on the desk, who had lived in England for several years, what 'uro' meant in Greek. 'Urine,' he told me.

12

Priests on Call, Robbers on Crutches

From one end of Europe, I went to the other. A couple of weeks later, I was heading towards the most north-westerly outpost of the Union. It was just a thirty-five-minute hop from Birmingham International Airport across St George's Channel to Dublin. I had considered catching a coach and crossing to Ireland by ferry, but gave up on the idea during an attack of laziness. Fortunately, Ryan Air did a fair impression of a coach firm. It was a sort of do-it-yourself airline: you could sit where you liked and you had to buy your own drinks. On this run they used a Boeing 737, the type of aeroplane that looks as if its engines are coming apart from the wing when it lands.

I was looking forward to seeing Dublin because I had missed it last time around. It was more than a year since I had flown in under the auspices of the Danish Energy Agency to sit at a conference table in Howth, a small fishing village at the northern end of the Dublin Area Rapid Transport system, or DART as they call it. Like most visitors on business, all I had seen was the inside of a conference room, a few boats in a harbour and an evening of fiddling in the local pub. We were much too busy with Europe's energy-efficient washing machines to bother about sightseeing.

My one abiding memory of that visit was the breakfasts, the central feature of which was the Fry. By this stage in my travels, I was pretty close to completing a European league table of breakfasts and there was little doubt that the Irish version would come out on top. If you spend any length of time in Irish B&B accommodation you will comfortably exceed all international guidelines for annual cholesterol intake. The whole collection of early morning food items swims towards you in a sea of saturated fats crying 'heart attack'. It's surprising that Brussels hasn't issued an edict against it. The bacon floats in a pool of lard, the sausages glisten with grease, the fried egg bobs in a coronary ooze, the tomatoes and mushrooms drift in an ocean of butter and the black pudding needs a life-raft. The Irish breakfast flies in the face of all known medical opinion and it's great. Continental breakfasts, eat your heart out. In Ireland real men don't eat croissants.

Starting each day with such a vigorous assault on the bloodstream was the perfect preparation for my treks around the streets of Dublin. I was staying in a place north of the River Liffey just off O'Connell Street, a wide thoroughfare studded with statues of Irish heroes and lined with the usual fast-food outlets and cheap souvenir shops. From the outside the Gate Hotel did not appear to encourage patronage. Its doorway was hidden away behind a matt grey exterior with no windows. Access was gained via a push-button intercom that made you feel as if you were entering a dodgy night club or an illegal gambling joint. Inside it was nothing more than a perfectly respectable hostelry with a smiling young woman behind the desk, the times of mass in the 'Information for Guests', and the usual concession to leprechauns in the bathroom: the only explanation I could think of for the curious Irish custom of positioning their mirrors at navel-height above the basin. Either that, or normal-sized Irishmen like to double up their ablutions and religious duties by shaving in a kneeling position.

When I handed my key in at the reception desk in the morning, after renewing my acquaintance with the inestimable Irish Fry, the middle-aged man in charge looked at me quizzically and said he was going to London next week. 'I'm flying to Stansted,' he declared. 'Can you tell me how do I get to Russell Square?'

He asked in such a matter-of-fact way, as if we were standing on the platform at Euston station and I was a ticket collector, that I was momentarily lost for words. In truth, I had absolutely no idea, but I couldn't tell him that. 'Umm, I expect there will be a bus into London,' I said lamely. He nodded sagely, his brow furrowed in concentration. 'Then you can get the tube.' He nodded again, digesting the information. 'I've not been to London before, you see,' he said hesitantly, 'and I don't want to get lost or do anything stupid.'

I felt sorry that I couldn't be more helpful, but assured him that there would be an information bureau at Stansted that would be able to help him. There was a pause, and I was half expecting him to ask whether I knew John Major or Kevin Keegan, when he nodded more definitely. 'The information bureau: that's what I'll be needing.'

The incident was symptomatic of Dublin, and Ireland in general. Although I had unconsciously been expecting all the EU countries to have great big anonymous cities for capitals, Dublin, like Helsinki and Stockholm, managed to combine its urban status with a hospitable and homespun air. For the British visitor, this is a particular relief. I think most of us who venture westward to the Emerald Isle do so with some degree of trepidation simply because all we ever hear about the place is news from the troubled Ulster counties of the North. I went to Northern Ireland once, and found the same feeling of warmth and familiarity. It was just the combat soldiers on the streets and the police stations that looked like fortresses that put me off. But as in the North, Dublin was equipped with lots of reassuring touchstones from home, like the familiar designs of the postboxes, although they were all painted green, and the fact that the shops shut at expected times. Outside on Parnell Street, khaki-green double-decker buses lumbered past driving on the left-hand side of the road.

The sun was shining and people were hurrying along to get to work by nine o'clock. It was warm and bright, and Dublin was already filling with tourists. I had no idea it was such an attraction to Europeans as well as Americans, but they must have all positively decided to come here because being an island on the outskirts of a continent it wasn't exactly on the way to anywhere else. Being a writer, I made a beeline for the Dublin Writers Museum which was tucked away behind a red-brick Georgian façade on Parnell Square.

One of the extraordinary aspects of this unpretentious little country on the edge of Europe is its contribution to literature. As the initial blurb inside the museum's first room put it, 'This unlikely spot has, by some quirk of socio-historical chemistry, given birth to an undue proportion of the world's greatest writers, both in its native Irish and in the language generically known as English.' Whoever they hired to pen the commentary, which must have been a daunting task, liked to get the odd swipe in about the English. You can imagine the glee with which the following was written: 'It has been claimed that the greatest weapon the English ever gave the Irish was their own language.' It's a good point, of course, but it's a shame this character forgot about the possessive apostrophe in the museum's title.

The place had an interesting collection of odds and sods from the galaxy of Irish literary greats: a first edition here, a first-night programme there; James Joyce's upright piano from his Trieste days; and the typewriter that Brendan Behan was supposed to have thrown through a pub window. The roll call sounded like a reading list for middle-aged self-improvement: Jonathan Swift, Oliver Goldsmith, Bram Stoker, W. B. Yeats, George Bernard Shaw, Oscar Wilde, Samuel Beckett. Upstairs, the Gallery of Writers was an airy, sun-drenched room with a painted ceiling on golden columns. It was lined with portraits and busts of the literati. Swift was pondering the injustices of life from beneath the red sock on his head, and Shaw looked like a kindly grandpa in his huge grey beard. A young Yeats looked as if he knew how clever he was behind his little round glasses, and Behan's head looked fit to burst due to an excess of alcohol. I found it depressing, because apart from appearing in student productions of a couple of their plays, I hadn't read any of them. I never set out to write books, it just sort of happened. If I'd meant to do it, perhaps I'd have taken a different route and absorbed a few of these characters' masterpieces on the way. Some of my friends express surprise when they come to my house and see that I don't possess many books, but I just tell them I'm too busy writing my own to read other people's.

I did a circle of Parnell Square, checked out the Garden of Remembrance in the middle – dedicated to those who gave their lives in the cause of Irish freedom – and passed the Sinn Fein bookshop. It was by the number 36 bus stop, next door to the Leinster Football Association. A poster in its window said 'Ban the RUC'. I made my way down O'Connell Street and crossed the river by a bridge that had the interesting distinction of being wider than it was long. Below the waterline on one side, a digital clock of green numbers told you how many seconds there were to go before the year 2000. It was more than a hundred million, but it was difficult to say precisely because several of the luminous bars had already given up the ghost. The odd lone street musician, who looked as if he really needed your contribution north of the Liffey, gave way to groups of respectable middle-class kids who expected payment for doing their violin practice in public. It was here that I entered the hallowed confines of Trinity College, the country's most famous university. Past the Corinthian columns and through the classical portico was a haven of peace from the busy streets outside. It was just like its Oxford counterparts apart from the plaintive cries of the seagulls.

Many of the literary figures commemorated in the Dublin Writers Museum had studied here and the main attraction that brings the crowds to Trinity College is also a piece of writing. *The Book of Kells* is an unfinished religious manuscript of indeterminate age. It is not the oldest old book in the College's vast collection, but it has been around for more than a thousand years. It is a sort of medieval coffee-table bible, weighing in at 680 pages of glorious full-colour artwork and text, produced on the vellum hides of nearly two hundred young calves. The book forms the central feature of an exhibition space set up with a little help from the European Regional Development Fund, and hordes of tourists were edging their way past the displays for a chance to see Ireland's most famous publication. Needless to say, when the time came the visitor only got the briefest of glances, but above the book, in the library's Long Room, the homage to literature continued with a long line of alcoves containing a multitude of other leather-bound volumes.

Among the manuscripts and marble busts sat a glass case that held Ireland's oldest harp, an oak and willow affair with twenty-nine strings. Legend has it that the harp belonged to Brian Boru, an Irish king who died while fighting the Vikings in 1014, but scientists have spoilt that one by dating the instrument to the fifteenth century. Whether or not it belonged to King Brian, the harp has been adopted as an emblem of the country's early bardic society to appear as a national symbol on state documents and Irish money. As it happens, the same harp has also been adopted as the badge of the country's best-known liquid export. Hence, foreigners can be forgiven for thinking that Irish banknotes are sponsored by Guinness.

It is appropriate that *The Book of Kells* is a religious tome because, as everyone knows, the Irish are a pretty religious lot. Where else in Europe can you see 'No Parking' signs prefaced with 'Priest on Call'? Christianity was brought to the Irish by Patrick, a Roman Briton who was kidnapped by Irish raiders and sentenced to seven years' swine herding before he escaped back across the Irish Sea. But after a moving dream, he gave up on his swine-herding career and became a Catholic missionary instead. Things went pretty well for Ireland with their new religion, until they were sold out by Pope Adrian, who granted overlordship of Ireland to Henry II of England in the twelfth century. The Greeks may moan about 400 years of Turkish rule, but that was nothing. The Irish got nearly twice as long under the English, and pretty mean we were to them, too, by all accounts.

It didn't start out so bad. For the first few hundred years, English control over the country receded until we were left with just an area round Dublin known as the Pale. 'Beyond the Pale' were just a bunch of Celts who weren't particularly interesting. It wasn't until the 1500s that we really got down to some serious repression. Catholicism was bad for the Irish and we knew it. Over the centuries we sent all sorts of Protestant missionaries to explain it to them, from Oliver Cromwell to the Black and Tans, but they never got the message.

In the eighteenth century, when the English gentry were Grand Touring it round the rest of Europe, Ireland was a backwater. Things had actually been getting a bit better since we gave them the potato, especially as we charged them rent for the land to grow it on, but as Charles Theodore Middleton described, the 'wild' Irish lived in 'mean huts or cabins built of clay and straw' and resembled the ancient Britons as described by Roman authors. We weren't interested in ancient Irish culture, not that there was much of it left by then. We went over there to civilise them by offering our own and they've had a chip on their shoulder about it ever since.

It should come as no surprise then that O'Connell Street is so full of statues and plaques about tyranny and slavery and rising up to melt the snows of lethargy. What is surprising is that they waited until 1966 to blow up the Dublin version of Nelson's Column that stood outside the General Post Office. Especially since this was where the Easter Rising took place in 1916. Today there is a bronze statue of the legendary warrior Cúchulainn in the sturdy grey GPO walls, commemorating the participants of April 1916 and their proclamation of an Irish republic. It took a couple of nasty civil wars and another thirty years before the country actually became a republic. They replaced Nelson's Column with a flowerbed.

The GPO is still a potent symbol of nationalism, so it was ironic to see a Union Jack hanging inside its refurbished interior. But it hangs along with the other flags of the EU countries on the balcony. This dilution of the link with Britain is one of the reasons why the Irish like being in the European Union. They're so keen that they have even adopted the EU design for vehicle licence plates, with the blue flag at one end, a concept pooh-poohed by every other country except Portugal. But like Portugal, Eire does quite well out of it all, and nowhere else in Europe are the benefits of membership more overt than they are in the Irish Republic. Everywhere you go, the visitor is confronted with blue plaques and notices informing you that this or that has been built with help from the European Regional Development Fund. On bridges and beside roads, at harbours and water-pumping stations, and in every other museum in Dublin, that tell-tale circle of yellow stars hovers like a halo over the latest act of munificence from Brussels. So common are these indicators, in fact, that it makes you wonder what the Irish did before they joined the EU.

The answer is, apart from producing literature, that they bred babies for export. As any demographer will tell you, Ireland has a unique place in European social history. Put simply, they still haven't recovered from the potato famine of the mid-1840s. On the eve of the terrible blight, the population stood at just over eight million. Then one million people died and another one and a half million emigrated overnight. They've been leaving in droves virtually continuously ever since. Today, despite still producing babies at an alarming rate, the population hasn't yet made it back to the four million mark. Until recently, you had to be pretty desperate to up roots and move *to* Ireland. One of those who did, a man named Beshoff, came in 1913 and set up a fish and chip shop in Dublin. It's still there on O'Connell Street. He came all the way from Odessa to do it.

The Irish never followed Dean Jonathan Swift's modest proposal concerning babies, however. He suggested that, as a means of reducing Ireland's poverty, the poor might offer some of their numerous infants for sale to the wealthy English as food, hence both relieving themselves of the burden of their education and making a bit of cash at the same time. Swift was one of the earliest of a long line of sharp Irish wits whose satire was aimed primarily at the English. But not exclusively. Down in Saint Patrick's Cathedral, where he was dean for more than thirty years in the eighteenth century, they have kept his wooden pulpit and an old bookcase with memorabilia in it. One of the books was open at his 'Sermon upon sleeping in church'.

Next door to the cathedral, through a tiny cottage garden with a sprawling rosemary bush by the steps, is Ireland's first public library, where Swift was a governor for many years. It was full of sagging black oak shelves, uneven floors and the smell of books in various states of decay. At the end and round the corner were three alcoves sealed with metal cage wire where they locked you in with rare books, but chief among today's exhibits was a glass case with more Swiftian memorabilia. Next to his pallid grey death mask was a venerable book about the history of rebellion and civil wars in England. Swift had scribbled rude comments about the Scots all over the margins. A modern explanatory note referred lovingly to his 'annotations'. Today, librarians shoot people for defacing books like that.

It is probably at least partly due to the acid wit of people like Swift that the Irish joke has evolved in England as a form of retaliation. We think the Irish are stupid. Here is an example.

An Englishman, a Scotsman and an Irishman are sitting in the pub celebrating the birth of the Englishman's first son. 'What are you going to call him?' asks the Scotsman. 'Well,' replies the Englishman, 'since he was born on Saint George's Day we're going to call him George.' 'Good idea,' says the Scotsman, 'we did the same. Our son was born on Saint Andrew's Day and we named him Andrew.' 'Same here,' exclaims the Irishman, 'my son's called Pancake.'

Here's another. An Irishman finds a monkey and asks a policeman what he should do with it. 'Take it to the zoo,' advises the policeman. The following day, the policeman sees the Irishman walking along the street hand-in-hand with the monkey. 'I told you to take that monkey to the zoo,' says the policeman. 'To be sure you did,' replies the Irishman, 'but that was yesterday. Today we're going to the cinema.'

Stupidity, naïveté, Irish logic, call it what you will, but one thing I'd found during my travels round Europe was that the propensity for one nation to poke fun in a superior way at its neighbour is by no means solely an Anglo-Irish preserve. Call the Irishman a Belgian and you'd have a French or Dutch joke, call him a Norwegian and the joke would be Swedish. Most European countries also have internal groups to ridicule for being a bit slow-witted. In France it's the Bretons, in Germany the Ostfriesen, in the Netherlands it's people from the province of Limburg. In Denmark it is the citizens of

Århus. Ole, my mentor in Copenhagen, told me this one: what does an Århuser do when he goes to the toilet? He takes the door off so that nobody can peep through the keyhole.

Groups who are careful with their money are another common target. In England this means the Scots, in Belgium the Dutch. Within Spain, it's the Catalans. A man in Madrid explained to me that these jokes always concern a guy named Jordi.

Jordi's wife has just died so he goes to the office of the local newspaper to arrange an obituary notice. 'What would you like to say?' asks the clerk. '"Maria's dead",' says Jordi, clearly distraught. 'But for the standard fee you can have ten words,' explains the clerk kindly. 'Ah,' says Jordi, 'OK then, add "Second-hand seat for sale".'

Religion didn't often crop up in these sorts of jokes, as far as I could see, but in this case Eire was a bit of an exception. I wasn't quite sure how I was supposed to react when a Dubliner told me this one in a pub one evening.

An innocent tourist walked across the no man's land between a Protestant and a Catholic area of Belfast, whereupon he was challenged by a masked gunman. 'Are you a Protestant or a Catholic?' demanded the gunman. 'Neither,' said the visitor, 'I'm a Jew.' 'That's as maybe,' replied the gunman from inside his balaclava, 'but are you a Protestant or Catholic Jew?'

Still on my literary kick, I went looking for Shaw's birthplace. I hadn't originally intended to, but the young man at the Writers Museum had sold me a double ticket at a knock-down price and I hadn't been able to resist the bargain. I found it in a Victorian part of town where the kerbstones were made of solid granite and leafy plane trees made the streets dim even at midday. The shadows followed me inside the little terraced brick dwelling. It reminded me of childhood Christmas visits to my grandparents' house in Sheffield: there were the same wine-red velvet tablecloths, the same round-backed shiny polished chairs, their seats stuffed with horsehair, and the chunky clock on the mantelpiece flanked by china dogs. At the fireplaces sat the same tongs and shovel and bellows and brush; on the sofa the same lacy white antimacassars that as a child I never understood. There were jugs and bowls in every bedroom, heavy drapes and net curtains at all the windows and a carved wooden hatstand in the hallway. A familiar dark musty smell pervaded throughout. Even the sepia family portrait photographs looked redolent of Victorian Middletons. Shaw had just the hint of a sneer in all of them, and in his early twenties a goatee that was to develop into his characteristic white whiskers.

To guide me round Shaw's house, the girl in charge had paused from discussing her exam results on the telephone to hand me a small tape recorder and headphones. A time machine, the commentary called it. It made everything easy, telling you where to stand and what to look at, and even gave you special sound effects to lend some atmosphere to the proceedings.

Time machine was about right. The only part of Dublin I found that came close to the recorded clamour of vendors on the street outside was back on the north side of the river, on a short stretch of Henry Street. It was here that I did a double-take, because the small gaggle of middle-aged ladies looked just like the ones occasionally seen selling sprigs of heather on the streets of Oxford. Only here they were with their menfolk and selling something more useful. If they updated the Dublin ballad about sweet Molly Malone, she wouldn't be wheeling her wheelbarrow through streets broad and narrow, she'd be standing on the corner of Henry Street crying, 'Cigarettes and tobacco at two pounds a pack.'

The cigarette-sellers were out-shouting the stallholders on Moore Street, where the vegetables, flowers and fish were replaced by stray giant seagulls drawn to the lingering smell of seafood for the evening shift. Elsewhere at the end of the day, shop keepers placed metal bollards in holes in front of their premises to protect against night-time ram-raiders. But such devices proved useless against the determined thief. Tucked away on page four of the *Irish Independent* one morning was a news story that seemed to confirm the English prejudice about the way things happen in Ireland. Beneath the headline 'Robber on Crutches' was the story of a disabled man who held up a twenty-four-hour shop in central Dublin by claiming to be in possession of a shotgun. Two hours after hobbling away with the loot, he returned to squeeze another thirty pounds from bemused staff. With appropriate understatement, the story concluded that the Gardai were expecting an early arrest. When I thought about it, I could imagine the same sort of incident happening in Belgium.

Overall, I gave Dublin mixed reviews. Tucked away behind every main thoroughfare was a warren of narrow alleys lined with corrugated iron fences, barbed wire and refuse. These bits looked as sorry and run-down as the grottier parts of Athens, but without the rabid dogs and mangy cats. In Dublin they had drunks instead. Most of the shopping streets looked the same as in Britain, but a few fashion shifts behind the times. Even the push-button street-crossing devices brought back memories of computer game noises in early 1980s student bars; when they told you to cross they sounded like the rapid-fire electronics of Space Invaders. In places, Dublin's role as European City of Culture in 1991 had spawned the apparently standard-issue pieces of street sculpture: tired shoppers sitting down surrounded by bags of shopping. But try as they might, they couldn't really succeed in covering up for a city that looked weary and rather down-at-heel.

There were, of course, pubs everywhere and old 'Guinness is good for you' signs provided an excuse, if you needed it, to cross their thresholds. Trust the Irish to invent a drink that fed you while you were getting quietly sozzled. These establishments did at least look more authentic than any of the mock-Irish theme pubs that have spread like a rash all across Europe. I had seen Plastic O'Grady's and Ersatz O'Reilly's in Paris and Rome, in Copenhagen and Luxembourg City, and even on the Helsinki–Stockholm ferry. They were Disney-fied versions of reality, all designed according to what the marketing men thought Irish pubs ought to look like. The real thing had sawdust on the floor and looked past its sell-by date. The only similarities with the themed version were the colour of the alcohol and the large TV screens, because the Irish have an affinity for gadgets. It's just that in the real Irish pubs the TVs are an afterthought, whilst in the synthetic variety the pubs have been designed around them.

Other types of feeding stops imported from overseas often came with an Irish twist. Try eating in an Indian restaurant where all the waiters are white boys with red hair and freckles; it just doesn't seem right. For fast food, McDonald's and Burger King had a foothold in the Irish market, but they obviously didn't serve enough grease, so a national chain called Abra*kebab*ra had grown to fill the gap. 'Magic food – super service' was their motto but having recently been in the Land of the Trojan Dog I decided against an Irish doner kebab. In among the standard fare lurked some local specialities, however, so I plumped for a venison burger. It was disappointing. I had to wait twenty minutes and when it came it didn't taste of anything at all. 'Bland food – crap service' more like. But the following morning I understood why they'd used the word magic. When I burped unexpectedly in the ticket queue at the bus station, the venison burger tasted bloody good.

It was time to leave Dublin and see a bit of the rest of Ireland. I bought a ticket to Waterford which the man behind the counter validated with a mechanical contraption that would have been considered a museum piece anywhere else in Europe, and jumped on to the bus leaving from bay number 2. The Liffey wasn't going anywhere as we sped out of the capital. It just sat there, its oily surface shimmering in the morning sun, and we soon left it behind as the bus ventured into a land where the signposts were covered in green mould. The sky was a pastel blue with nearly all the cloud types possible neatly stacked up like the diagrams you see in geography textbooks.

We passed through Naas, the chief town of County Kildare, which didn't seem to be much more than a main street. We nipped on and off bits of dual carriageway, where the signposts gave distances in kilometres, to winding country roads where things were still measured in miles. As expected, the countryside was overwhelmingly green, with splashes of bright red poppies on the dual carriageway verges. There was a great sense of space, punctuated every so often with a new house where the poppies had invaded the piles of dug earth to give them the colour of tandoori paste.

We stopped at Carlow, which was bigger than most places and had a large square box on the outskirts that said it had a Braun factory inside. Beside the bus stop, opposite the Superquin supermarket, was a memorial to a local boy who had died in 1960 while serving with the UN forces in the Congo. Elderly gentlemen with tweed caps climbed on and off the bus. The two boys in the seats behind me had finished comparing their exam results and moved on to discuss the girl situation. Somewhere outside Carlow we passed a slip road exiting a motorway that had a large notice saying 'Danger – wrong way – turn back' for anyone thinking they might take an inappropriate short cut.

The display of cloud types had given way to a total cover of dirty cotton wool. Fields of wheat were being cut and tractors pulling trailers piled high with straw bales chugged along the country roads. Thomastown had a pretty riverside location but the main street found it difficult to cope with our bus and a beer tanker at the same time. Gradually the fields got smaller and the hedges larger until we joined the long queue to get into Waterford. A series of notices declared that it was twinned with Saint Herblane in Brittany, had a sister city in Rochester, New York, and was partnered with a district in Kenya. Whatever Waterford has in common with any of these places, I didn't find it.

The bus stopped at the joint rail and bus station on the north bank of the River Suir, although at this point it was wide enough to look like an estuary. I wandered into the train station on the look-out for something to eat. The departures and arrivals board looked home-made, a hotchpotch of chunky hand-painted letters beside times depicted in those square gold and black stick-on numbers you see on new housing estates. A couple of small plaques on the wall by the door said that it had won the medium station category two years running in the Anglo-Irish best station competition. Something must have happened subsequently in the cafeteria because it offered as dispiriting a selection of eats as any British Rail station, but without the glossy packaging. Wrinkled pasties and sad cakes on white plates lined up with a few dejected sandwiches and I decided I could postpone the hunger pangs for a while.

I had more luck across the Brother Edmund Ignatius Rice Bridge, where I bought a pork pie with a side of ham inside for lunch and ate it looking at the breweries and grain silos lined up on the quayside. A couple on a motorcycle stopped at the kerb and a young woman asked me in Italian-English whether they were going the right way for Wexford. I didn't have any idea until she showed me the map. They were driving in the opposite direction. The woman consulted her partner, whose leathers creaked as he turned around, and she translated his comment: 'Perhaps because we have to drive on the wrong side of the road.' The rest of Waterford was busy and bustling. There were tourist emporia selling woollens and tea towels, and more up-market versions that sold Irish Dresden china and every-thing you could possibly imagine that could be made from glass. Away from the river they had built a nasty new shopping mall in which the municipal waste bins were referred to as 'street furniture'.

I caught a local bus run by Suirway Bus and Coach Services for the thirty-minute trip down to Dunmore East, a little place that managed to fit a busy fishing harbour and a beach resort into two dimples in the lower lip of the river mouth. As usual, I hadn't been very organised about this jaunt and I was a bit worried about finding accommodation at the height of the tourist season, but I found a bed in the dormitory-style hostel behind the old harbour house. The place was run in a very leisurely fashion by staff who were almost entirely local teenage girls. They were all very open and chatty and nervous in an endearing way. They all greeted you with 'How are you today?' as if they were genuinely concerned for your welfare and whatever you asked for they said, 'No problem,' as if it really wasn't.

The village was strung out along the main road that climbed up and down just inland from the cliffs. It was one of those laid-back little places where they sell home-made cakes and jam in the local newsagent's, along with a couple of postcards and a bucket and spade. There was a pub and a church, and many of the thatched cottages had turned to the bed and breakfast trade. I spent a relaxed few days wandering the cliff paths and watching the sea anglers pluck their dinners from the green-blue Atlantic, lounging on the springy coastal turf to watch the sun go down before dining on seafood in the old harbour house restaurant.

I shared the dormitory with two Dutch guys who were backpacking their way round the British Isles. I was interested to know what had drawn them to Eire. 'The wide open spaces and the beer,' said the Dutchmen almost in unison. Had it been up to expectation, I wondered. 'Definitely,' came the reply. 'It is one of the few areas of Europe that is still wild,' said one, I think referring to the wide open spaces. 'And the beer is excellent,' chipped in his mate, 'and unlike in England the pubs never close.'

Dunmore East's harbour was continually buzzing with activity. It was tucked in behind the mole which had a lighthouse shaped like a stunted Doric column at the end. Along the quayside, nets, ropes and cables were laid out to be worked upon beside half a dozen decaying containers lined up and then forgotten. Sitting in the water were dozens of small trawlers, their masts bristling with antennae and lights. At any time of the day or night one of them seemed to be unloading at the quay in front of the auction house crowded with men in yellow waders. A small crowd of holidaymakers would usually gather round to watch as stacks of white plastic Co-operative boxes were swung up from the hold by a boom, for a fork-lift to transfer into the shed. The catches had already been sorted, each box containing a different fish beneath a layer of crushed ice. I recognised sole and plaice, the blue patterned sheen of shiny mackerel that matched the sky, large crayfish and small sharks. An old-timer who was helping to line up the boxes as they were landed pointed out monkfish and turbot, rays and ling. While the trawler-men were unloading their catches, squawking gulls descended on to the rolls of nets at the stern to tug at what titbits had been left behind.

Away from the harbour, a cliffside park led round the headland to the sandy beach. There were blackcurrant bushes and large fuchsias and hard green sloes in the hedgerows. Everywhere I looked, rocks and fences and concrete seats were splotched with yellow lichen. A mother was changing her baby's nappy on a flat boulder, while behind her a group of local boys was seeing how many times they could get the adjective 'fuckin' ' into a sentence as they made their way down to the sea with their towels to bathe.

The beach was only a beach when the tide was out from the sea wall that towered as tall as a house. When it did go out, it left a fair bit of seaweed strewn across its dark sands but this didn't perturb the families who had come to play. Laid out in various shades of white, most of them were Irish. As I knew from my conversations in the dormitory, the few continental Europeans who had made it down to this remote spot hadn't really come for the beaches. They stood on the sea wall wearing jumpers and licking their ice creams as they marvelled at the chalky northerners on the beach below. I joined them one afternoon, with a book and a cornet, to observe a nation at leisure.

Mums and dads and grandparents sunned themselves and read the paper, while the next generation got down to all the normal seaside activities. There were a few rudimentary sandcastles, a junior long-jump competition, and beach tennis for the under-tens in which no point lasted longer than a single shot. One boy was digging for treasure (or was it Australia?), while another was being buried up to his neck by his brothers, an exploit that came to an abrupt end when his sister appeared carrying a bucketful of water. A gentle breeze, tinged with the smell of the sea and seaweed, blew over the proceedings, making the one windbreak that had been set up redundant. This also explained the poor performance of the two windsurfers out beyond the gentle lapping of the mini-waves. They shared the water with a plethora of rubber dinghies and a canoeist.

Dogs who wanted to play, but weren't appreciated on the beach, hovered at a loss on the edges of the games. When they tried to join in, they usually got the brush-off. All except one, that is. A large black bulldog had decided that the best game to play with a Frisbee was trying to get it into your mouth. A group of youngsters looked on forlornly as the great black beast took a good ten minutes to verify the impossibility of the task, before abandoning the luminous yellow object and trotting off for a paddle. As it did so, a small boy, still in shock, was carried past by his father, a scarlet stream of blood on his leg after a fall on the rocks.

The scene could have been almost anywhere in Europe, except for the absence of a teenage contingent who had all gone to the Oasis concert in Cork, and the fact that everyone, even the tiniest tots, was wearing a swimming costume. It was not surprising that a nation which still wavered over the modern realities of divorce and abortion hadn't discovered topless sunbathing yet.

On my last day, a huge white ocean liner appeared to sit at anchor a few hundred metres out and motor launches plied back and forth to ferry its passengers in for a day in rural Ireland. The sun was bright again and I overheard an American woman complaining about it because she hadn't brought her hot weather gear. 'They told us it was going to be cold in Iceland too, but when we got there it was real hot.'

Some of the day-trippers had a look at the harbour and plodded off to see the church and eat an ice cream overlooking the beach, while others jumped on to the organised transport to visit the glass factory in Waterford. But by half past five they were all back on board and the *Royal Princess* headed out into the Atlantic with a wisp of grey smoke from its rear funnel smeared on the blue horizon. Then it disappeared beyond the curve of the earth and East Dunmore was left with its longer-term visitors.

For me too, it was time to move on. I could have dallied for ever in Ireland because the pace was so unhurried and civilised and the soda bread was the best I'd tasted. But I still had Austria and Germany to visit, and I was looking forward to all that beer and sausages.

13

Death in Vienna

The last time I'd been in Vienna was in 1989, when a UN agency hired me to put together an atlas of the iron and steel industry in Africa. My boss was an African who wore Yves Saint Laurent suits with no shirt and paced around the office barefoot. You don't come across many black people in Austria, and Mr Im-Bham was an awe-inspiring sight. He was huge in every direction, well over six feet tall, and well over six feet wide. One of his assistants told me a story of how the two of them had been driving in the city one day and were pulled over for speeding. Mr Im-Bham climbed out of his car and stood towering over the little Viennese policeman, who suddenly lost confidence when confronted with this enormous black presence. As the police officer stuttered his accusation, Mr Im-Bham boomed, 'I eat people like you for breakfast,' and the little speed cop jumped on to his motorbike and roared away without another word.

Another African gentleman acted as Mr Im-Bham's second-in-command. Although he didn't appear to do anything except read the paper, he was very friendly to me and proved to be an endless source of invaluable advice on the subject of vitamin supplements. Otherwise, the Im-Bham office was staffed by a small entourage of typists and assistants, all of whom were female and all of whom were really rather beautiful. The day I arrived, Mr Im-Bham outlined the requirements for the job and then gave me a piece of his own advice. 'I don't mind what you do,' he said, 'as long as you observe the golden rule: don't touch my secretaries.'

Other than the daily entertainment provided by Mr Im-Bham and his followers, I didn't really enjoy Vienna. The weather was cold and so were the people. My job had an impossible deadline so I had to work long hours (those were the innocent days when I thought that words like 'urgent' meant the same in UN-speak as they did everywhere else on the planet). My hotel was in an uninspiring part of town and I was usually so tired after a day in UNO City that I had little energy left to go exploring the Austrian version.

One of the job's advantages, however, was that I was given business-class plane tickets, and this meant that I could change my itinerary, at no extra cost, to make stop-offs anywhere along the London–Vienna route. At the end of one visit, I decided to stop for the weekend in Prague. Unfortunately, the night before I was due to leave Vienna, I was stood up by a woman who obviously wasn't as interested as I'd thought she was, and I went on a binge to drown my sorrows. The following morning, feeling very awful indeed, I managed to catch my plane. It was mid-November and bitterly cold, but warmed by my terrible hangover I wandered the fairytale city of Prague in a daze.

The streets of the Czech capital seemed strangely muted. Apart from a heavy militia presence, there weren't many people about. On Saturday evening, I ambled around Wenceslaus Square and saw a few candles flickering beside a flowerbed. Grey men inside cardboard uniforms eyed me suspiciously from beneath their tin hats, but there was no one else abroad. This was my first visit to what was then communist Eastern Europe and I didn't know what else to expect. Apart from the amazing architecture, I found the place was desolate.

Still suffering from the aftermath of the mother of all hangovers, I flew home the following day and sat next to a British journalist from ITN on the plane. He was full of excitement. The Czechs had risen up against their oppressors this weekend, he told me; the end of communism was nigh.

I had been in Prague at the start of the Velvet Revolution and I'd missed it. I've never forgiven Vienna for that.

So it was with a lingering sense of hostility that I set out for the Austrian capital in September 1996. My trip did not start well. I missed my plane at Heathrow.

I felt very stupid. Experienced travellers aren't supposed to miss their flights. It had only happened to me once before, many years previously in Algeria, but on that occasion it hadn't been my fault. This time I simply should have caught an earlier bus to the airport. My plane ticket was a cheap one, unchangeable under any circumstances, the travel agent had emphasised. I threw myself on the mercy of the KLM staff. What great people the Dutch are: they put me on the next flight.

The cute little airport at Vienna was just as I remembered it: quiet, clean and unhurried. I even remembered the bar at Gate A in the arrivals/departures lounge, only I don't think it was called the Bye Bye seven years before. The place was a stark contrast to the bedlam that had passed for a departure lounge at Dublin on a Friday afternoon a few weeks earlier. I jumped on to the S-Bahn, the overground train system, that took me into town and joined the throng of people taking the air on the pedestrianised Kärntner Strasse. It was lined with smartly dressed late middle-aged couples who looked extraordinarily out of place doubling as organ-grinders on a Sunday lunch time. Such people always look sad and down-at-heel in Britain.

This time, I had decided to put up in a hotel right in the middle of Vienna and since this was my last sortie into Europe (I was proceeding to Germany after Austria), I went for a splurge. I wanted the full Habsburg grandeur so I had thrown caution to the wind and booked into a former palace in the old city. It was full of crimson fabrics and crystal chandeliers. There were discreet fairy lights in the lift and an embossed waste paper bin in my room. The floors were covered by red Persian carpets and the windows dressed by sumptuous velvet drapes. The soaps and sewing kit came in fetching little scarlet boxes that I wanted to own. The only problem I had with staying in such a smart hotel was that I found it difficult to leave my room. I was so intent upon getting my money's worth that I spent one evening just padding barefoot back and forth through the ankle-deep carpets listening to Strauss on the radio. But on the day of my arrival I had more pressing business. I wanted to visit the Prater, Vienna's famous park on the site of a former imperial hunting ground on the banks of the Danube.

I caught the U-Bahn (the underground) from Stephansplatz and emerged a few hundred metres from a giant Ferris wheel, the Riesenrad, Vienna's answer to the Eiffel Tower or the Atomium. Crowds were milling to and from their Sunday afternoon outings in the Prater. I was heading for the funfair and the great wheel. From this distance, its iron ribs looked as thin as the spokes of a bicycle wheel, turning in its slow, deliberate fashion to give the passengers in its little red boxcars their brief view over the city. I bought a ticket and joined the queue at the foot of the giant structure, shivering slightly in the autumnal gusts. A small display board carried black and white photographs of the Riesenrad gently revolving through its hundred years of history. Grimy images of its sorry broken girders, on a smashed and dreary backdrop of post-war Vienna, led on to stills of Orson Welles and Joseph Cotten meeting in the film *The Third Man*. A small leaflet had been produced on the occasion of its hundredth birthday, with boxes in twelve languages giving a brief history of the giant wheel. It was built in 1896, and its English engineer also designed sister wheels for London, Blackpool and Paris, but these were soon dismantled and sold for scrap, so only the Wiener Riesenrad remains.

The man at the concrete platform was only allowing people on to every third car and we made way for a man on crutches to board first. About ten of us walked into the wooden box the size of a small railway guard's van. In its middle was a low wooden bench, but most of its space was for standing to look out of the windows. The sliding door was slammed shut and, for a moment, I couldn't be sure whether it was the boxcar that was moving or whether someone was winding a screen, painted with Viennese scenery, slowly up the window. But then a passenger stepped across from one side of the car to the other and a perceptible sway betrayed our motion. We had taken off, to rise in a majestic arc, the city sinking away gently below us.

The man with the crutches had propped them on one side of the car and was limping from window to window with his video camera, recording the receding landscape. Behind him, great thick metal support girders were appearing to look in on their new customers. Down below, the friends, families and lovers in the funfair were gradually diminishing to become the black dots that Harry Lime had gazed over in *The Third Man*. For a few moments we were on top of the wheel and all of Vienna was laid out below us. Beyond the Danube stood the gleaming, futuristic, curved glass towers of UNO City and I wondered whether Mr Im-Bham was still there with his bevy of secretaries. It also struck me that although the EU was ten years younger than the UN, and didn't have quite as many members, it had created a bureaucratic jungle in Brussels which was just as impenetrable as anything dreamt up in New York. The sun was looking watery and approaching the end of its shift. A slight wind could be heard sucking at the wooden slats, and on either side of us, slightly below on the wheel, an empty red car lent extra emphasis to the feeling of gently swinging weightlessness. I closed my eyes and heard the jaunty tune of zither music behind the creaking of the boxcar.

Back on the ground, the wind had picked up: a whispering herald of the icy blasts that grip Central Europe in winter. I bought something to eat, chosen at random from the list on a van opposite the ghost train. Five little spicy sausages, about a kilogram of brown mustard, and a pile of fried onions were handed across the counter on a small cardboard plate. From the spelling of the name on the list, I guessed it must be a Czech dish. I ate it watching small children transfixed by the moving model of King Kong, a crocodile with a leg in its mouth, and a suitcase that opened and shut to reveal a brightly painted human skeleton.

I made my way back towards the U-Bahn as the sun finally gave up the ghost and the wind strengthened to bite deeper. The funfair music and the clamour of its customers were painted garish colours by flashing neon and the family parties were giving way to groups of Viennese youth. The giant wheel almost lost its spokes against the darkening skyline, leaving just a ring of illuminated cabins floating in the evening air. In contrast to most of Vienna, which looks prosperous and well kempt, Wien Nord station was as run-down and grimy as any you could see in the former communist countries of Eastern Europe. They say that Vienna is where the West thinks it's East, and vice versa, and the sense of being on that frontier was heightened by the nearby roadsigns to Budapest and Prague. The wind followed me beneath the arches to whip up old newspapers along the line of kiosks selling pizza slices and new newspapers. Over the door of one of the kiosks, a large, weakly illuminated ice cream cornet advertised a business whose season was fast coming to an end. On top of the cornet sat an elderly pigeon, probably drawn by the light's heat, which struck me as ironic. It must have been a favourite spot because the ice cream was streaked with bird shit.

It felt good to be engulfed by the warm man-made draught that hit me as I descended into the underground system. On the train, the same recorded voice that I remembered from seven years before was still telling you, in unhurried tones, the name of the next station and the numbers of connecting tram services. Hanging from a string beside my seat was a magazine to look at.

The thing that surprised me about the free magazines on the U-Bahn was that nobody stole them. They wouldn't have lasted five minutes on the London underground. It could have been because the magazines contained complete rubbish, but I couldn't tell because I can't read any German. I don't think so, however. Above ground, passers-by could buy daily newspapers from see-through plastic pouches attached to lampposts. There was a small metal box for your money, but you didn't have to push a coin through the slot to open the plastic pouch. Anyone could simply filch a newspaper without paying, but they didn't. The Viennese were just a very law-abiding lot. I had come across the same upright character in the Scandinavian capitals, but somehow here in Vienna it made the people less endearing. They were courteous enough, but they combined it with a sense of self-importance more akin to the Parisians.

Nevertheless, Vienna seemed a pretty safe place. There were gaggles of drunks and drop-outs at the railway stations, but there were fewer social misfits on the streets than in a lot of other European capitals. It was almost as if the authorities had banished street crime. They had filed it safely away in a museum instead. It was in Leopoldstadt, the city's second district, housed in an old soap-boilers' works.

When I walked into Vienna's Crime Museum through a big black door, I was met with the same trust in civic behaviour. It was all of five minutes before a woman with a beehive hairdo appeared to take my money. In the meantime I could have walked off with all their postcards.

The museum was slightly frustrating because all the explanations were in German, but I gathered that the exhibits and pictures traced the history of Austrian crime and the judiciary from the Middle Ages through to recent times. There was a heavy emphasis on death, both by murder and execution. Umpteen engravings of people stabbing each other were complemented by diagrams of fallen figures in house plans that looked like Austrian versions of Cluedo. Some life-sized cardboard cut-outs re-enacted the attempt on the life of Kaiser Franz Joseph I in 1853. Looking down on the scene from a comfy seat in the clouds was God, clearly thinking, oh dear. The young Franz Joseph was standing by a wall innocently enjoying the view when his assailant, who wore a heavy black moustache and Brylcreemed black hair, attacked him with a knife. The Cluedo answer would have been Groucho Marx, with the dagger, on the balcony.

The murderous theme continued with numerous glass cases containing cracked skulls, and murder weapons to show what they had been cracked with (hammers mostly). Other equipment of the Viennese murderer through the ages included the saws employed to facilitate corpse disposal and original sacks used for dumping. There were death masks of people who had been hanged for their misdemeanours, most with their eyes closed but their mouths still slightly open in surprise. As the exhibits moved into the present century, the engravings were superseded by gory photographs. Inevitably these were more realistic. Nothing was left to the imagination. There were grisly murder scenes splashed with blood, and pictures of dismembered corpses lying on pathology slabs. It was the murder scene shots that really brought home the full horror. They were pictures of normal surroundings, like bedrooms and offices and park benches, but with real dead bodies in them. It was disturbing. The place should have displayed a health warning at the entrance, yet most of my fellow visitors were families. In one room, an entire wall was taken up by a blown-up photograph of a naked woman minus her arms and legs. It was disgusting. As I stood with my mouth agape, two small boys walked in and giggled at the woman's pubic hair. They were soon followed by their mother, and the boys moved on, pretending not to have noticed the huge photograph. The mother walked past it with hardly a glance.

The Viennese have an obsessive fascination with death. Gruesome though the Crime Museum was, I thought I would follow this up with a visit to another establishment listed in the Vienna museums pamphlet: the Undertaker's Museum. Gaining access to the place was not straightforward, however. It was only open from noon until 3 p.m., and ominously enough, you had to make an appointment.

One morning I dialled the number and after a few rings a man answered. In an attempt to emulate the rather formal Austrian approach to social discourse, I had been prefacing all my dealings with the local population by the polite enquiry, 'Do you speak English?' Everyone seemed to, until now.

'I am sorry sir, I am not speaking English,' the voice on the other end of the line declared. I realised what a pointless question it was, because I was going to speak to him in English whatever. I tried to make it as simple as possible: could I visit the museum today?

'At twelve o'clock?' the voice asked, thankfully in perfectly good English. Yes, I told him. 'One man?'

'Yes, one man only,' I replied.

'*Gut*, one man only at twelve o'clock.' I thanked him and hung up, glad that he hadn't asked me how tall I was.

The place was a short U-Bahn ride south of the centre. It was in an anonymous apartment block with a courtyard at the back. Through the opening I glimpsed a parked hearse before I entered through the front door, on the dot of twelve o'clock. Inside the narrow foyer I was faced with three glass doors. A porter emerged through the one on my left to ask my business. He requested that I wait while he used the telephone to announce my arrival. I stood there. The room to my right, which looked like some sort of conference facility, was very 1950s in its lights and other fittings. The porter said I would be attended to in a few minutes.

Eventually, a small grey man appeared down the stairs I could see through the glass door in front of me. He opened it and came through with his hand outstretched. 'You are the Englishman,' he proclaimed, as if he was making an important disclosure.

The man was in his fifties and looked like an undertaker. He had a good head of grey hair, a neat grey moustache, square metal-rimmed glasses and a grey cardigan. But he was obviously off-duty because his tie was slightly askew to reveal that the top button of his shirt was undone. He led me back via the door through which he had just come and we walked up the spiral staircase. I assumed that this was the man I had spoken to that morning, but despite what he had said on the telephone his English was very passable.

'English or American?' he asked. I told him English, and he nodded because this was indeed what he had thought. We walked along a corridor and the grey man produced a set of keys from his pocket, selected one, and used it to open a door. He put his hand into the darkness and flicked some switches. Neon lights flickered and held to illuminate a small ante-room with table and chair and somewhere to hang my jacket.

'This museum is built in nineteen hundred and sixty-seven,' he told me. 'It is the house of the only funeral director in Vienna. There are twenty-three thousand funerals a year: earth and fire.'

'Only one funeral director in all of Vienna?' I asked, somewhat surprised.

'Yes,' he said firmly with a slight bow of the head, 'and twenty-three thousand funerals a year: earth and fire.'

We walked through an opening framed by heavy black curtains into a larger room with display cases full of black uniforms down one side and what looked like a large carpet, with a yellow cross in the middle, hung on the opposite wall. I was obviously going to get a guided tour.

My undertaker friend showed me an old photograph of a typical apartment entrance shrouded with black curtains similar to those we had just passed through. In old Vienna, he explained, such curtains were hung to indicate the presence of the deceased to those who wanted to pay their last respects. Standing by the curtains in the photograph was a man dressed in formal attire holding a staff. It was his job to welcome any visitors, I was told. After two days lying on display, the deceased is then conveyed in procession to church. The display cases along the wall contained black dress uniforms for the coachmen and pallbearers. Coachmen wore triangular hats, apparently, pallbearers two-pointed. 'These are for rich peoples only,' the grey man explained.

We turned to the carpet. It was a coffin drape, for the journey from the church to the cemetery. It was just the first of several hung on moving screens that opened on hinges across the length of the room like vault doors to a darker place. My guide opened each one in turn and explained their origins. This one was for master carpenters, the next for members of the Austro-Hungarian veterans' association. He pointed out the small artillery symbols in the corners of the latter, which dated from 1876. Each drape was made of sumptuous black velvet with silk embroidery. The next my guide described as 'super-black, for very rich people only'. He pointed to the corner symbols, small poppies, 'the symbol of the big sleep'.

This was followed by a blue and silver affair, 'for people not married, virgins and children'. Finally came one without a cross in the middle. It consisted of a central circle from which purple and green stripes radiated like a stylised sun. 'This is for a special class of people,' he told me, 'still used today.' But when I asked him to explain this special class, his English finally failed him.

The next room contained more bizarre apparatus: a nineteenth-century system of pulleys and a rope, one end of which was tied to the hand of the deceased in the coffin. At the other end was a bell which would ring in the grave-digger's house should the corpse turn out not to be deceased after all. My undertaker friend gave the rope a smart tug and the bell clanged very loudly indeed, a noise which seemed highly inappropriate in an undertaker's museum. He smiled, gently rocking on the balls of his feet, then stopped the bell. A more recent version was illustrated in a nearby photograph. It showed a store room full of corpses on slabs. Each corpse was attached to an electric bell.

The fear of premature burial was a very real one that gripped most of Europe in the last century, and for some the spectre of being buried alive was so terrible that they left instructions on what should be done with their bodies in the event of death. In many cases this involved delaying burial. Others opted to make assurance doubly sure. I was shown a long knife for the purpose. 'There are three doctors at the deathbed,' my mentor informed me. He had trouble explaining why three doctors were needed, but if I understood him correctly, there was the family doctor and an official doctor and a third doctor who possessed a knife like the one in the case before us. 'Doctor number three makes stick in the heart,' he said simply. 'For one hundred crowns,' he added before moving on.

I was shown a seventeenth-century engraving of a plague doctor wearing a leather cloak that covered the entire human body and a mask that had a long nose, like a cartoon duck, which was filled with herbs and spices. There were pictures of coffin wagons through the ages, including a tram version used when all the horses were off fighting World War I, and a number of real coffins. There was even a wooden model designed under a decree passed by Emperor Joseph II in 1784. It was reusable. A simple black iron lever was pulled to activate the false bottom. With a clank, the flaps opened. 'Bye bye,' the little grey man said with a smile. 'Next.'

In the last room was a selection of cremation urns. My question was anticipated: 'Eighteen per cent of people in Vienna'. A couple of glass specimens, which looked like the dust covers you see over carriage clocks on old-fashioned mantelpieces, were full of charred grey fragments. I pointed to them with a look of surprise on my face. 'Horse ash from test fire,' I was told.

Inevitably, I suppose, most museums in Austria managed to get a musical angle on their exhibits, and the Undertaker's Museum was no exception. Among the final exhibits I was shown were Franz Schubert's original death certificate, an invitation to Beethoven's funeral, and Haydn's death mask.

'Does anyone still have death masks made?' I wondered. The grey man screwed up his top lip and shrugged his shoulders in disappointment. 'In two or three years, one is made,' he answered sadly.

My tour over, I was led noiselessly back to the foyer to get my jacket. The undertaker said he had a leaflet in English and produced some postcards. I noticed the leaflet said the collection could be visited 'during a guided tour without entrance fee', so I selected half a dozen of his postcards while he stood rocking on the balls of his feet being invisible, a skill that comes with the trade I suppose. I gave him the money for the postcards, pulled on my jacket and thanked him. As I turned to leave, he said, 'Please sir, a little money for the visit.' It was a statement. Somewhat embarrassed, I apologised and asked him whether twenty schillings would be appropriate. I handed him a fifty, and the note disappeared into his pocket with no further comment. He'd done that before, I thought to myself.

The Viennese interest in death, and their somewhat fatalistic attitude to life, is bound up with a lack of self-assurance that applies to all Austrians. To a large extent, this reflects the traumas of the twentieth century, a period when the country has regressed from being a European superpower to a small state with a large identity problem.

Austria was ruled by the Habsburgs for more than six hundred years. They were interested in European unity and created an empire for the purpose largely through strategic matrimonial arrangements. It was Napoleon who sounded the alarm bells for the beginning of the end of Austrian dominance, but it wasn't until the aftermath of World War I that Austria was reduced to what we see today: a small sliver of a country deep in the heart of Europe.

The Habsburgs left Vienna as their legacy to the world, a city of imperial splendour where even the Spar supermarkets have stuccoed ceilings and twiddly bits on the walls. Over at Schloss Schönbrunn, Maria Theresa's very yellow pad originally designed to out-Versailles Versailles, you can walk through the mirror room where a six-year-old kid called Mozart gave his first concert before the Empress. The interior decor, though very rococo, is actually much more restrained than that at Versailles and better for it.

As it happened, 1996 was a year of anniversaries in Austria. As well as being the centenary of the Prater's giant wheel, it was also 1000 years since the first mention of *Ostarrichi*, in a document issued by the Holy Roman Emperor Otto III. Restaurants were marking the end of Austria's first millennium with traditional dishes each month, and outside in the grounds of Schloss Schönbrunn they had set up an exhibition of 1000 famous Austrians. I wandered through the drizzle in search of the open-air gallery and nearly gave up when the rain started to get serious.

When I did find it, the exhibition consisted of 1000 Identikit wooden silhouettes in chipboard, each set in a concrete base with a metal plaque attached. They stretched into the distance either side of a scaffolding corridor draped with white material on which quotes from the Austrian famous were printed. Having owned large parts of Europe, Austria could lay claim to people who had been born all over the Continent, from Bonn to Budapest, from Brussels to Rome. Hungarians would question the inclusion of Liszt and both the Germans and Czechs would quibble over Kafka. Obviously they included Ludwig van Beethoven because it was only the Viennese aristocracy who would put up with his bad manners, but perhaps the best-known of all Austrians was conspicuous by his absence. Clever people, these, I thought to myself as the raindrops trickled down my neck; they've turned Beethoven into an Austrian and Hitler into a German. It was Adolf, of course, who made the most recent attempt to bring together the Continent into one big, but not so happy, family.

Austria's relationship with its northern neighbour has been a long and complex one. When Charles Theodore Middleton wrote his *Complete System of Geography* in 1779, he put Austria into the chapter entitled 'Empire of Germany' and included an engraving of Vienna which he called the capital. (Incidentally, the stiffness of Austrian manners and the cold, uninteresting style of conversation was a real turn-off for the few Brits that ventured to Vienna during the Grand Tour.) In more recent times, the boot has been on the other foot, and it is still tempting to think of Austria simply as a bunch of second division Germans. On several occasions this century they have been pretty keen to sign up with the *Deutsche Volk*, and of course they managed it in the late 1930s. But following that little episode, the Austrians have now decided that they aren't just Germans in disguise after all. After fifty years of being provincial, Austria is ready to join in with the EU ideal as a nation in its own right.

Given its disorienting recent history, Austria was a gift for a man named Freud to get to grips with personal psychoanalysis. Sigmund was Jewish and the Austrians have been pretty slow to catch on to the fact that anti-Semitism isn't very fashionable any more. This helps to explain why it took them until 1971 before they opened Freud's old flat on Berggasse as a museum. It was raining again the morning I found the building and climbed the wrought iron staircase to the mezzanine apartment where Freud had lived and worked for nearly fifty years before he fled Vienna in 1938. I pressed the bell beside the door which was opened immediately by a dishevelled man in a black polo neck and dark blue cords. He had unruly black hair and small round glasses. I paid him my entrance fee and he handed me a ring folder full of clear plastic envelopes containing a very detailed guide in English to the numbered items displayed in the apartment. It seemed fittingly designed to make you feel like a doctor doing the rounds.

The museum consisted of just three rooms: Freud's waiting room, his consulting room and his study. Only the first contained furniture. The other two were largely empty except for an extensive collection of old photographs and memorabilia around their walls. Blown-up versions of a series of photos, taken not long before Freud vacated the premises for England, gave the visitor a good idea of what confronted Freud's patients in the first half of the century. The absence of furniture in most of the flat was described in my dossier as 'a symbol of the history of psychoanalysis in Austria after 1938'. I could tell I was going to enjoy this.

If the great detail in the pages of my ring folder seemed a little on the anally retentive side, this was appropriate. Freud was a hoarder. After the panoply of honorary certificates that papered the walls in the waiting room, his consulting room was a cross between an ethnographic museum and an opium den. The old photographs showed phallic Egyptian icons and oriental figurines looking on from sideboards and glass cases. Ancient Egypt obviously held a particular fascination for him, because above the consulting couch hung a large water-colour of the rock temple of Abu Simbel, while on another wall a painting showed Oedipus giving the come-on to a large-breasted Sphinx. During analytical sessions, Freud liked to sit beside a wooden figure of an Egyptian deity with a falcon's head. The couch itself looked very comfortable and was draped in Turkish rugs.

His study had been more of the same, plus books, only here the rugs had started to inhabit the sideboards and the icons had invaded the floor. Among the items on display in the cabinets lining the room were the records of his matriculation exams held in Vienna in 1873. His moral conduct had been exemplary, his German excellent, and everything else very good. Quotations from Freud's letters supplied in my ring folder showed that he had also mastered the bitter-sweet Viennese sense of humour. The notes given to accompany his certificate of appointment to the rank of Professor Extraordinarius in 1902 quoted the following from a letter he wrote concerning the consequent flood of congratulations. It was 'as if the role of sexuality had suddenly been recognised by His Majesty, the interpretation of dreams confirmed by the Council of Ministers, and the necessity of the psychoanalysis therapy of hysteria carried by a two-thirds majority in Parliament'.

In the elucidation given for exhibit 121, a photograph of a public book-burning in Berlin, was: 'What progress we are making. In the Middle Ages they would have burned me; nowadays they are content with burning my books.' The year was 1933; they were early days.

That evening I wrote up my notes on a coffee house crawl to sample what they call the *Kaffeehauskultur* of Vienna. The tradition supposedly dates from Ottoman times when retreating Turks left behind their bean supplies and coffee was adopted as one of the few desirable aspects of an otherwise undesirable Asian culture. I sampled several, starting in the Café Central, a cavernous building that looked more like a church, and ending in the Hotel Sacher Café where Graham Greene wrote his outline for *The Third Man*. I can't now remember in which one it was that I took note of the unusual design of Austrian toilet bowls. Was it just a coincidence, I wondered, that their thrones incorporated a rather Freudian inspection platform for your contributions?

The Hotel Sacher Café was sumptuous and red, with crystal chandeliers and silk wallpaper, and full of the quiet hubbub of intimate chatter. Waitresses in starched pinnies floated around to take your order and one brought me a small coffee and a six-foot glass of brandy on a little silver tray. Also there, on a snow-white plate, was a slice of their renowned Sacher-Torte, a luscious chocolate cake with a hint of apricot. The recipe is a closely guarded secret dating from 1832, when an apprentice cook created it for Prince Metternich. The cake may not have changed in all that time, but the myth of Vienna as a bastion of old-fashioned values took a rude jolt when I noted that the corrugated dollop of cream beside it had recently been occupying a can.

But the cake is rich and delicious, and if you aren't about to go to Vienna to sample it, the Hotel Sacher, in very twenty-first-century style, runs a worldwide delivery service accessible on the Internet. I didn't need to bother, of course. Whilst all the other shops in Vienna enjoyed the most restrictive opening hours in Europe (why Austrian shops, as in many other Continental countries, shut on Saturday afternoons is beyond me), the Hotel Sacher ran a *confiserie* that was open for the sale of take-away Sacher-Torte long after dusk. There was something very appealing about spending twenty pounds on a chocolate cake at 11.30 at night.

The train pulled out of Vienna Westbahnhof and trundled through the suburbs which became gradually more hilly and forested. The rain had continued unabated for several days, and even little streams were gushing Sacher-Torte-brown water. It was more than half an hour before I caught a glimpse of the Danube again, at Melk. A Sunday morning football match was in progress below an imposing monastery-cum-fortress, whose walls were arranged in yellow and white hoops.

The scenery was green and lush, with a gentle roll. Every other field was growing maize and small plots of the stuff had started to invade the town of Pöchlarn. We entered a tunnel several minutes long and emerged to get another brief sighting of the mighty river, wide and brown, before it disappeared again behind the trees. The conductor announced imminent stations in German and English: 'Ladies and gentlemen, our next stop: Amstetten.' The station was stained the yellow-brown colour of nicotine.

The agricultural theme continued, dotted here and there with sturdy square farmhouses surrounding interior courtyards. The sun tried to peek through the clouds at St Valentin and we crossed the River Enns, a tributary feeding the greedy Danube with a swirling mass of dark water fresh from the mountains to the south. We turned away from Europe's second-longest river at Linz and an hour or so later we arrived in Salzburg.

The tourist information kiosk on the platform was frighteningly efficient. I walked in and asked the woman behind the counter if she could find me a hotel near the station. 'Yes, sir, what price did you want to pay?' I told her around 500 schillings and she tapped the information into her computer terminal. 'A single room sir?' 'Yes please.' Tap, tap, tap. 'With or without bathroom?' 'With.' Tap, tap. After ten seconds, she said, 'We have two possibilities close to the station, one for 520 schillings a night which is ten minutes' walk, the other for 550 schillings, just seven minutes from here.'

She swivelled round on her chair and plucked two glossy leaflets from the bank of papers behind her. 'In both cases breakfast is included,' she continued. 'These are the brochures.'

I looked at the photographs of bedsteads painted with Alpine flowers and dining rooms decorated with paintings of Mozart. I picked the nearer of the two. The woman asked for my name and she tapped a few more keys on her keyboard. 'It is booked now, they are waiting for you,' she said as if I had better start walking without delay. Then she produced another leaftet from under the counter and spread a map before me. 'We are here,' she told me, marking the station with a cross, 'and the Pension Adlerhof here. So, you must take the first turning on the left. It is the third house on the right.'

Six minutes and fifty-four seconds later I opened the door to the Pension Adlerhof to be met by a smiling man who stood behind the counter with a piece of paper in his hands. He was trying to pronounce my name.

It was another twenty minutes' walk to the middle of Salzburg, a baroque masterpiece dominated by local boy made good, Wolfgang Amadeus. There was Mozart House, Mozart Museum, the Mozarteum and a Mozartplatz where a statue of the great man stood, pen in hand, gazing at the Café Glockenspiel. The shop windows were bursting with costly merchandise that bore his name. Mozart liqueurs jostled with Mozart cigars and Mozart busts were available everywhere. But most ubiquitous of all were the Mozart chocolates: small round balls, wrapped in expensive foil bearing his portrait, that were obtainable in boxes of all shapes and sizes. My favourite was shaped like a grand piano.

It was evening, and I bought a small box so that I could sample one before dinner. The round balls turned out to be truffles, and I was pleased to note that they were almost as good as Belgian chocolates. Like the Belgians, the Austrians don't contaminate their chocolate with vegetable fat as we do in Britain, so it tastes much more real. As I was wandering through the series of majestic squares that make up the centre of old Salzburg, I was reminded of a story told to me by Mr Armstrong, the Euromythology man from DG Ten in Brussels. As a new boy to the EU game, the Austrian nation had been horrified not long after joining by a scare story stemming from the long-running saga of the Commission's attempts to legally harmonise the recipe for European chocolate. With the chocolate directive in melt-down due to complaints by those countries that wanted to use vegetable fat, someone had taken out a patent for chocolate containing ox blood. The Austrian media were full of stories about having to make their precious chocolate out of dead animals.

As I was quietly smiling to myself over this one, a young one-legged man on crutches sped past me. It took me a second to register this as an unusual event: one-legged men on crutches aren't supposed to speed anywhere. I turned my head to see him disappearing down a side street, using his crutches to propel himself along on a roller-blade. I couldn't decide whether this was because I was thinking about the Commission or about Belgium. It was another Magritte moment.

Either way, I was hungry. I found a beer hall full of polished wood and stags' antlers and ordered some beer. I had a decision to make that night. Since I only had a day in Salzburg, I had to decide whether to do the Mozart bit, or to focus on a more contemporary musical theme and take a *Sound of Music* tour. I ordered goulash with potato dumplings so that I could think it over.

Soon after I sat down, the table next to mine was occupied by a group of about a dozen men of varying ages. They were an international party, and judging from the main topics of conversation, most of which was in English, they were natural scientists of some kind. The group was dominated by an Englishman who wore a green British Lichen Society sweatshirt. He talked a lot, and loudly, the way people do when conversing with foreigners: as if the increased volume would make a difference to their understanding. If he'd been listening to what he was saying he would have talked a lot less.

But he had little competition. As it transpired, most of his fellow diners were from Scandinavia, a naturally garrulous lot. 'I had a mosquito in my bedroom last night and it got me four times,' the Englishman said brightly, holding up four fingers so that his Nordic companions could appreciate the full scale of his suffering. 'Did anyone else experience the same problem?' There were abrupt shakes of the heads that were trying to concentrate on their menus; then one of the group, who sounded as if he was probably Austrian, said that it was unusual to find mosquitoes in Salzburg in September. 'Interesting insects, mosquitoes,' the Englishman went on, but thankfully I was distracted by the arrival of my goulash.

When the waiter came to take the group's order, the British Lichen Society representative enquired as to the nature of a certain dish and when he was told it was beef, he asked, with extra volume, 'I hope it's English beef?' And he looked around the table with a great big idiot smile on his face to make sure that all appreciated his joke. The Scandinavians looked bored. The waiter suppressed a withering look and answered politely that he thought the cow had been reared in Austria. The group ordered dinner, and to give them an appetite, the Englishman told them about cows in India and the various parasites that lived on and in them.

'Have you ever been to India?' he asked one of the Nordics. There was a mumbled 'no'. 'Fascinating country,' the Englishman declared, 'I went for a month and came back with constipation.' He looked around, obviously wondering whether the word needed explanation, but he thought better of it. 'Constipation,' he added for greater effect. 'No one ever does that.'

I returned to my important decision and pondered the pros and cons, but at that moment the Englishman began to lecture his assembled victims about Mozart. 'Clever man, Mozart, a genius really ...' That did it. I opted for the *Sound of Music* tour.

As I paid the bill, the group had reached the coffee stage. 'It's never too late for coffee,' I heard. There was a barely audible response. 'Keeps you awake does it? I can drink it at any time.' Even from my table I could discern the vaguely murderous look he received from his Scandinavian associate. He turned to another victim. 'Does it keep you awake?' he chirped. Sensing a bloodbath, I concentrated hard on the bill that had arrived in front of me, concerned that I might be drawn into something I might regret. It's best to pretend you aren't British when faced with this type of latter-day Englishman abroad.

It was raining again the next day when I assembled with a large number of mostly American tourists at Mirabellplatz for the *Sound of Music* tour. We hurried out from under a tree and climbed aboard the bus to take our seats. A rather serious-looking young woman with long, slightly frizzy blond hair climbed aboard after us and picked up the microphone to apologise earnestly for the inclement weather before welcoming us to the tour. She outlined our itinerary which would last approximately four hours. It would consist of visits both to places frequented by the von Trapp family in real life and to locations used in the Hollywood version of their story. This was an important distinction. The young woman was very keen to acquaint us with the facts concerning the film, of course, but also with what really happened.

As the bus wound its way through Salzburg, she started with some background information. 'Baron von Trapp was very bald in the war,' she told us. There were giggles from the two girls in the seat behind me. 'He was a submarine captain.' She told us about his wife who died and about Maria, the nun whom he had hired as a governess for his children in the film, but in reality only for one of his numerous offspring. 'In reality,' she explained gravely, 'it was not such a big love story. Perhaps it was not possible at that time, but they did get married in 1927.' We saw the convent where Maria had lived prior to becoming Mrs von Trapp.

Our guide said that we were approaching a railway station. 'I have told you that there were some differences between the reality and the movie,' she reminded us. 'This is the train station where they escaped from, but this is a difference ...' she paused for dramatic effect and looked at us knowingly. 'In the movie they didn't escape by train but by car.' There was a murmur of understanding from inside the coach. We were starting to get the hang of things.

Having done the sights in town, we crossed the River Salzach. Our guide apologised for the fact that its waters were dark with sediment. Usually it was white like the salt traditionally mined in the region, she told us. We left Salzburg and took in a couple of impressive houses used as locations in the movie for the von Trapp family home. We stopped to get wet while looking at the glass gazebo in which the kids had sung about being sixteen going on seventeen. It was just a gazebo, sandwiched between a large beech tree and a yellow wall. By this time the heavens had really opened and the usual walk in the gardens was abandoned.

We were out of town now and passing a mountain shrouded in cloud. 'This is the mountain they used for Switzerland in the movie,' we were informed. 'But in reality Switzerland is six or seven hundred kilometres away.' There was silence for a few minutes as we continued through the driving rain. Our guide was discussing an issue of some importance with the driver, then she came on the microphone again. 'No, Switzerland is two or three hundred kilometres away. But still, it is very distant.'

The two girls behind me were in stitches. Earlier, one had told her friend that she had eaten dinner recently with some Austrians in Vienna, and they were all very perplexed when she said that she would be taking this tour. *The Sound of Music* was a flop in Austria apparently. Maybe this explained the deadpan approach of our tour guide. If she'd realised that the film is about the only thing most foreigners know of Austria, apart from Arnold Schwarzenegger and the odd ski resort, she might have tried a bit harder.

Some minutes later we were in lush green pastureland with occasional well-kept houses, backed by coniferous forests that faded out into the low clouds. The guide came back on the microphone. 'In this field Maria was running and she was singing "I have confidence".'

We splashed on past a couple of lakes and through the odd small settlement full of old farmhouses. 'You can see the old farmhouses, half wooden, half brick,' and then, just to confirm, 'the wooden half is upstairs, the brick half is downstairs. It was built this way because the wooden half was easier to warm up in the winter.' She paused. 'But many of these farmhouses are now *pensions* because farmers noticed that with tourism they made more money than with sheep and cows.'

The rain was positively monsoonal now and we aborted a roadside stop for a view that wasn't available. Next came the low-down on 'Edelweiss', the only real song in the movie. 'Edelweiss is under nature conservation now but also it is a symbol of the true love because a young man has to climb up the mountain high to pick it and give it to his true love.' For the first time on the trip, the young woman smiled, but she continued in grave tones. 'But now, because of nature conservation, he would have to pay a fine, and for this reason true love is not allowed any more in Austria.'

Behind me the two girls were wetting themselves. Outside, the deluge continued. We were warned that we were approaching another field, despite the fact that I'd been gazing at nothing but fields for the last twenty minutes. 'Here is the meadow where Maria was singing "The hills are alive", and from here she ran to the convent in Salzburg.' The guide paused. 'So she must have run very fast in reality.' She looked concerned, but carried on. 'Surely she must have been exhausted when she arrived.'

The bus stopped for an hour in Mondsee so that everyone could examine the church used for the wedding scene in the movie. The rain had eased off to just a downpour but I still spent the remainder of my time in a café with some strong black coffee and a piece of apple strudel. On the journey back to Salzburg, the guide asked if we would like to hear some music. Everyone called 'yes' and she slipped a cassette into place. To everyone's amusement, it began with the strains of 'Climb every mountain'. In reality the mountains were totally enveloped in cloud and some of the ragged cotton-wool balls were even sitting in the fields. When 'Doe, a deer' came on, the girls behind me joined in with the chorus. I made a mental note to write a letter of thanks to the British Lichen Society for the inspiration I'd received from their representative.

14

Wedding in Berlin

Salzburg is hard up against the border with Germany so we must have entered the country almost as soon as the train had crossed the swirling Salzach. There were enormous piles of cut logs nestling among yellow mountains of woodchips at Freilassing but the real mountains were still invisible behind the thick veil of clouds. Squat Alpine chalet houses with shallow roofs led us out through the foothills to glimpses of the glassy Lake Chiemsee a few field-lengths away to the right of the tracks. Men in short trousers and long socks climbed on and off the train wearing tweed hats with feathers in their bands. I saw a few dirty sheep and some brown and white cows grazing the pastures, and gradually the church steeples with cupolas gave way to towering spires like sharpened candles. The River Inn outside Rosenheim was swollen and surging and green-blue like the ocean, an unusual colour for a river. When we pulled into Munich and I climbed out of the train, the crisp, dry, cold air told me I was a long way from the sea.

Munich Hauptbahnhof was a huge gleaming monument to prosperity on two levels. Dotted around the sparkling information counters and shop fronts were giant video screens advising you on what to buy next time you go down to the corner shop. 'I'll have a litre of milk, and twenty Marlboro Lights please. Oh, and I'll take one of those new Golf GTIs as well.'

There was a selection of hotels around the station and I walked into one on a street off the main thoroughfare, since that extra 100 metres usually knocks 20 per cent off the bill. The place looked as if it was built back in the days when Formica was the latest fad in interior decor. It was efficiently run and spotlessly clean and my room was equipped with the standard Germanic bed linen: a folded duvet and an immense, flat, square pillow that looked like a giant piece of ravioli. I got bed and breakfast. The only annoying thing about the place were the notices at the breakfast bar. One announced that orange juice was 3.60 deutschmarks extra, and the other said 'Please do not take our food'. The latter caught me off-guard the next morning when I was the first to arrive for breakfast. I stood there for a full minute trying to work out how I was supposed to eat it before I realised that they were appealing to guests to control their criminal tendencies.

That wasn't the only surprise Munich had in store for me. I'm not sure what I was expecting, but whatever it was, it wasn't what I got. Sure, it was affluent and clean and everyone looked rich and well dressed, as if they had just driven into town from the BMW showroom. But the town centre was also full of beautiful old buildings that looked as if they had escaped from Italy. On reflection, I realised that the only images I remembered seeing of the city were from the Munich Olympics, so unconsciously I had been expecting the whole place to be covered by a groovy curved glass roof.

Not a bit of it. Even the ordinary shop fronts had painted friezes and stuccoed façades, and the Marienplatz could have given the Grand'Place in Brussels a run for its money. Walking round churches isn't my absolute favourite form of recreation, but some of Munich's offerings were breathtaking. Inside its red-brick exterior, Frauen-kirche was serenely unadorned, with slender columns and simple wooden pews, and all the more impressive since you have to enter through a semi-circular tent-like curtain that was suddenly dark and soft before propelling you into its elegant interior. Just across town, Asamkirche was the complete opposite. Its multi-coloured marble, statues and pillars set in a mock rock face looked like the entrance to a fairground attraction. Go through the door and you think you're in a music hall or a casino. It was more florid than the State Apartments in Versailles, and more outlandish than the Palácio da Pena at Sintra. It was the sort of thing Salvador Dali would have designed if he'd been alive in the eighteenth century. It was rococo-baroquo gone loco.

Munich also had by far the most up-market street entertainers I had seen anywhere on my travels around Europe. One evening on Kaufingerstrasse there was a conjuror, in full DJ, whose skill would not have embarrassed any cabaret act, and two mime artists. One was sprayed entirely in gold (I genuinely thought he was an avant-garde statue before someone put money into his slot and he started moving), and another was dressed as an angel, wings and all, shooting heart-tipped arrows into a cocked hat from the top of a stepladder draped in celestial cloth. And as the twilight faded, from underneath an arch off the Marienplatz, a rendition of 'Ave Maria' from a woman in a padded wind-cheater, accompanied by two men on a mandolin and a small cello, was enough to bring tears to the eyes. It would not have sounded out of place in an opera house.

Another surprise came in a beer hall where I went to sample what you do expect from Germany, and Bavaria in particular: lederhosen and beer and sausages and more beer. The Germans drink more beer per head than any other Europeans, nearly 149 litres a year, more than five times what the Italians drink, and this was the sort of spot they liked doing it in. I wasn't disappointed by the look of the place. It was full of black wooden benches and panelling, thick beams and dried hops hanging over the bar. Stags' horns adorned the stone walls along with framed selections of old playing cards. Women in frilly blouses and blue dresses, and butch waiters in black waistcoats, motored back and forth across the quarry-tiled floor carrying trays laden with huge glass tankards brimming with dark brews.

The table I chose was serviced by a small, middle-aged troll. She had reddish hair and a ruddy face to go with it. She didn't look like a troll when I first sat down at the huge wooden table, but she did an hour and a half after I had ordered because I was still waiting for my food. She was flustered and overworked but also grossly inefficient, not a combination I had expected to find in Germany. The young couple next to me smiled broadly when I told them this outsider's perception of their nation. 'Efficient?' the young man exclaimed, as if this was a new concept to him, and he laughed. Well, everything's relative, I thought to myself.

My mind kept wandering back to an engraving in Middleton's *Complete System of Geography*. It showed a small group of wretches gazing longingly down from a wicker basket hung from the ceiling of a hall not unlike this one. The caption read: 'Method of punishing the idle in the poor house at Hamburgh, by suspending them in a basket over the table where the more industrious are at their meals'. They should have reintroduced the punishment for waitresses like the troll.

By the time the couple's meal had arrived, and they had cleaned their plates, even they thought her level of incompetence amounted to poor service. They attempted to hurry things along on my behalf. But each time, the stumpy woman became more unfriendly and she threw her arms in the air in a show of exasperation at the unreasonable pressures she faced in carrying beer and food back and forth between counter and table.

I would have walked out in disgust, but the couple engaged me in conversation. They would shortly be visiting England, the young man told me, and he had been reading up about it in preparation. Last night he had read the story of Captain Webb, the first man to swim the English Channel. It would be their first time in Britain, apparently. Their previous holidays had all been on this side of Europe. 'We usually visit northern Italy two or three times a year,' he said. Now they thought they'd like to see what life was like on the outskirts of the Continent. 'Outskirts' was his word. It made me feel very peripheral. Since they were heading for Cornwall, I gave them advance warning of such delights as pasties and cream teas and clotted cream, and soon turned the conversation to the EU, but not before another attempt to attain my dinner which was met with the customary curt response.

'Germans don't like the EU,' I was told. 'They think it will cost them a lot of money and there are no benefits. But the politicians want it and actually Germany needs it because we are relying very much on exports.' He also added that the German people had had their hands full with the little process of reunification over the last six years. They themselves obviously weren't terribly interested, but they did recommend some places I ought to see in Bavaria.

When my food finally arrived it was cold and unpleasant. The troll soon followed it up with the bill. The place had quietened, but she was still scowling. Another stereotypical perception of the Germans is that they lack a sense of humour. They even have a word for an unsmiling person: a *Moltke*. It is derived from General Helmuth Graf von Moltke who is supposed to have smiled only twice in his life. That was twice more than the troll.

Among their recommendations, the couple endorsed the views of several German people I know in England who had told me to go to the Englischer Garten in Munich, though none of them could tell me why it was called the English Garden. They just kept saying I should go because people tend to take their clothes off there. I never made it because the weather was so bad, but I did make a mental note to re-examine my friendships with these people because it seemed that they all thought I was a voyeur. Instead, I went to two places that I reckoned would give me a more typically German experience. The first was the BMW museum.

It was located out by the Olympic Park, so I saw the outlines of the glass roof after all. The museum consisted of a wide, spiral, futuristic pathway that you walked up. Lining the walkway were all the sorts of gleaming exhibits you might expect from a major motor manufacturer: motorcars and motorbikes, a sidecar without the motorbike that set the world speed record for three-wheeled vehicles in 1954, and numerous complicated engines with names like *Doppelstern-motor*. I have to say that motor vehicles don't particularly excite me. I don't know how they work and I don't want to know. I'm not interested in washing them, or caressing them, or taking bits of them out and cleaning them. All I want from them is that they take me from A to B and don't break down on the way. So while some men stood poring over engines with saliva dripping from their lower lips, and lying on the floor to fully appreciate the suspension of the 2002 turbo with four cylinders, 1990-c.c., 5800-r.p.m., 70-litre fuel tank, low-slung front spoiler and an exhaust gas turbocharger, I was left a bit cold by them all.

More interesting were the numerous space-age video screens positioned at strategic intervals along the walkway that you could plug into with your very own headset. The videos had titles like 'The Engineer', and 'The Works Council'. My favourite, 'The Owners of BMW', documented the exciting role of share-holders and capital investments in the history of the company. Another looked at the business of recycling automobiles and began with a touch of humour: a man trying to obliterate an East German Trabant with a sledgehammer. The vehicle was clearly indestructible. As the voice-over pointed out, the body was made of something called Duroplast which had been designed to be indestructible. In the West, the 'Trabi' has long been a joke, a symbol of everything that was bad about the former East Germany. It was slow, polluting and unattractive to look at, but I had never realised that it was made of this immortal material. In the video, the superior BMW voice-over slagged it off because it couldn't be destroyed, but I bet they wish they'd invented it.

Other screen banks presented offerings that were less obvious in their connections with BMW. They showed continuous loops of clips from old films like *Dr Phibes' Cabinet of Terror*, *The Creature from the Black Lagoon*, and *Frankenstein and the Monster from Hell*. Up on level 3, their significance was revealed. A series of corporate videos dispelled all these mythical nightmares of human ingenuity going haywire. The message was clear: the future was safe in the hands of the motor vehicle manufacturer from Bavaria. BMW would create a car to save the world and wipe your bottom for you at the same time.

After laughing at BMW's vision of the future, I went to Dachau for a look at the past. This 1200-year-old Bavarian town is twenty minutes outside Munich on the S-Bahn, between Walpertshofen and Karlsfeld. It's also where the Nazis built their first concentration camp. There was quite a crowd of sightseers on the train and we all piled out of the station to board the number 722 bus which would take us to the site. Bus drivers the world over helpfully call out the names of stops that they know their foreign passengers are aiming for, but it still came as a bit of a shock when the driver of bus number 722 shouted, 'Concentration camp.'

A line of cars had stopped behind the bus as people disembarked, and their drivers watched us closely as we did so. It was a weird feeling. I didn't want to make eye-contact because I felt more like a voyeur than I had wandering around the prostitutes' shop windows in Amsterdam. Did the car drivers feel we were rubbing salt into their wounds just by coming here? Did they feel pangs of guilt, or were they angry that we had come to look at something most people would prefer to forget? My gaggle of sightseers took stock of what appeared to be just a leafy German suburb with the usual bicycle lanes and recycling bins. Across the way, 100 metres up the road, stood a line of watch towers that gave the game away.

In March 1933, Munich's then chief of police, Heinrich Himmler, announced that a concentration camp would be built on the site of the old munitions factory at Dachau. Twelve years later the camp was liberated by US troops. What happened in between is the subject of what is now called the Concentration Camp Memorial Site. Many of the buildings have been preserved: some reconstructed to show how those taken into 'protective custody' lived, others to indicate the conditions in which they died. In one of the main buildings, a museum has been set up to illustrate the machinations of the unholy regime. History before and since the Nazis is full of stories of people trying to kill each other, but this particular set of Germans were the first to try genocide on an industrial scale. The museum was appropriately spartan with plain white walls and a grey polished floor. The blown-up photographs and documents were displayed on matt black boards. Most of the visitors moved through the gallery in silence, as if they were inside a church, but there was one small German school party being lectured at by their teacher in hushed tones. Most of the teenagers listened attentively, but like any school group there were some who looked bored. I wasn't as moved by the exhibits as I'd expected to be. I'd seen too many old documentary newsreels and too much Hollywood footage for it to be new or shocking.

The Dachau Concentration Camp Memorial Site receives about a million visitors a year and the visitors' book was full of scribbles from many nationalities, as had been the inmates themselves, which surprised me. Most victims of the Holocaust had come from Europe, of course, but a handful had hailed from as far afield as Africa, China and South America. The book's comments section had been left mostly blank. A few visitors had put their inability to comment into phrases like 'Beyond words', but some had been more strident: 'Germany should be ashamed for ever,' said one. 'How many ordinary Germans did it take to make the Final Solution work?' asked another.

The release of tension on emerging into the weak sunshine outside on the parade ground was palpable. Some of the school party started running, older visitors lit cigarettes to calm their nerves. I still felt a tinge of guilt and embarrassment at having been a voyeur in a private place of other people's suffering. Whatever your reaction, this place, or others like it, had to be a must on any modern-day Grand Tour of Europe. The last exhibit in the gallery had been a simple quotation that gave the reason why: 'Those who cannot remember the past are condemned to repeat it.' Surely, I thought to myself, European citizens would still be coming here in a hundred years' time, in 500 years' time, for a salutary reminder of how low things European had sunk, and how important it was for us all to get it right this time. Having spent much of the previous year touring the Continent's cultural highlights, it just struck me as ironic that we still think of ourselves as so civilised.

*

The train leaving from platform 3 would take me all the way to Berlin, a seven-and-a-half-hour journey. German Railways had provided a *Fahrplan* to all its customers showing distances, arrival and departure times and those for connecting services. I settled into my seat in carriage 16, a modern, open-plan car with a butterscotch colour scheme and automatic touch-doors, and broke out my map. I had brought an old 1:1,000,000 dating from before German reunification so that I could see where the border had been. My train had come from somewhere called Mittenwald, a town deep in the Bavarian Alps which, according to my map, was near a mountain that bore the unfortunate name of Wank.

Augsburg, our first stop outside Munich, was equipped with a station building that was as bad a Stalinist concrete monstrosity as anything ever designed in Moscow. It looked uncomfortably spartan next to an elderly yellow and terracotta tiled edifice. The ticket collector arrived to check our tickets. His name was Herr Schneider according to his lapel badge and he looked very smart in his shirt, tie and Deutsche Bahn cap. As he proceeded along the carriage Herr Schneider removed the 'reserved' tickets from above the seats that had been occupied. Outside, hops grew in the agricultural scene, dangling like a long line of fox furs from their aerial supports.

We pulled into Nuremberg, sat there for eight minutes, and pulled out again. An eighteenth-century Englishman who passed through the city on the way to Italy noted that its main business at that time was the drug trade – narwhal teeth, elk's feet and the skulls of people slain in battle. Two hundred years later, Nuremberg was the place for Nazi mass rallies and where their organisers were subsequently tried. I went in search of a coffee in the dining car. The automatic touch-doors of the former West German carriages gave way to Bullworker pulls between the carriages and push/pull flap doors to enter the corridors of their older, former East German counterparts. In the restaurant car, the espresso was made with instant coffee powder, just lots of it.

We followed a series of gravel pits that led us into Bamberg. Although we were still well inside what had been West Germany, Bamberg was nevertheless a frontier town of a kind. It sat on the Main, the river Germans call the Weisswurst Äquator. It marks the divide between what northerners think of as the more sophisticated North and the sausage-eaters of the South. As we proceeded

272

northward, haystacks covered in shrink-wrapped plastic sat in the meadows between a series of neat little villages with cascades of flowers draped from the balconies of their houses. The valley was narrowing and the thick conifers of the Thüringer forest were closing in. We rolled through Ludwigsstadt which according to my map was the last village in West Germany before what had been the East–West border. It looked prosperous and orderly and had a nice little green cemetery. The thin yellow worm of a road marked on the map had wiggled up to Ludwigsstadt and then stopped before reunification, but now they were busy forcing a road through the increasingly narrow defile next to the rail line, rejoining the arteries of a severed country. It was a tight squeeze. The train wound its way through the dense, dark Thüringer Wald rising steeply up the precipitous slopes. Slowly the pass widened a shade and slate screes could be seen between the trees. They had used the slate to face the houses at Probstzella, the first settlement in the former East.

The train trundled on, passing what looked like an old wooden watch tower in a green pasture where the crossing had finally broadened to become a narrow floodplain. We disappeared into a tunnel for a few minutes and emerged to pass through more little villages, some boasting plots of maize and small apple orchards. Many of the houses were brick with wooden beams visible in their walls like old Tudor buildings in Britain. There were no flowers on their balconies. We crossed over a river, where a fisherman stood waist-deep in the water with his rod, and followed the river into Saalfeld where the yellow and lime-green corrugated metal walls of a new factory stood in stark contrast to the dirty dereliction of the old brick structures that otherwise lined the track. There were dead railway carriages in the sidings and a beaten-up old Trabant parked or abandoned in a wasteground car park.

Rudolstadt was dominated by a lofty great austere castle with a single turret which reminded me of pictures I'd seen of the infamous Colditz Castle where the Germans had put troublesome POWs during World War II. The town cowering below the castle had a medieval feel to it. Lots of the houses sported Gothic mini-towers. On the outskirts there were a few faceless apartment blocks and a small industrial zone.

We were deep in Thuringia, traditional heartland of old Germany, and the rails held tight to the River Saale all the way to Jena, where thick overground pipes like obese strings of spaghetti followed us on to the platform lined with conker trees. Jena is famous for its Carl Zeiss cameras and optical equipment, and is the site of the university where the philosopher Hegel was on the staff. It was Hegel who came up with the dialectic between thesis and antithesis leading to synthesis, an idea that inspired Karl Marx, a student at Jena a few generations later. Karl and his mate Friedrich applied the concept to the materialist world to produce the inevitable progress of communism. It was appropriate in a way that it was in Germany that the application of their ideas cut an entire nation in half. Appropriate too that as history continued to run, the very dialectic of a divided Germany eventually led once more to its synthesis, to reunification as one state. But we all know which side came out on top and the evidence was there for all to see. Germany may have been resynthesised politically, but there was still a way to go before the economic and social divides would heal over. The *Wessis* of the former West Germany baulk at the cost of bringing their eastern brethren the *Ossis* up to scratch, while it has been hard for the former East to admit defeat.

We approached Leipzig past a string of needle-thin village church steeples and a procession of mushroom-shaped electricity pylons marching out from the defunct lignite power stations across the flat brown fields. I consulted my map again and compared it to the one on the carriage wall. The city to the east, marked as Karl-Marx-Stadt on my map, had had its pre-war name of Chemnitz restored as if the ironically titled German Democratic Republic had all been a bad dream. For many it was, of course, but I still couldn't help feeling a tinge of sympathy for the *Ossis*, for the humiliation some of them must have felt. Having seen the oppression of Eastern Bloc communism in action in Mongolia ten years before, I never thought I'd feel a sense of nostalgia at its passing.

But depressing reminders of the regime's down side surrounded the city of Leipzig. Here was the legacy of East German heavy industry in all its derelict splendour. The track was lined by grimy brickwork, abandoned factories and dilapidated warehouses with rusting iron window frames and every window smashed. The weather was in harmony with the scene of industrial decay: it was grey and dreary and raining. But out beyond the station I could see tall cranes involved in the reconstruction, and Leipzig already had a new, trendy, grey box building producing something for Miele. The train sat for fifteen minutes, half in and half out of the huge curved station roof, before leaving the way we had come as if the driver had changed his mind and didn't want to go any further.

It was ticket inspection time again. Herr Schneider had been replaced by a younger man with a small moustache and tassels on his black slip-ons. His shirt was tucked into his boxer shorts and you could see the 'Earthbound' label above his trouser belt. I pulled out my lunch, filched from the Munich hotel breakfast bar in spite of (actually because of) the notice advising against such action. I had packed the bread roll and tube of liver pâté in a sanitary towel bag from the bathroom, a ruse which I now realised was a bad one because it didn't improve my appetite.

In the seat opposite me, a new passenger who had embarked at Leipzig was settling himself in. He was in his fifties with blond hair, a hard face and a pock-marked chin. He wore a short-sleeved white nylon shirt, several buttons of which were undone to reveal a large gold medallion at his chest. He too had tassels on his black slip-ons. He had carefully placed his black Delsey shoulderbag on the seat-back table in front of him and now pulled a portable telephone from its depths. The phone was covered in a see-through plastic wallet which he brushed over lovingly with his hand before propping the device on the window ledge beside him. Next to emerge from the bag was a portable cassette player. It took him some time to unravel the wires, select a cassette, and set up the machine. But then he sat gazing out of the window with a smile on his face, happy with his little display of Western gadgets.

After the hills had petered out around Leipzig, the landscape continued flat all the way to Berlin. We crossed the River Elbe which had low grassy banks and wasn't that wide, and pulled into Wittenberg. It was here, in 1517, that Martin Luther nailed his theses to the church door, so launching the Reformation. I guessed the huge church dome that looked like a World War I German helmet, with a pointed spike on top, must have been the place. The station itself was full of the standard filthy brown siding buildings with broken windows and multi-coloured graffiti, and beyond the Gothic dome, the skyline was punctured by the modern industrial steeples of a chemical works that pumped little clouds of pollution into the afternoon air.

I pulled out some sheets photocopied from my namesake's geographical compendium. Middleton's description of Germany was as apt today as it was then: 'a country whose affairs and transactions are interwoven with those of every nation in Europe, of which it may be termed both the head and the centre'. Although he couldn't help getting in a dig at the national appetite ('No people eat and drink to greater excess than the Germans') he was keen to emphasise the country's links with Britain: 'it is our original country; that from hence came our ancestors, whose language, customs, laws, we in good measure still retain, together with what constitutes the chief glory and happiness of the British Isles, viz. their form of government.

'Upon these accounts,' he concluded, 'no Englishman can call this country foreign, nor its natives foreign to him.' What a difference a couple of wars make, I thought to myself. But then, this was the sort of sentiment the whole EU was designed to rekindle. In a way it had. I had sensed a feeling of unity across Europe during my travels, but I had also come across a distinctive form of hostility reserved especially for the Germans. When I returned home from my stint in Denmark I remarked to a German friend in England that the Danes didn't think much of her fellow countrymen. 'Of course not,' she replied immediately, 'everyone hates the Germans.' Those weren't the exact words I would have used, but they did rather catch the flavour of the thing. Middleton included a section on Germany's military adventures across Europe through the ages; today's German invasions are touristic. Greeks and Spaniards had complained to me about the annual influx of German visitors; in Austria, Denmark and even as far afield as Eire, they moaned about Germans buying holiday homes and retirement pads in their countries. In Sweden, German tourists stole the elk warning signs. Yet all these people were quite happy to receive the tourists' deutschmarks; it's just that they would have preferred it if the Germans had sent the money but stayed at home. I suppose in a way joining the EU was one way of achieving just that.

It was pancake-flat across the Fläming and into Berlin Hauptbahnhof. Birch trees had started to mix it with the conifers in the sandy soil and I wondered whether the horses in the fields knew they were no longer communists.

*

I had a mission in Berlin. My old friend Steve, the American anthropologist I had met up with in Stockholm, was marrying a Berliner. But I had a few days before the ceremony to have a look round.

Steve had booked me a hotel and he met me at the station armed with a Berlin street map and travel pass. He and Astrid were expecting all sorts of friends from Britain and Steve had organised their visits with a relaxed efficiency born of years arranging academic conferences. But his level of organisation didn't quite reach the heights perceived by one of his guests when he first arrived. His respect for Germanic efficiency momentarily reached new peaks on the bus ride in from Tegel Airport as he passed numerous signposts to the northern Berlin suburb of Wedding.

My hotel was located just south of the Kurfürstendamm, West Berlin's most fashionable avenue, known colloquially as the Ku'damm. The area was affluent, safe and tidy. There were lots of hairdressers and pavement *Kneipe* bars, and shops selling fresh flowers, dried flowers and stylish metal objects. Clean kids rollerbladed through the parks wearing all the right protective padding, and the cars on the traffic-calmed streets were all sparkling and new. The parking ticket machines were powered by gleaming solar panels. Even the tarmac looked smart.

My hotel was pretty smart too, and unmistakably German. It came with a couple more pieces of information for guests that I could add to my list of bizarre advice from European hotels. On the inside of the wardrobe door, hidden among the fire escape notices, was the following announcement: 'The breakfast is obligatory in our hotel. If breakfast is not taken, the price per night raises.' Later, to my surprise, I noticed that every sixth sheet of toilet paper was printed with the word *Danke*.

A good way to get an overview of Berlin is to take a boat trip on the River Spree that snakes its way through the city. Steve and Astrid seemed very relaxed about their forthcoming marriage, so we agreed to take one together. We met late the following morning at the Richard-Wagner-Platz U-Bahn station and strolled towards the mooring through the gardens of Schloss Charlottenburg, built in Prussia's early days as a kingdom. As we rounded a corner of the rambling palace I was met with an entire flowerbed planted with the multi-coloured buddleia that I'd seen in the grounds of the fort at

Lourdes and again in the Generalife in the Alhambra almost a year before, when I was starting this book. I took it as a good omen. By this time the seeds I had stolen from the Generalife had produced a healthy plant standing 50 centimetres high in my garden at home, which just goes to show how long it takes to write a book. I knelt down to examine the flowers and tried to explain my satisfaction to Steve and Astrid, but I think they just thought I was stupid.

Our boat, the *Condor*, took us from west to east through the kaleidoscope of change that was Berlin. I read somewhere that despite being bombed to blazes, sapped of a large part of its pre-war population, and cut in half for thirty years, Berlin today still has a gross domestic product equal to that of whole countries like Eire and Greece. Small wonder then that everyone else in Europe remains in awe of German might. Economically, anyway, it was a case of 'if you can't beat 'em, join 'em'. Since the fall of the Wall and the reunification of the two Germanys – a transition Germans refer to as *die Wende*, 'the turning point' – Berlin had become Europe's largest construction site. When the city was chosen as the capital of the reunited country, the no man's land that had been the Berlin Wall suddenly became prime real estate. Strips of bare ground, once a haven for bite-on-sight dogs and landmines, were now bristling with cranes and earth-moving equipment. Gigantic barges laden with rubble and earth plied back and forth from the construction sites. Dredgers and diggers and a temporary forest of cranes had invaded the denuded territory, early colonisers paving the way for the 'climax community' (to extend the vegetational metaphor – it's a geographical term, meaning permanent cover in tune with the climate of the time) of the new German capital. The Reichstag had been eviscerated and surrounded by scaffolding in readiness for its resurrection, and next to it the Spree itself had been moved a little to the left in preparation for a new U-Bahn tunnel.

We coasted beneath the bridge leading into the dirty glass canopy of Friedrichstrasse S-Bahn station, one of the entry/exit points when the city was divided. Under the watchful eyes of East German security men and their dogs, visitors would line up on the platform to go through immigration. The S-Bahn had been run by the East, and after the building of the Wall, the stations in the West were boycotted by West Berliners. Astrid, who had grown up knowing nothing but a divided city, was always told by her mother not to use the system because her money would be going into Eastern pockets. Western U-Bahn trains continued to transit beneath GDR territory between Wedding and Kreuzberg, but they shot through ghost stations without stopping.

Beyond the Brandenburg Gate, the once great Potsdamer Platz, centre of old Berlin and stop-off point on the Paris to St Petersburg highway, was having a facelift. Actually, more like an entire body transplant. A huge red cabin had been erected on stilts beside the site for people to view the work in progress and peek into the future through the interactive video screens and corporate exhibitions. Steve told me that some parts of the operation were open to guided tours, whilst in others, temporary stages had been erected for open-air construction site performances. Things had moved on since the rubble-women who cleared post-war Berlin by hand for a few extra rations each day. Today's site-workers were navvies from Britain and Ireland, Portugal and Eastern Europe, shipped in to work twelve-hour days and six-day weeks pouring concrete. They earned at least three times the hourly rate they would get at home, assuming they could find the work.

Unless the money runs out, they should have jobs for some time to come. Beyond Museum Island, its black brick walls still spattered with fifty-year-old bullet-holes, and with the lofty pinnacle of the Alexanderplatz TV tower receding behind us, we passed kilometres of riverside dereliction before disembarking. We walked over Oberbaumbrücke, a feat that had been impossible for nearly thirty years thanks to the Wall. Its fairytale twin turrets had been renovated and traffic was once more speeding back and forth, but the warehouses on the banks either side looked sad and empty.

We caught the S-Bahn to Treptower Park and walked into one of Berlin's many green oases to find the Soviet war memorial. It was a vast pedestrian avenue of Stalinist majesty. A weeping woman, probably Mother Russia, looked through her white granite tears along a poplar-lined pathway towards two soldiers, heads bowed beneath polished red structures bearing anti-fascist slogans in Russian and German. We walked up to them and took in the continuation of the avenue, another 100 metres of grassy verges leading to a small hillock. On its top stood a statue of another soldier carrying a baby on his shoulder. Five thousand Soviet troops were buried around the monument, built with stones from Hitler's chancellery. The place had an eerie feeling, shrouded in silence, and it made you feel very small indeed. Astrid, a mercurial, no-nonsense woman, didn't like it and said so. We soon left. She said she didn't come very often to what had been East Berlin. It clearly made her uneasy.

On the S-Bahn back into town, I sympathised. We passed through Ostkreuz, a confusion of crumbling red-brick tenements populated by dreary people who looked decidedly poor. It was as if no one had told them that the Wall had come down. The station master looked like Orson Welles with a pigtail, and a band of bald extras from *Mad Max* boarded the train wearing jackboots and sleeveless sheepskin jackets that revealed muscled arms covered in devil tattoos. They were passing round a bottle of yellow liquid that might have been orange squash, but probably wasn't. It was more likely to have been nitroglycerine.

It wasn't just the fact that both Astrid and Steve had been living in Britain for the past few years that made Astrid's marrying a Westerner likely. If she'd been living in Berlin, the chances were high that she would have done the same. She came from the southern suburb of Zehlendorf which had been in the American sector of Berlin, and if it hadn't been an American, it would probably have been a fellow West Berliner. Shortly before my visit to the new German capital, I read a newspaper article that contained some statistics on Berliners getting hitched. Of the 16,000 Berlin couples who had made the pledge since the collapse of the Wall, just 377 involved East Berlin women wedding Westerners. The number of women from West Berlin marrying men from the East was 185. Physically, the Wall may have gone, but for many Berliners, on both sides of the former divide, it was still there in their heads. Or at least, for the younger generation. For Berliners who remembered, the fall of the Wall was a return to normal.

Having seen so many areas where the Wall had been, I was keen to see what was left. Large parts had been dismantled, of course, and many of these broken up for sale. A big stretch had been sold to Disneyland, another put in a glass case and placed in Berlin's gleaming Europa-Center. For the individual collector, small fragments were on sale as souvenirs all over Berlin. But rumours had started to circulate that many were not genuine. It was not surprising really; they were just old bits of concrete. On Pariser Platz, just east of the Brandenburg Gate, I got talking to the one Aryan face among a long line of Turks and Sri Lankans selling communist mementoes. The man showed me how genuine pieces had many layers of coloured spray-paint on one side, interspersed with coats of white-wash where the authorities had constantly painted over the graffiti. There was also a more technical method for determining authenticity, he told me. East German concrete was the densest in the world. Any standard test of tensile strength would easily distinguish between the genuine and the fake.

Well, not quite, I learnt later from another expert. Communists loved concrete and used it to build everything. The second man informed me that he had seen people breaking up sections of East German road to pass off as pieces of Wall.

Occasional stretches of the real thing had been left in place, but some were still as difficult to approach as in the East German communist days. One morning I returned to the railway station where I had first arrived in Berlin. The Hauptbahnhof was in the eastern part of the city, and had been renovated to become a small island of Western prosperity patrolled by railway police. Outside, it was surrounded by the drab and dreary East. One part of the Wall, known as the East Side Gallery because of its high-quality colourful graffiti, had become part of an encampment for young social outcasts like the nitroglycerine drinkers. They were all pink hair and tattered clothes, and even their dogs had Mohican haircuts. As I tried to approach the multi-coloured section, one punk came up to me with a curled lip that he probably thought was a smile, and asked for a donation. I could hardly refuse, but I didn't venture much closer.

I found a more accessible section beneath the red cabin that overlooked the building site of Potsdamer Platz. It too was flush with multi-coloured graffiti and littered with old spray cans. Behind it, an old East German watch tower stood looking forlorn on a piece of wasteground. As I was pushing my way through the opening in the fence, a middle-aged German man clutching a camera asked me something in a deferential voice as if he thought I was this section's equivalent of the youth who had fleeced me on the East Side Gallery. I apologised for not speaking German and he looked hugely relieved. Not counting the obvious scams in Athens, I had been mistaken for a local in Paris, Brussels and Rome during the course of this book, which had made me feel like a real European citizen. But given the circumstances, it was with mixed feelings that I added Berlin to the list.

From Potsdamer Platz I strolled down towards Friedrichstrasse, once the most dynamic street in the Kaiser's Berlin. Back in August 1961 it had been amputated by the Wall and then issued with a drip: Checkpoint Charlie. Most of the paraphernalia that came with the Wall – the minefields, the self-triggering machine guns, the dog runs, watch towers and barbed wire – had all long gone. In their place, Friedrichstrasse was another linear building site bristling with cranes. Just a few reminders of the old times were left. An historic sign, in the languages of the four powers that controlled post-war Berlin and German, announced to the reader that they were leaving the American sector and beside it a more recent notice, only in English, claimed that for one deutschmark the Turks lurking beneath it would stamp your passport with one of the original exit stamps.

Behind the wire fence that surrounded the construction site, an old GDR checkpoint booth stood with a few broken windows and a new roof. On top of that, someone had placed a gaudy golden replica of the Statue of Liberty, and pinned to the fence nearby was a notice with a lot of stuff about the symbolism of freedom and tyranny.

The East German authorities always said that the Berlin Wall was built to protect their citizens from the evil influences of the West. The Anti-Fascist Protection Barrier they called it. Several hundred of their citizens didn't know what was good for them, so they tried to break out, through, over and under the barrier. Curiously enough, however, during the twenty-eight years between the building of the Wall in 1961 and its demolition in 1989, no one ever attempted to break *into* the German Democratic Republic.

A few metres away to the south, on the edge of what had been West Berlin, was a museum dedicated to the many astonishing attempts to breach the Anti-Fascist Protection Barrier. The museum was full of motor vehicles with hidden compartments, makeshift chairlifts, home-made hang-gliders and even a helicopter. Short descriptions of the escape attempts were interspersed with emotional soundbites from world leaders, such as 'Blood is a liquid that dries very fast' from General de Gaulle. In one alcove, a continuous filmloop showed J. F. Kennedy declaring *'Ich bin ein Berliner,'* a pronouncement which always brings a wry smile to the faces of those who know that its colloquial translation means 'I am a doughnut.'

The ways devised by the happy citizens of the German Democratic Republic to escape their communist homeland ranged from the ingenious to the bizarre. The central exhibit in the first room was a 600-amp welding machine with a hidden compartment, successfully used to smuggle out twenty-nine people between 1971 and 1973. Nearby were photographs of two suitcases which joined together to provide just enough space for a young woman to secrete herself on a train luggage rack. Then came a home-made mini-submarine. It took five hours to pull its inventor 25 kilometres across the Baltic Sea to Denmark. There was a large stereo which was carried across the border with a girl inside, and a 'Trojan cow' that worked in the same way. It was a life-sized plastic model brought over for a dairy exhibition.

Unsurprisingly, the museum was full of overtly pro-Western propaganda about the evils of communism and the wonders of democracy, but I began to wonder just how much the museum's curators really appreciated the reasoning behind these breaks for freedom when they felt the need to annotate the story of one tunnel, dug by students, with the following: 'All the students worked for nothing. Their only reward would come if the tunnel remained undetected to the end.' Did they really expect any other incentive to be involved?

Not all the attempts to escape from East Germany were successful, of course. At least 255 people were killed trying to cross the Berlin Wall, and another 371 died in their attempts to cross the East–West border elsewhere. Nearly two hundred people lost their lives on unauthorised Baltic voyages.

My wanderings in the eastern part of the city gave me a taste of what they had been running from and further evidence of the scale of the task faced by Germans in reuniting their country. It was also more than just a German story. Despite the dubious ways in which the Nazis had approached issues of ethnic origin, East Germans had always been recognised as West German citizens by virtue of their bloodline. Hence, theoretically at least, all biological Germans east of the Iron Curtain had been members of the European Union since it first began in 1957. While for some, recent talk of the 'reconstruction of Germanness' was worrying, for others it was just another compelling reason to make the EU work. There were wider implications too. With most of the other former communist states of the defunct Eastern Bloc now queuing up to join the party in Brussels, the German experience was an enlightening precedent.

Beyond Unter den Linden, which had already been restored to its Prussian imperial splendour, some other aspects of the West's triumph were less appealing. The East German TV tower, still dominant on the Berlin skyline, had been allowed to retain its silhouette which looked like a tapered candle topped with a golf ball and barber's pole. But inside, its characteristic Eastern Bloc space-race feel had been ripped out and replaced by the same furnishing and decor that you can see everywhere else in the supposedly superior West. Alexanderplatz itself was little changed, but for the invasion of Mazda, Sanyo, Sharp and Panasonic logos on the office blocks and a plastic Burger King in front of the fountain. They had put a preservation order on the Lego housing blocks along Karl-Marx-Allee, but they hadn't been able to resist the temptation to slap a gigantic Coca-Cola sign on its Stalinist grandeur. Skulking round the curious World Time Clock at the foot of the TV tower, a disaffected East German youth, who had grown up longing for all those smart Western consumables, now realised that, though within reach, he couldn't afford them.

Further into the East, the pavements were still decorated with weeds and dog shit and old bits of car door. Other facets of the former communist regime now appeared to be worthy of artistic appreciation. A red banner hanging above the mock-classical frontage of the Volksbühne suggested it was showing an exhibition about cement. Elsewhere, the same stuff was being chipped off the brick façades of apartment blocks. Many of them were covered in netting, and workers in overalls shovelled grit from piles on the pavements.

I stopped off to look at a Jewish cemetery where the man at the gate told me in sign language that I ought to be wearing a hat. When I indicated that I hadn't got one, he disappeared into his gatehouse to return with a black nylon skullcap. The gravestones were concealed beneath a thick forest of sycamore trees, and ivy had run riot. In places, the stonework on the graves was being restored, but elsewhere giant headstones lay toppled among the creepers.

The district was populated with Vietnamese cigarette-sellers look-ing bored on street corners, and people with green hair rode their bikes past the Turkish grocers and kebab shops. Open entries gave vistas on to deserted and run-down courtyards in the four-storey terraces but the postwoman with her yellow trolley was delivering nonetheless.

Astrid and Steve's wedding passed off well. Astrid had been lucky to live in Zehlendorf because, being in the former American sector, the registry office could offer a bilingual ceremony, in German and English. It was short and sweet, and afterwards the varied assortment of guests moseyed down Teltower Damm in bright sunshine towards the flat where Astrid's parents had laid on a buffet lunch. Some of the more recent arrivals from Britain had trouble avoiding the red pavement cycle lanes, so we detoured through a shady park for the final stretch.

By late afternoon, I had to leave to cross town for my flight home from Tegel. After checking in at the little airport, I was perusing a newspaper stand when a lady asked me in German for directions. I apologised in English, and she repeated her question so that I could understand. I directed her to the check-in stands and paused to wonder how many years it might be before I would be able to answer her in German.

Epilogue

As my plane was buffeted through the cloud layer and emerged to soar into a clear blue European sky, I looked back over my year of Continental experiences. It was good finally to be going home because I was exhausted, but I had certainly confirmed many of my preconceptions about some parts of Europe and their people. The Finns were introspective, and the Germans and Austrians well disciplined, but then everyone was better behaved than the Italians. Athens was the Continent's capital of smog and Amsterdam its capital of snog. For me the Luxembourgers still lacked an identity but I'd discovered what made the Parisians all walk around with their noses in the air. By contrast, I'd met an inefficient German and a talkative Swede. I'd decided that the Belgians weren't boring at all, just a bit bizarre, and the Irish were no more stupid than any other nationality.

There had been other surprises too. I hadn't realised the full extent of the Viennese obsession with death, and I'd felt sorry for the former East Germans. I'd been disappointed to learn that the Dutch hadn't invented the windmill, disturbed by the Swedish penchant for eugenics, and amazed to discover that the von Trapp family hadn't escaped from Austria by car, but by train.

Despite being written off as a 'less favoured' has-been, Portugal had provided me with Europe's most idyllic spot (Sintra), its most enjoyable museum (the Gulbenkian), and its best fried chicken. Overall my best food award had to go to Belgium, although the best breakfasts were made in Eire. Luxembourg got the award for best exhibition of reptiles.

When it came to the cultural monuments, many of Charles Theodore Middleton's recommendations still held good. The modern-day Grand Tourist can't be disappointed by the Alhambra, the first glimpse of the Acropolis, everything in Venice except the smell, and most things in Rome despite the traffic. To these should be added some modern musts: the Eiffel Tower, of course, the Prater's big wheel, and the Belgian iron crystal atom that has been magnified 165 billion times. Others that I'd taken the trouble to visit I wouldn't bother with a second time: the Little Mermaid in Copenhagen, the Manneken-Pis in Brussels, and the Expo '92 site in Seville. I'd been disappointed that the underwear museum in Brussels had shut down and that apparently there never had been a museum of excrement in Amsterdam. Go and mellow out in a coffee shop instead to appreciate Dutch attitudes. Likewise, visit the Wine and Spirits Historical Museum in Stockholm to fully understand the Swedes. In Portugal you must attend a bullfight, and in Finland have a sauna in a forest.

I was happy enough with the itinerary I'd followed, although there would always be interesting variations. Scandinavia would have been very different if I'd gone in the summer when the sun never sets. I wouldn't have had to wear those Arctic rubber boots nor invest in the thermal underwear that I'll probably never wear again. And I could have done Greece in the winter: Athens in the snow would have been peculiar. The Continent's tremendous variety was one thing that had really struck me. Despite the ubiquitous tacky souvenirs and the plastic fast food, my travels as a Brussels scout had shown me that Europe was still a kaleidoscope of cultures. I'd learnt a lot about my continent and it had turned out to be just as different and bizarre as anything on offer in more far-flung destinations. In Greece toilet paper was something to collect and in Germany they were thankful if you wiped your bottom on it. In Sweden an elk was both a driving hazard and a flavour of salami, while in Belgium a horse was an entrecôte waiting to happen. In Rome pavements were for driving on while in France they were for dogs to crap on. In Finland the sausage is a vegetable and in Portugal they use carrots to make jam.

Given this diversity, it was understandable that I had come across the full spectrum of attitudes towards the idea of European unity. At one end of the spectrum, countries like Portugal, Eire and Greece were pretty keen on the idea because they were poor and therefore had a lot to gain economically. They had an unlikely ally in Luxembourg which, although rich, was tiny and hadn't got much to lose culturally. I didn't come across anyone quite as anti-European as some Brits can be, but most of the member states I'd visited did have some gripes with the Commission in Brussels. As it happened, an unusually large number of these gripes appeared to be concerned with cheese.

Indeed, it seemed to me that most of the problems of the European Union stemmed from the way the whole enterprise was run. The entire EU set-up needed a shake-down. MEPs would never be taken seriously until they could decide which of their two parliaments they should do away with, while the Eurocrats would continue to be regarded as dangerous fanatics until they stopped shuffling their papers for long enough to remember why it was they were shuffling them. This was a shame, because after travelling the highways and byways of the Continent, I was certainly convinced that the European Union was fundamentally a good idea.

I looked out of my window down towards the flat land made of cotton wool. The captain came on the airwaves to tell his passengers that our landing would be delayed due to the congestion at Heathrow. I would have to wait for another twenty minutes before arriving home on my small island in a cold sea full of herrings.